Embedded
SQL for DB2

Application Design and Programming

Books and Training Products From QED

DATABASE

Data Analysis: The Key to Data Base Design
The Data Dictionary: Concepts and Uses
DB2: The Complete Guide to Implementation
and Use
Logical Data Base Design
DB2 Design Review Guidelines
DB2: Maximizing Performance of Online
Production Systems
Entity-Relationship Approach to Logical Data
Base Design
How to Use ORACLE SQL*PLUS
ORACLE: Building High Performance Online
Systems
Embedded SQL for DB2: Application Design
and Programming
SQL Spoken Here for DB2: A Tutorial
SQL for dBASE IV
Introduction to Data and Activity Analysis
ORACLE Design Review Guidelines
Managing Projects: Selecting and Using PC-
Based Project Management Systems
Using DB2 to Build Decision Support Systems
How to Use SQL for DB2

SYSTEMS DEVELOPMENT

Handbook of Screen Format Design
The Complete Guide to Software Testing
A User's Guide for Defining Software
Requirements
A Structured Approach to Systems Testing
Practical Applications of Expert Systems
Expert Systems Development: Building
PC-Based Applications
Storyboard Prototyping: A New Approach to
User Requirements Analysis
The Software Factory: Managing Software
Development and Maintenance
Data Architecture: The Information Paradigm
Advanced Topics in Information Engineering

MANAGEMENT

Strategic and Operational Planning for
Information Services
The State of the Art in Decision Support Systems
The Management Handbook for Information
Center and End-User Computing
Disaster Recovery: Contingency Planning and
Program Analysis

MANAGEMENT (cont'd)

Winning the Change Game
Information Systems Planning for Competitive
Advantage
Critical Issues in Information Processing
Management and Technology
Developing the World Class Information
Systems Organization
The Technical Instructor's Handbook: From
Techie to Teacher
Collision: Theory vs. Reality in Expert System
How to Automate Your Computer Center:
Achieving Unattended Operations
Ethical Conflicts in Information and Computer
Science, Technology, and Business

TECHNOLOGY

Data Communications: Concepts and Systems
Designing and Implementing Ethernet Networks
Network Concepts and Architectures
CASE: The Potential and the Pitfalls
Open Systems: The Guide to OSI and its
Implementation
VAX/VMS: Learning DCL Commands and
Utilities

PROGRAMMING

VSAM Techniques: Systems Concepts and
Programming Procedures
How to Use CICS to Create On-Line
Applications: Methods and Solutions
DOS/VSE/SP Guide for Systems Programming:
Concepts, Programs, Macros, Subroutines
Systems Programmer's Problem Solver
VSAM: Guide to Optimization and Design
MVS/TSO CLISTS
MVS/TSO: A Working Approach to Native
Mode and ISPF
VAX/VMS: Learning DCL Commands and
Utilities

SELF-PACED TRAINING

SQL as a Second Language
DB2: Building Online Production Systems for
Maximum Performance (Video)
Introduction to UNIX (CBT)
Building Production Applications with ORACLE
(Video)

For Additional Information or a Free Catalog contact

QED INFORMATION SCIENCES, INC. • P. O. Box 82-181 • Wellesley, MA 02181
Telephone: 800-343-4848 or 617-237-5656

Embedded
SQL for DB2
Application Design and Programming

Jonathan S. Sayles

QED Information Sciences, Inc.
Wellesley, Massachusetts

© 1990 by QED Information Sciences, Inc.
P.O. Box 82-181
Wellesley, MA 02181

Library of Congress Catalog Number: 89-10679
International Standard Book Number 0-89435-308-X
Printed in the United States of America
90 91 92 10 9 8 7 6 5 4 3 2 1

Library of Congress Cataloging-in-Publication Data

Sayles, Jonathan.
    Embedded SQL for DB2: Application Design and Programming

    1. SQL (Computer program language) 2. COBOL
(Computer program language) 3. IBM Database 2
(Computer system) I. Title.
QA76.73.S67S287   1989   005.75'6
ISBN 0-89435-308-X

Contents

Preface   xi

Chapter 1.   Overview of SQL/COBOL Programming   1
1.1.   What Is a DB2 Application Program?   2
        1.1.1. SQL/COBOL Application Overview   3
        1.1.2. SQL/COBOL Application Development Process   6
1.2.   Why Use DB2 Application Programs?   7
1.3.   Comparison of a DB2 Application Program
        With a VSAM Program   9
1.4.   WORKING-STORAGE — Where You Define
        Your Host Program Variables   15
1.5.   PROCEDURE DIVISION — Where You Code
        Your SQL Statements   17
1.6.   Program Preparation   18
1.7.   Chapter Summary   20
1.8.   Review Questions   21
1.9.   Answers to Selected Questions   21

Chapter 2.   Introduction to Embedded SQL Statements   23
2.1.   Overview of Embedded SQL Coding Rules   24
2.2.   Embedded SQL Differences from Interactive SQL   24
2.3.   Singleton SELECT (SELECT INTO) Exercises   27
2.4.   DB2 Update Statements   31
2.5.   INSERT   31

2.5.	INSERT	31
2.6.	UPDATE	33
2.7.	DELETE	34
2.8.	INCLUDE	36
2.9.	WHENEVER	38
2.10.	Sample Program I — SAMPLE01	40
2.11.	Workshop I	46
2.12.	Workshop II	52
2.13.	Employee and Video Store Database Tables	59
2.14.	Answers to Selected Exercises	62
	2.14.1. SELECT (part 1)	62
	2.14.1. SELECT (part 2)	63
	2.14.2. INSERT	64
	2.14.3. UPDATE	65
	2.14.4. DELETE	66
Chapter 3.	**SQL/COBOL Program Preparation**	67
3.1.	Program Preparation Overview	68
3.2.	Required Datasets	72
	3.2.1. COPYBOOK.COBOL	72
	3.2.2. SOURCE.COBOL	72
	3.2.3. MODIFIED SOURCE	74
	3.2.4. DBRM.CNTL	74
	3.2.5. LOADLIB	75
	3.2.6. EXTERNAL DATA FILES and Other Run-Time Required Files	76
3.3.	Declaring WORKING-STORAGE Table Descriptions — DCLGEN	76
3.4.	Precompile Using JCL	79
3.5.	Precompile Using the DB2I Panels	80
3.6.	Compile/Link-Edit JCL	80
3.7.	Compile/Link-Edit Using the DB2I Panels	84
3.8.	BIND JCL	84
3.9.	BIND Using the DB2I Panels	88
3.10.	Running Your Program with JCL	89

3.11. Running Your Program from the DB2I Panels 92
3.12. Running Your Program from within a CLIST 93
3.13. DB2 Precompile/Bind Timestamp Problems 94
3.14. Review Questions 95
3.15. Answers to Selected Questions 99
    3.15.1. Filled in Job Steps 100
3.16. Workshop III 101

Chapter 4. Using Host Variables 107

4.1. Host Variable Review 107
4.2. Coding Requirements 109
4.3. Host Variable Assignment Compatibilities 110
4.4. Allowable Data Declarations of Host Variables 112
4.5. Host Structures 115
4.6. Null Indicator Variables 118
4.7. Null Indicator Structures 120
4.8. Host Variable Considerations 122
    4.8.1. Called/Calling Programs and Host Variables 122
    4.8.2. Overflow Problems 123
    4.8.3. Truncation Problems 123
4.9. Host Variable Exercises 123
4.10. Exercise Solutions 126

Chapter 5. Handling SQL Return Codes 129

5.1. Handling Run-Time Errors and Exceptional
    Conditions 129
    5.1.1. DB2 and the SQLCA 130
5.2. The SQLCA Fields and Their Uses 132
    5.2.1. SQLCAID 133
    5.2.2. SQLCABC 133
    5.2.3. SQLCODE 133
    5.2.4. SQLERRM (SQLERRML and SQLERRMC) 134
    5.2.5. SQLERRP 134
    5.2.6. SQLERRD 134

	5.2.7. SQLWARN Flags	135
	5.2.8. SQLEXT	136
5.3.	The WHENEVER Statement	136
	5.3.1. GENERAL-CONDITION	139
	5.3.2. UNCONDITONAL-ACTION	139
5.4.	WHENEVER Considerations	141
	5.4.1. WHENEVER Pluses	142
	5.4.2. WHENEVER Minuses	142
5.5.	DSNTIAR — The SQL Return Code Module	143
5.6.	Review Questions	144
5.7.	Exercise Solutions	146
	5.7.1. USING WHENEVER	146
	5.7.2. CUSTOM CODE	146
5.8.	Workshop IV	147

Chapter 6.	**DB2 CURSOR Operations**	157

6.1.	Why CURSORs?	158
	6.1.1. Singleton SELECT versus Symbolic Cursor Processing	158
6.2.	What Is a CURSOR?	159
6.3.	Defining a CURSOR for Retrieval	160
6.4.	OPENing a CURSOR	162
6.5.	Retrieving Rows (FETCH) with CURSOR	163
6.6.	CLOSEing a CURSOR	166
6.7.	Using a CURSOR in Retrieval Operations	167
6.8.	Updating a Table Using a Symbolic Cursor	174
	6.8.1. Global UPDATE Processing	174
	6.8.2. Localized UPDATE Processing	175
	6.8.3. When Can't You Update Using a Cursor	176
6.9.	Defining a Cursor for DELETE	178
	6.9.1. Localized DELETE Processing	178
6.10.	Using Multiple CURSORs	186
6.11.	Review Questions	187
6.12.	Solutions	189

6.13. Workshop V   190
6.14. Workshop VI   195
6.15 Workshop VII   203
      6.15.1. REFINTEG   205
6.16. Workshop Tables   213

Chapter 7. Performance-Oriented Application Design   215

7.1. Performance Considerations: When and Why   215
7.2. How DB2 Accesses Your Data   217
      7.2.1. TABLESPACE SCAN versus INDEX SCAN   217
      7.2.2. The Different Types of Index Access   219
7.3. Using SQL Statements Effectively   225
7.4. SQL Statement/Index Usage   226
      7.4.1. Performance Guideline #1 — Employ the
             Best Tool for the Job   226
7.5. Recoding SQL Statements to Take Advantage
      of Available Indexes   228
      7.5.1. Using UNION in Place of OR   228
      7.5.2. Useing Table Joins in Place of Subqueries   229
      7.5.3. Avoid Datatype Conversion Problems   231
      7.5.4. Avoid Arithmetic Expressions in a
             WHERE Clause   232
      7.5.5. Avoid Using LIKE in Embedded SQL
             Statements   232
      7.5.6. Indexes on Columns DECLAREd
             FOR UPDATE OF   233
7.6. The EXPLAIN Statement   234
7.7. Using EXPLAIN   240
7.8. Overview of BIND   243
7.9. BIND Options for Locking   244
      7.9.1. ISOLATION LEVEL: CS/RR   244
      7.4.2. Resource Acquisition/Release   246
7.10. BIND Options for DB2 Object Authorization   248
7.11. Review Exercises/Workshop VIII   249

Appendix 1   259
Workshop I: 259
Workshop II: 264
Workshop IV   270
Workshop V   277
Workshop VI   290
Workshop VI   298

Appendix 2   311
Database Definition Statements   311

Appendix 3   319
Common DB2 Return Codes   319

Appendix 4   339
SQL/DB2 Limits and Capacities   339

Appendix 5   343
SQL/DB2 Reserved Words   343

Appendix 6   345
Guide to the IBM Database 2 Reference Manuals   345

Preface

This is a book about SQL[1] programming, COBOL programming, and DB2 application design and development. The purpose of this book is twofold:

1. To provide the reader with the skills necessary to develop, test, and implement COBOL application programs that access DB2 data through embedded SQL statements.

2. To provide the reader with useful guidelines about how to design efficient SQL/COBOL applications in a DB2 production environment.

This book assumes a working knowledge of interactive SQL, DB2, and relational database concepts and facilities. Such knowledge may be obtained by reading "SQL Spoken Here" and the many books about databases available from QED Information Sciences. This is not a book for business endusers of DB2 systems. It is aimed at application designers, programmers, and developers who will be writing SQL/COBOL applications that execute in standard IBM MVS/XA and MVS/ESA environments.[2]

---

[1]"SQL" stands for Structured Query Language.

[2]"MVS/XA" stands for Multiple Virtual Storage — Extended Architecture. "MVS/ESA" stands for Multiple Virtual Storage — Enterprise System Architecture.

IBM DATABASE 2 (DB2) is a database management system that provides a relational model of data. Because DB2 provides many rich and powerful functions to its users, it is important to understand:

1.   How the various functions are performed.

2.   What effect the functions have on the performance of a DB2 system and the applications executing in this environment.

To that end, this book contains material of a fairly technical nature, particularly in chapter 7 "Performance Oriented Application Design." The reason for this is that the more programmers and programmer/analysts understand the DB2 system, the better they are able to achieve an optimal performance. Because data is based in tables and the access to these tables is done through a set-level language (SQL), there are several unique design aspects that the programmer should be aware of to achieve the best performance.

The development of database applications using DB2 has been with us for just a short while now. The smoke has yet to clear. Many misconceptions and few standards have found their way into installations writing systems in COBOL that access DB2. I've wanted to write a book that addressed this problem for a very long time, and I hope *Embedded SQL for DB2: Application Design and Programming* will provide technical and design skills to make things a little clearer, and your life a little easier.

I hope you enjoy this book. If you have comments on how it could be improved, please feel free to contact me in care of QED. Information Sciences, 170 Linden Street, Wellesley MA 02181.

Acknowledgments

In writing this book, I find that I am indebted to many people who have contributed in both a direct and indirect fashion.

First, I need to thank Beth Roberts of QED. Her patience with my many shortcomings as a professional author are closing in on legendary. And her pursuit of quality shows in the work on every page.

I also need to thank Frank Tozier and Seth Eisner for their technical support and advice. They have come to my rescue on more than one occasion.

As always, my friends and colleagues at The Systems Group, Dot Mariano, Carl Foster, Gabe Gargiulo and Roberta Ruthen were their usual highly helpful and professional selves.

And I need to thank the hundreds of students who have studied DB2 Applications Programming with me. "From your pupils, you'll be taught" is no exaggeration, and I could fill this book with footnotes on the enlightening experiences I have shared with them.

Finally, I dedicate this book to my father, David G. Sayles, who gave me most of any creative and literary gifts that I possess, and whose clear, wry, humble and humorous approach to teaching and writing continues to inspire me.

Chapter 1

Overview of SQL/COBOL Programming

After completing this chapter you will be able to describe the features of an SQL/COBOL program, describe the differences between an SQL/COBOL program and a VSAM/COBOL program, outline the steps in program preparation/preprocessing, and list the two parts of a COBOL program affected by embedded SQL statements. Topics include:

1.1. What Is a DB2 Application Program?
1.2. Why Use DB2 Application Programs?
1.3. Comparison of a DB2 Application Program with a VSAM Program
1.4. WORKING-STORAGE — Where You Define Your Host Program Variables
1.5. PROCEDURE DIVISION — Where You Code Your SQL Statements
1.6. Program Preparation
1.7. Chapter Summary
1.8. Review Questions
1.9. Answers to Selected Questions

This chapter is meant to give you an overview (a view of the "forest") on developing application programs that contain embedded SQL statements. It is a chapter that presents a conceptual view ("what it is"), not the specifics ("how do I do it?") on SQL/COBOL programming.

Details on each tree in the forest will follow in chapters 2 through 7. Let's begin.

1.1.   WHAT IS A DB2 APPLICATION PROGRAM?

A DB2 application program is simply an application program written in a third-generation language such as COBOL, PL/I, Fortran, or C, that contains SQL statements. The SQL statements access data stored in DB2 tables. The SQL statements can *supplement* or *replace* standard I/O operations such as OS file READs and WRITEs, VSAM file processing, or IMS database calls. If you know or have used interactive SQL in SPUFI[1] or QMF,[2] embedding SQL statements in application programs will be a relatively straightforward procedure for two reasons:

1.   Embedded SQL statements are very similar to their interactive counterparts — the same nine verbs, statement format, etc.

2.   Third-generation language programs are relatively unchanged due to the presence of SQL statements.

Application programs that contain embedded SQL statements can be executed in the following standard IBM environments:

---

[1] SPUFI stands for SQL Processor Using File Input, an option on the DB2I interactive panels that allows you to code and test SQL statements online.

[2] QMF stands for Query Management Facility, IBM's interactive report writer and query editor product for DB2 and SQL/DS databases.

- TSO Background (batch mode)
- TSO Foreground (Online)
- CICS Online region
- IMS DC Message Processing region (MPR)
- IMS DC Batch Message Processing region (BMPR)
- OS Batch job (must use Call Attach Facility)[3]
- IMS Batch job — (must use Call Attach Facility)

Also, IBM currently offers language support for application programs that execute under one of the above environments, shown in Figure 1.

LANGUAGE	CICS	IMS	TSO	BATCH (CALL ATTACH FACILITY)
C	NO	YES	YES	YES
COBOL	YES	YES	YES	YES
ASSEMBLER	YES	YES	YES	YES
FORTRAN	NO	NO	YES	YES
PL/1	YES	YES	YES	YES

Figure 1. IBM language support for embedded SQL statements.

As you can see, you can run DB2 application programs with embedded SQL statements in most of the mainstream system development and production IBM environments.

1.1.1. SQL/COBOL Application Program Overview

An example of a simple COBOL program with embedded SQL is shown in Figure 2.

---

[3]Call Attach Facility is a facility which allows a program written in assembler language to access DB2 in a more direct and controllable fashion.

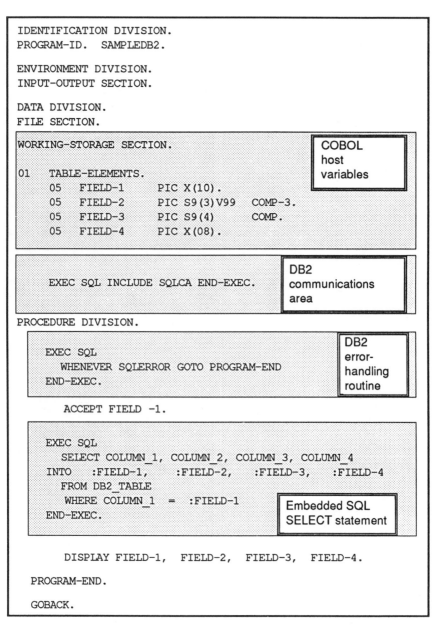

```
IDENTIFICATION DIVISION.
PROGRAM-ID.  SAMPLEDB2.

ENVIRONMENT DIVISION.
INPUT-OUTPUT SECTION.

DATA DIVISION.
FILE SECTION.
```

```
WORKING-STORAGE SECTION.                         COBOL
                                                 host
01   TABLE-ELEMENTS.                             variables
     05   FIELD-1      PIC X(10).
     05   FIELD-2      PIC S9(3)V99   COMP-3.
     05   FIELD-3      PIC S9(4)      COMP.
     05   FIELD-4      PIC X(08).
```

```
                                            DB2
     EXEC SQL INCLUDE SQLCA END-EXEC.       communications
                                            area
PROCEDURE DIVISION.
```

```
                                            DB2
     EXEC SQL                               error-
         WHENEVER SQLERROR GOTO PROGRAM-END handling
     END-EXEC.                              routine
```

```
         ACCEPT FIELD -1.
```

```
     EXEC SQL
         SELECT COLUMN_1, COLUMN_2, COLUMN_3, COLUMN_4
     INTO   :FIELD-1,    :FIELD-2,   :FIELD-3,    :FIELD-4
         FROM DB2_TABLE
         WHERE COLUMN_1  =  :FIELD-1      Embedded SQL
     END-EXEC.                            SELECT statement
```

```
         DISPLAY FIELD-1,  FIELD-2,  FIELD-3,  FIELD-4.

PROGRAM-END.

GOBACK.
```

Figure 2.   COBOL program with embedded SQL statement.

As you can see from the above example, there are two areas of your program affected by SQL processing:

1   WORKING-STORAGE SECTION — where you describe your program's input/output areas for DB2 data.

2. PROCEDURE DIVISION — where you write the executable SQL statements to access and manipulate DB2 data.

You can embed any SQL statement in an application program:

•   DATA DEFINITION STATEMENTS:

    —CREATE
    —DROP
    —ALTER

•   DATA CONTROL STATEMENTS:

    —GRANT
    —REVOKE

•   DATA MANIPULATION STATEMENTS:

    —SELECT
    —INSERT
    —UPDATE
    —DELETE

•   TRANSACTION CONTROL STATEMENTS:

    —COMMIT
    —ROLLBACK

However, the vast majority of your work will involve Data Manipulation statements (SELECT, INSERT, UPDATE, DELETE).

1.1.2. SQL/COBOL APPLICATION DEVELOPMENT PROCESS

In order to execute your program, you will have to "prepare" it. The SQL/COBOL program preparation process has several steps that are unique to the DB2 environment. This is shown in Figure 3.

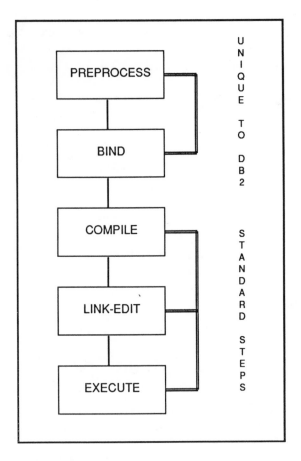

Figure 3. Program preparation process.

These steps are all run as separate Job Control Language (JCL) step executions, and we will be covering them in depth later on in this chapter and in chapter 3.

Now, let's take a quick look at when (or why) you would want to use application programs with embedded SQL.

1.2. WHY USE DB2 APPLICATION PROGRAMS?

Even though embedding SQL statements in application programs is not intrinsically complex or difficult in comparison with using other database and file access systems like VSAM, IMS, or IDMS, it is still much easier to access DB2 data using an interactive product such as QMF, SPUFI, or DB-Proedit.[4] You don't have to worry about defining input/output areas, testing return codes, program preparation, or any of the standard third-generation language encumbrances, statement syntax, procedural algorithms, logic bugs, etc.

So, when would you use a DB2 application program in an application development effort, instead of an interactive, user-friendly, development tool such as QMF?

Application systems use DB2/SQL programs for at least four categories of processing activities:

1. Enforcing data update integrity — DB2 does not enforce application-specific rules pertaining to allowable data values. For example:

    > Part numbers for "Frammises" shall be within the range of A0000 to H9999.
    >
    > Frammis Part Numbers can only be updated at month end
    >
    > Frammis suppliers can only be from Arkansas, Rhode Island, Virginia, and Schenectady, New York.

---

[4]DB-Proedit is an interactive DB2 table editor available from Online Software.

To enforce these and other types of "Domain Integrity" rules (the term "domain" refers to the allowable set of values for a given column), you can use application programs. So, for data entry and data update processing, you will often use application programs to avoid ending up with garbage on the database.

2. Mass INSERT, UPDATE or DELETE processing. Typing in multiple interactive SQL statements to INSERT and DELETE rows, or UPDATE values in columns can be cumbersome, time consuming and error-prone. Most applications use batch SQL/COBOL programs for large-scale update processing requirements.

3. Complex reporting activity. QMF has definite limits on the level of complexity and diversity for reports available through it (control breaks, formatting, etc.). You may have to use programs to handle custom reporting needs that are beyond the software limitations of QMF.

4. Online processing — or requests that must run quickly and efficiently. Any frequently scheduled or critical transactions or activities are best served by application programs running under the supervision of CICS, IMS DC, or TSO/ISPF. Because SQL statements are compiled ahead of time when they are embedded in application programs, much run-time overhead associated with interpretative processing of SQL requests in QMF and SPUFI can be avoided.

You can probably think of other processing requirements in production DB2 applications that are best controlled by programs. These might include any portion of an application needing the tight data access control available through the procedural logic or a third-generation programming language.

Now, let's take a look at a native VSAM/COBOL program with file access commands and see how it differs from an embedded SQL COBOL program. If you haven't coded VSAM calls before, read this section anyway. It is fairly apparent from the program code what is going on, and most of the points I will be making apply to many IBM file processing techniques.

1.3.   COMPARISON OF A DB2 APPLICATION PROGRAM WITH A VSAM PROGRAM

Recall from section 1.1 that what embedded SQL statements do in most application programs is file access. Shown in Figure 4 is a VSAM/COBOL program with random retrieval, insert, and update processing. Figure 5 shows an SQL/COBOL program with the corresponding embedded SQL statements to accomplish the same processing. Study these two programs for a few minutes. There are at least a half dozen or so differences between the SQL/COBOL program and the VSAM/COBOL program. Can you spot some of them?

As you can see from the examples in Figure 4 and 5, there are several ways that VSAM/COBOL programs differ from SQL/COBOL programs. Specifically:

•   DB2 tables do not require external file references or specifi- cations of any kind. This means:

— No JCL DD card for your table(s)
— No SELECT/ASSIGN entry in the ENVIRONMENT DIVISION
— No FD entry in the DATA DIVISION

You only need external file handling statements for your non- DB2 files (such as OS or VSAM transaction files, or report files).

```
IDENTIFICATION DIVISION.
PROGRAM-ID.  SAMPLVSM.

ENVIRONMENT DIVISION.

SELECT VSAM-FILE          ASSIGN TO INOUTVS
                          ORGANIZATION IS INDEXED
                          RECORD KEY IS VS-KEY
                          ACCESS IS RANDOM
                          FILE-STATUS IS VS-STATUS.


SELECT TRANS-FILE         ASSIGN TO UT-S-TRANS.

DATA DIVISION.
INPUT-OUTPUT SECTION.

FD    VSAM-FILE
      LABEL RECORDS ARE STANDARD
      RECORD CONTAINS 100 CHARACTERS
      DATA RECORD IS RECORD-VS.

01    RECORD-VS.
      05    VS-KEY        PIC X(10).
      05    FIELD-1-VS    PIC S9(3)V99    COMP-3.
      05    FIELD-2-VS    PIC S9(4)       COMP.
      05    FIELD-3-VS    PIC X(08).
      "             "             "


FD    TRANS-FILE
      LABEL RECORDS ARE STANDARD
      RECORD CONTAINS 80 CHARACTERS
      DATA RECORD IS RECORD-VS.

01    RECORD-TRANS.
      05    TRANS-SRCH    PIC X(10).
      05    FIELD-1-VS    PIC S9(3)V99    COMP-3.
      05    FIELD-2-TR    PIC S9(4)                COMP.
      05    FIELD-3-TR    PIC X(08).
      "             "             "


WORKING-STORAGE SECTION.

01    FIELDS-WS.
      05    VS-STATUS     PIC X(2).
      05    REPORT-FLD    PIC X(133).
      "             "             "
```

Figure 4.   VSAM/COBOL program example — part 1 of 2.

```
PROCEDURE DIVISION.
*** READ ALL TRANS RECORDS AND PROCESS UNTIL E-O-F   ***
*** OPEN ***
```

```
     OPEN INPUT TRANS-FILE.
     OPEN I-O VSAM-FILE
          IF VS-STATUS NOT = ZEROS
               DISPLAY 'ERROR MESSAGE . . . .'.
```

```
*** READ NEXT TRANS
```

```
     READ TRANS-FILE
          AT END MOVE 'Y' TO EOF-SW. . . . . .
```

```
*** RANDOM RETRIEVAL
```

```
     MOVE TRANS-SEARCH TO VS-KEY.
     READ VSAM-FILE.
          IF VS-STATUS = ZEROS
               PERFORM UPDATE-RTN

          ELSE
          IF VS-STATUS = '23'
               PERFORM ADD-RTN
          ELSE
               DISPLAY 'ERROR MESSAGE . . . .
```

> Branch to separate processing routines based on return code from VSAM

```
 ADD-RTN.
*** INSERT — MOVE statements and other logic goes here
```

```
 WRITE RECORD-VS.
      IF VS-STATUS NOT = ZEROS
           DISPLAY 'ERROR MESSAGE . . . .'.
```

```
 UPDATE-RTN.
*** UPDATE — MOVE statements and other logic goes here
```

```
 REWRITE RECORD-VS.
      IF VS-STATUS NOT = ZEROS
           DISPLAY 'ERROR MESSAGE . . . .'.
```

```
*** CLOSE ***
```

```
 CLOSE VSAM-FILE, TRANS-FILE.
      IF VS-STATUS NOT = ZEROS
           DISPLAY 'ERROR MESSAGE . . . .'.
```

```
PROGRAM-END.
  GOBACK.
```

Figure 4.   VSAM/COBOL program example — part 2 of 2.

```
IDENTIFICATION DIVISION.
PROGRAM-ID.  SAMPLDB2.

ENVIRONMENT DIVISION.
```

****NOTE****
no ENVIRONMENT
DIVISION entry for
DB2 table

```
        SELECT TRANS-FILE ASSIGN TO UT-S-TRANS.
```

```
DATA DIVISION.
INPUT-OUTPUT SECTION.
```

```
FD    TRANS-FILE
      LABEL RECORDS ARE STANDARD
      RECORD CONTAINS 80 CHARACTERS
      DATA RECORD IS RECORD-VS.

01    RECORD-TRANS.
      05    TRANS-SRCH    PIC X(10).
      05    FIELD-1-VS    PIC S9(3)V99    COMP-3.
      05    FIELD-2-TR    PIC S9(4)       COMP.
      05    FIELD-3-TR    PIC X(08).
      "             "                     "
```

****NOTE****
no DATA DIVISION
entry for DB2 table

```
WORKING-STORAGE SECTION.

01    TABLE-ELEMENTS.
      05    FIELD-1       PIC X(10).
      05    FIELD-2       PIC S9(3)V99  COMP-3.
      05    FIELD-3       PIC S9(4)     COMP.
      05    FIELD-4       PIC X(08).
      "             "                   "
```

****COBOL****
host variables
(fields used as
input/output areas for
DB2 data)

****DB2/SQL****
communications area
— copied into program
at precompile

```
      EXEC SQL INCLUDE SQLCA END-EXEC.
```

Figure 5.   SQL/COBOL program example — part 1 of 2.

```
PROCEDURE DIVISION.

    EXEC SQL
         WHENEVER SQLERROR GOTO PROGRAM-END
    END-EXEC.

*** OPEN   **********************************

    OPEN INPUT TRANS-FILE.

*** READ ALL TRANS RECORDS AND PROCESS UNTIL E-O-F   ***

    READ TRANS-FILE
         AT END MOVE 'Y' TO EOF-SW. . . . . .

*** RANDOM RETRIEVAL

    MOVE TRANS-SRCH TO FIELD-1.
    EXEC SQL
       SELECT COLUMN_1, COLUMN_2, COLUMN_3
       INTO  :FIELD-1,  :FIELD-2,   :FIELD-3
         FROM DB2_TABLE
         WHERE COLUMN_1 = :FIELD-1
    END-EXEC.
       IF SQLCODE  =  ZEROS
             PERFORM UPDATE-RTN
       ELSE
       IF SQLCODE  =  +100
             PERFORM ADD-RTN.

ADD-RTN.
*** INSERT — MOVE statements and other logic goes here

    EXEC SQL
         INSERT INTO DB2_TABLE VALUES
             (:FIELD-1,  :FIELD-2,  :FIELD-3,  :FIELD-4)
    END-EXEC.

UPDATE-RTN.
*** UPDATE — MOVE statements and other logic goes here

    EXEC SQL
         UPDATE DB2_TABLE SET
             COLUMN_2  =  :FIELD-2,
             COLUMN_4  =  :FIELD-4
         WHERE COLUMN_1  =  :FIELD-1
    END-EXEC.

*** CLOSE ***

    CLOSE TRANS-FILE

PROGRAM-END.
   GOBACK.
```

****NOTE****
DB2 return-code
error trapping mech-
anism

****NOTE****
Open for
TRANS-FILE only

Branch to separate
processing routines based
on return code from DB2

Figure 5.   SQL/COBOL program example — part 2 of 2.

- In SQL/COBOL programs, DB2 manages all the physical file activities for your data. You don't open or close tables within your program the way you open and close VSAM and OS files.

- In VSAM/COBOL programs logical data access is at the record level. You read, update, delete, and insert records at a time.

- In SQL/COBOL programs logical data access is at the field element level.[5]

- VSAM programs define the input/output data areas in the File Section of the Data Division. SQL/COBOL programs define the "input/output areas" made up of COBOL variables for SQL statements as elementary level fields in WORKING-STORAGE.

  Both programs use COBOL statements to initialize search fields and set up input/output (I/O) calls. This usually consists of moving some values from an input file or screen to search arguments in the data access statement (VSAM file-handling statement, DB2 SQL statement).

- Both programs test a return code from the File Manager (VSAM or DB2) to ascertain the success, failure, and exception condition status of the data access requests. In VSAM you use a status code, in DB2 a WORKING-STORAGE field called SQLCODE.

- SQL/COBOL programs can handle error conditions automatically. The WHENEVER statement generates conditional tests for DB2 execution errors and exception conditions.

---

[5]Even though you think of your results table as containing rows (which are the rough equivalent of records), you will in fact access only the data elements (columns of a table) needed to satisfy the business requirements of your program.

• One of the mechanisms used in automatic DB2 error condition handling is the fields in the SQLCA — SQL Communications Area. The SQLCA is a COBOL 01 level data structure containing elementary level fields that reflect the status of a DB2/SQL statement execution. The SQLCA is required for a DB2 application program and is copied into WORKING-STORAGE using the SQL INCLUDE statement.

Interestingly enough, IMS programs that access DL/I databases function in a very similar fashion:

• Like DB2, you need no external file references and opens/closes for IMS databases. There is also a return code similar to SQLCODE for interrogating the status of IMS calls.

• Like VSAM, IMS promotes record (segment) level access to your DL/I data.

I suppose since all of these products are offered by the same vendor (IBM), similarities in the architecture and file processing protocol should be expected.

Let's get a little closer to the trees now, and take a look at the entries in the WORKING-STORAGE SECTION of an SQL/COBOL program.

1.4.   WORKING-STORAGE — WHERE YOU DEFINE YOUR HOST PROGRAM VARIABLES

As you can see from Figure 6, you define variables to hold DB2 data in your program's WORKING-STORAGE SECTION and reference those variables in your SQL statements contained in the PROCEDURE DIVISION. IBM calls these variables "host variables," and we will refer to them as such from now on.

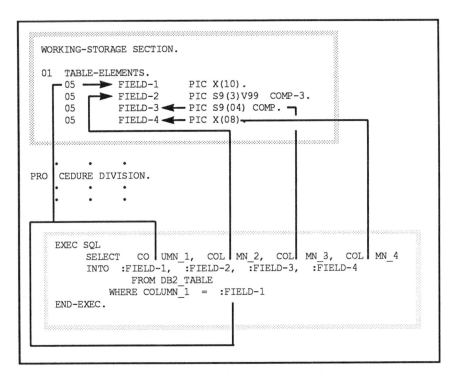

Figure 6. Host program variables being referenced in SQL statements.

Host program variables serve two functions in application programs.

- They are the I/O areas DB2 returns values into after a successful SELECT execution, and where DB2 takes data from on update processing.

- They are used in place of literal values (search arguments) in your SQL statement's WHERE clause.

Host program variables are critical links between your program and DB2. As such they:

1.   Must correspond positionally with the DB2 table/column data they will access;

2.   Must match their associated DB2 table/column datatypes exactly;

3.   Should match their associated DB2 table/column size definition;

4.   Have specific definition requirements for COBOL coding (PICTURE clause, USAGE, LEVEL, etc.);

5.   Are defined in your program's WORKING-STORAGE SECTION or LINKAGE SECTION, not the FILE SECTION.

We will learn the specifics on how to code COBOL host variables that meet these criteria in chapter 4. For now, let's move on to the PROCEDURE DIVISION components of a SQL/COBOL program.

1.5.   PROCEDURE DIVISION — WHERE YOU CODE YOUR SQL STATEMENTS

Figure 7 shows a partial example of SQL statements embedded in the PROCEDURE DIVISION of a COBOL program. These SQL statements will be covered in depth in chapter 2. As you can see, embedded SQL statements are formatted slightly differently from their interactive counterparts, but their basic structure and processing remain the same.

If you know interactive SQL, then the above embedded statements should be familiar to you, except for WHENEVER. As mentioned in section 1.3, WHENEVER is used to automate the handling of error conditions that may arise during DB2 data access. WHENEVER is similar to the CICS "HANDLE CONDITION" statement and will be discussed in detail in chapter 5.

```
PROCEDURE DIVISION.

        EXEC SQL
              WHENEVER SQLERROR GO TO PROGRAM-END
        END-EXEC.


        EXEC SQL
              SELECT COLUMN_1, COLUMN_2, COLUMN_3, COLUMN_4
              INTO  :FIELD-1,  :FIELD-2,  :FIELD-3,  :FIELD-4
                  FROM   DB2_TABLE
                  WHERE COLUMN_1  =  :FIELD-1
        END EXEC.


        EXEC SQL
              INSERT INTO DB2_TABLE VALUES
                  (:FIELD-1,  :FIELD-2,  :FIELD-3,  :FIELD-4)
        END-EXEC.

PROGRAM-END.
    GOBACK.
```

Figure 7.   PROCEDURE DIVISION — SQL statement coding.

1.6.   PROGRAM PREPARATION

In chapter 3, we will take a close look at the process illustrated in figure 8. Preparing COBOL programs for execution that contain SQL statements is not difficult, but it is different from the same procedures used for COBOL programs without SQL statements in them. Because of the differences, it deserves its own chapter, and we will only touch on the process here.

One of the first steps in a development effort is to build a set of COBOL copybooks that describe your DB2 table's columns. This is done using the DCLGEN Panel of the DB2I facility, and will be discussed in chapter three.

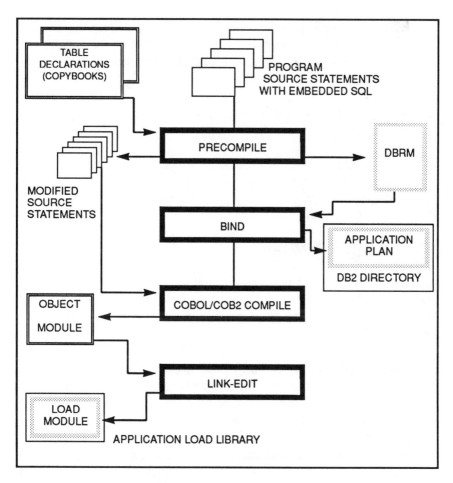

Figure 8.   Program preparation.

After DCLGEN is completed, you execute several jobsteps to:

• Precompile your program — Precompile scans your COBOL source code for SQL statements and places all SQL code into a database request module (DBRM). Precompile also modifies your program's source code so that it can be compiled and link/edited.

- BIND the DBRM — BIND makes executable machine code out of the SQL statements in your DBRM. This executable code is called an "application plan" and is stored in the DB2 Directory.

- Compile your program — turn your source statements into object code

- LINK your program — resolve external CALL statements and place your program (now in executable format) in an application load library.

1.7.   CHAPTER SUMMARY

In this chapter you have gotten a first glimpse at the "What," "When," and "Why" of DB2 embedded SQL application programming. The "How" begins in chapter 2, and continues for the rest of the book.

You have seen that embedding SQL statements in COBOL programs is little different from coding standard Input/Output logic and file access, although you may be able to replace some looping constructs — because of the set-level processing capabilities of SQL. You have also seen that the application development procedures for program preparation are altered due to the presence of SQL statements (which the COBOL compiler would take great exception to, so they must be preprocessed). You have seen that interactive SQL statements are very similar to embedded SQL statements in format and process. Finally, you have seen that in designing applications that contain SQL statements, you will have to learn to think "relationally" — field element level data access, not row (record) access.

Please answer the questions in section 1.8 before continuing with the rest of the text.

1.8.   REVIEW QUESTIONS

1.   What is a DB2 application program, and how is it different from a standard COBOL application program?

2.   Why use DB2 application programs?   When would you choose to process application requirements using QMF instead?

3.   Where do you define your DB2/host program variables?

4.   Where do you code your executable SQL statements?

5.   List the IBM environments which support SQL/COBOL applications:

   * _____

   * _____

   * _____

   * _____

   * _____

   * _____

   * _____

1.9.   SELECTED ANSWERS

1.   A DB2 application program is simply a program in some third-generation language that uses SQL statements to access DB2 data. It is different from standard COBOL programs in that there are no references to external files for

DB2 tables and the SQL statements require preprocessing.

2.   There are at least four reasons for choosing embedded SQL programs:

- Enforcing data update integrity;
- Mass INSERT, UPDATE or DELETE processing;
- Complex reporting activity;
- Online processing — or requests that must run quickly and efficiently.

3.   In the COBOL WORKING-STORAGE SECTION.

4.   In the COBOL PROCEDURE DIVISION.

5.   The IBM environments which support SQL/COBOL applications include:

- TSO Background (batch mode)
- TSO Foreground (online)
- CICS Online region
- IMS DC Message Processing region (MPR)
- IMS DC Batch Message Processing region (BMPR)
- OS Batch job (must use Call Attach Facility)
- IMS Batch job (must use Call Attach Facility)

Chapter 2

Introduction to Embedded SQL Statements

This chapter presents the topic of embedded SQL data manipulation language statements from a perspective of contrasts and comparisons with interactive SQL statements. Through the exercises in this chapter you will learn how to code embedded SQL statements to access and manipulate DB2 data. Topics include:

2.1.   Overview of Embedded SQL Coding Rules
2.2.   Embedded SQL Differences from Interactive SQL
2.3.   Singleton SELECT (SELECT INTO) Exercises
2.4.   DB2 Update Statements
2.5.   INSERT
2.6.   UPDATE
2.7.   DELETE
2.8.   INCLUDE
2.9.   WHENEVER
2.10   Sample Program I — SAMPLE01
2.11   Workshop I
2.12   Workshop II
2.13   Employee and Video Store Database Tables
2.14   Answers to Selected Exercises

This chapter contains several sets of SQL statement exercises, as well as a sample program and two workshops. The answers to the SQL exercises are found in section 2.13. The answers to the workshops can be found in Appendix A. Appendix B contains the SQL Data Definition Language statements to define and load the Video Store database tables and the Employee database tables, which are referred to in both the exercises and the workshops for this chapter.

Now that we've looked over the major parts of a SQL/COBOL program, it's time to get into the details. We'll begin by coding embedded SQL statements — learning how to put them into COBOL programs and how to use COBOL host variables within the statements. We'll be stressing the similarities and differences between embedded and interactive SQL formats.

2.1.   OVERVIEW OF EMBEDDED SQL CODING RULES

The rules for coding embedded SQL statements are easy to remember and are outlined for you in Figure 9.

2.2.   EMBEDDED SQL DIFFERENCES FROM INTERACTIVE SQL

An example of an embedded SELECT statement is shown in Figure 10. Can you distinguish the "SELECTed DB2 COLUMNs" from their respective "selected INTO" host variables? Host variables are the major difference between interactive and embedded SQL. For instance, when you use SPUFI or QMF you do not have to worry about where the results table data is put. The software took care of that for you. But when you embed SQL in an application program, *you* are responsible for correctly defining and using sending and receiving fields (host variables) for your DB2 table data.

- Begin each statement with EXEC SQL — on one line

- Delimit each statement with END-EXEC. — on one line

- Code all statements between columns 12 and 72

- Code INCLUDE statements in the WORKING-STORAGE SECTION

- Code WHENEVER in the PROCEDURE DIVISION

- Code SQL Data Manipulation Language˙ statements in the
  PROCEDURE DIVISION;

      —   SELECT
      —   INSERT
      —   UPDATE
      —   DELETE

- Do not use host program variables that begin with SQL or SQL
  reserved words (a complete list of SQL reserved words can be found in
  Appendix E)

- Prefix your host program variables with a colon (:) when you reference
  them within an SQL statement

- Do not prefix your host program variables with a colon when you reference them outside of an SQL statement

- Avoid continuing words form one line to another

˙You can also code SQL Data Definition Language (DDL) or Data Control
Language (DCL) statements in an application program (CREATE, DROP,
ALTER, GRANT, etc.); however, there are few practical uses for these in
most business applications. Also, several performance issues (DB2
System Catalog locking/contention, etc.) surround using Data Definition
Language statements. For this reason, all of the exercises and work-
shops in this book demonstrate embedded Data Manipulation Language
statements only.

Figure 9. Rules for coding embedded SQL statements.

```
EXEC SQL
      SELECT COLUMN_1,   COLUMN_2,   COLUMN_3,   COLUMN_4
      INTO  :FIELD-1,  :FIELD-2,  :FIELD-3,  :FIELD-4
      FROM DB2_TABLE
           WHERE COLUMN_1  =  :FIELD-1
END-EXEC.
```

Figure 10.   Embedded SELECT statement example.

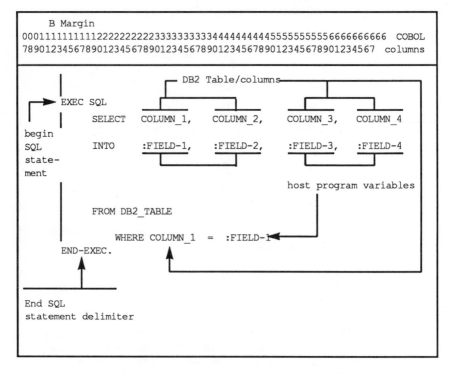

Figure 11.   Embedded SELECT statement example — showing
COBOL columns.

Figure 11 illustrates the same embedded SELECT statement, this time showing the COBOL coding columns for reference.

Besides the INTO clause of the SELECT statement, host variables are often used in place of literal values in the WHERE clauses as search arguments.

Where you used to code:

```
WHERE COLUMN = value . . . .          WHERE DEPT = 'MKT'
```

You will now code:

```
WHERE COLUMN = host-variable . . . .        WHERE DEPT = :DEPT-WS
```

Of course, you must initialize the host variable in your WHERE clause, by MOVEing some search argument value to the COBOL field before executing the SQL statement. This search argument value would most likely come from some external source like an online screen or transaction file.

Figure 12 juxtaposes interactive SQL statements with their embedded SQL counterparts. Study this diagram[1] carefully before you continue. Note the use of the NULL keyword in the INSERT statement example.

2.3. SINGLETON SELECT (SELECT INTO) EXERCISES

Now it is time to test your understanding of how to code embedded SQL statements. Figure 13 contains several incomplete

---

[1]Section 2.12 is this chapter contains the tables that this example uses.

INTERACTIVE SQL	EMBEDDED SQL

SELECT NBR, LNAME
 	
    FROM EMPL
        WHERE DEPT = 'FIN' OR
            JOB IN ('PROG', 'VP');
	EXEC SQL
	    SELECT NBR, LNAME
	    INTO :NBR, :LNAME
	        FROM EMPL
	            WHERE DEPT = :DEPT OR
	        JOB IN (:JOB1, :JOB2)
	END-EXEC.

SELECT AVG(PERF), MAX(PERF)
    FROM EMPL;
	EXEC SQL
	    SELECT AVG(PERF), MAX(PERF)
	INTO :AVG-PERF, :MAX-PERF
	        FROM EMPL
	END-EXEC.

SELECT LNAME, HOURS * RATE * 1.1
 	
    FROM EMPL, PAY
        WHERE EMPL.NBR = PAY.NBR
            AND EMPL.NBR = '07';
	EXEC SQL SELECT LNAME,
	        HOURS * RATE * :ADJUSTMENT
	        INTO :LNAME, :NEW-NET-PAY
	            FROM EMPL,PAY
	        WHERE EMPL.NBR = PAY.NBR
	            AND EMPL.NBR - :EMPL-WS
	END-EXEC.

UPDATE EMPL
    SET PERF PERF * 1.1
    WHERE DEPT IN
        (SELECT DEPT
            FROM EMPL
            GROUP BY DEPT
                HAVING AVG(PERF) > 4);
	EXEC SQL
	UPDATE EMPL
	    SET PERF = PERF * :ADJUSTMENT
	    WHERE DEPT IN
	        (SELECT DEPT
	            FROM EMPL
	            GROUP BY DEPT
	                HAVING AVG(PERF) > :MIN)
	END-EXEC.

DELETE FROM PAY
    WHERE HOURS < 20;
	EXEC SQL
	    DELETE FROM PAY
	        WHERE HOURS < :MINIMUM-STD
	END-EXEC.

INSERT INTO PAY VALUES
    (11,NULL,27.88,150,NULL);
	EXEC SQL
	    INSERT INTO PAY VALUES (
	        :NBR,
	        NULL,
	        :RATE,
	        :DED,
	        NULL) END-EXEC.

Figure 12.   Comparison of interactive and embedded SQL.

embedded SQL statements which you must transform into executable statements by adding code. Create the embedded
SELECT so that it accomplishes the same thing as the interactive
SELECT. Name your host program variables the same as your
column names (only remember to prefix them with a colon). In
some cases (if you are SELECTing arithmetic expressions or
functions), you will need to make up your own host variable
names. Be sure to re-read the rules for coding embedded SQL
statements in section 2.1 if you're a little fuzzy on all the Do's and
Don'ts.

You will start with the embedded SQL form of SELECT statement
called a Singleton SELECT.[2] You can use a Singleton SELECT
only if your results table will contain a single row. In chapter 6, we
will learn how to code SELECT statements that use symbolic
CURSORs to handle multiple row results tables. The format for
Singleton SELECT is shown below:

```
EXEC SQL
      SELECT DB2_TBL_COL_1, DB2_TBL_COL_2
      INTO
                :HOST-VAR_1,    :HOST-VAR_2
          FROM     DB2_TBL
          WHERE DB2_TBL_COL  =   :HOST-VAR
END-EXEC
```

Singleton SELECT example.

---

[2]Singleton SELECT — SELECT statements in this format may return at most
one row when they are executed. If more than one row results from execution,
you will receive a run-time DB2 error. Because of this, the only time you can
safely use a Singleton SELECT statement is when you are SELECTing a DB2
column function (SELECT MAX(PERF), AVG(PERF) FROM EMPL), or when
your WHERE clause qualifies the row using a unique indexed column with the
equal condition (SELECT * FROM EMPL WHERE NBR = '03').

INTERACTIVE SQL	EMBEDDED SQL

SELECT NBR, TITLE, STAR
   FROM MOV
   WHERE TITLE = 'COCOON';
	EXEC SQL
	   SELECT NBR, TITLE, STAR
	   INTO
	   FROM MOV
	       WHERE TITLE =
	END-EXEC.

SELECT *
   FROM PROJ
     WHERE NAME = 'SYSTEM R';
	EXEC SQL
	   SELECT *
	   INTO
	
	     FROM PROJ
	      WHERE NAME =
	END-EXEC.

SELECT NBR
   FROM INV, CUST
     WHERE ID = CUSTID AND
       LNAME = 'WEST';
	EXEC SQL
	
	END-EXEC.

SELECT LNAME, HOURS, RATE
     HOURS * RATE – DED
   FROM PAY,EMPL
   WHERE EMPL.NBR = PAY.NBR AND
   EMPL.NBR = 10;
	EXEC SQL
	
	END-EXEC.

SELECT DEPT, AVG(YTD), MAX(YTD)
   FROM EMPL, PAY
     WHERE EMPL.NBR = PAY.NBR
       GROUP BY DEPT
         HAVING AVG(YTD) > 20000;	

SELECT TITLE
   FROM MOV CORR_VAR
     WHERE NOT EXISTS
       (SELECT * FROM I_M
         WHERE M_NBR = CORR_VAR.NBR);	

Figure 13.   Interactive and embedded SELECT exercises.

Remember to look up the tables in the Video Store Database and Employee Database found in section 2.12 before doing these exercises. Remember to look at the tables as described in section 2.12 before doing the exercises in this chapter.

2.4.   DB2 UPDATE STATEMENTS

Recall from chapter 1 that one of the frequent uses of embedded SQL in applications is to maintain the data integrity of your DB2 data. You can verify data entry and update with cross-edits, range edits, value/conversion checks, numeric tests — the entire scope of 3GL logic is at your disposal in application programs with embedded SQL.

To maintain DB2 data, you use the SQL INSERT, UPDATE, and DELETE verbs. They are all extremely easy to use and follow their interactive formats closely. The only major difference in embedded and interactive update statements is the use of host program variables in place of literals and as search fields.

2.5.   INSERT

With INSERT, you would typically be scrubbing (editing) data from an input file and bulk-loading a DB2 table in batch processing mode. Or you might insert single rows into a table with data from an online screen. These types of application requirements lend themselves to programs over, say, the DB2 LOAD Utility, because of the tight control you can maintain over your inserted data, scrubbing the records exhaustively with COBOL edits.

The format for embedded INSERT statements is shown below. You can INSERT literal values, data in host program variables, arithmetic expressions, and the keyword NULL. If you INSERT using the keyword NULL, all rows you INSERT will contain a NULL in that column — unconditionally. This may not be accept-able to your application requirements, so in a later chapter I will show you how to insert NULLs conditionally. Figure 14 shows some INSERT exercises.

```
***   COBOL MOVE statements to initialize your
***   host program variables go here.

EXEC SQL
      INSERT INTO DB2_TBL VALUES
      (:HOST_VAR,
       :HOST_VAR,
       literal,       ('XXX' or 20.00 etc.)
       NULL,          (note — no colon prefix)
       :HOST_VAR      (note — all columns separated
END-EXEC.              with comma except last)
```

Embedded SQL INSERT statement example.

INTERACTIVE SQL	EMBEDDED SQL

`INSERT INTO MOV`
`  VALUES`
`(23,  'BOTTOM GUN',  'PG13',`
`     'COMEDY', 'FRED GWYNNE',`
`     12,.41);`
	`EXEC SQL`
	`    INSERT INTO MOV VALUES`
	`    (`
	
	`                          )`
	`END-EXEC.`

`INSERT INTO INV`
`  VALUES`
`(33, '12', 24.00, 89001, NULL)`
	`EXEC SQL`
	
	`END-EXEC.`

`INSERT INTO PAY`
`(NBR, HOURS, RATE, DED, YTD)`
`  VALUES`
`(31, 14, 23.99, YTD * .1, 44000);`	

Figure 14.   Interactive and embedded INSERT exercises.

2.6.   UPDATE

UPDATE is used to change existing values in a DB2 table with data from an input file or screen. The syntax is very easy and should present no difficulties. A larger concern is the "scope" of UPDATE. Recall that SQL is a set-level language. This means that a single data access command acts on a set of rows — not a single row — at a time. This means that a single execution of UPDATE could conceivably change the values in the entire column (every row) in a DB2 table. If you are coming from a background in sequential file processing, VSAM file processing, or IMS or IDMS database processing, where a single execution of an update command can only update a single record on a file, this can be disconcerting, to say the least.

```
***   COBOL MOVE statements to initialize your
***   host program variables go here.

EXEC SQL
      UPDATE DB2_TBL VALUES
      SET  TBL_COLUMN   = :HOST—VAR,
           TBL_COLUMN   = literal,
           TBL_COLUMN   = TBL_COLUMN,
           TBL_COLUMN   = NULL
        WHERE TBL_COLUMN =   :HOST—VAR
END—EXEC.
```

Embedded SQL UPDATE statement example.

There is a technique for limiting the scope of UPDATE to a single row. You will learn how to use it in chapter 6. Until then, realize the importance of carefully constructing your WHERE clause to pinpoint your statement's updates, so that only the rows that should be affected — in fact are affected, and no others. Figure 15 shows some UPDATE exercises.

INTERACTIVE SQL	EMBEDDED SQL
| ```
UPDATE MOV
  SET QTY = 8
    WHERE NBR = 9;
``` | ```
EXEC SQL
  UPDATE MOV
    SET



END-EXEC.
``` |
| ```
UPDATE MOV
  SET PRICE = PRICE * 1.15;
``` | ```
EXEC SQL




END-EXEC.
``` |
| ```
UPDATE MOV
  SET RATING = 'X',
    WHERE TYPE = 'HORROR';
``` | ```
MOVE INP-RATING  TO HVAR-RATING.
MOVE INP-TYPE    TO HVAR-TYPE.
``` |

Figure 15. Interactive and embedded UPDATE exercises.

2.7.   DELETE

DELETE is used to remove existing rows from a DB2 table. Like UPDATE, DELETE is easy to use. And like UPDATE, DELETE can be dangerously powerful. DELETE discards *all* rows that meet the conditions you specify in your WHERE clause. This could, in fact, mean every row of the table (although DB2 flags unconditional row deletion with a warning).

```
***    COBOL MOVE statements to initialize your
***    host program variables go here.

EXEC SQL
       DELETE FROM DB2_TBL
       WHERE TBL_COLUMN =    :HOST—VAR
END-EXEC.
```

Embedded SQL DELETE statement example.

DELETE, like UPDATE, has an alternate form which limits the scope of record deletion to a single row. You will learn how to use this alternate form of DELETE in chapter 6. Figure 16 shows some DELETE exercises.

INTERACTIVE SQL	EMBEDDED SQL

`DELETE FROM MOV`
`   WHERE NBR = 9;`
	`EXEC SQL`
	`        DELETE FROM MOV`
	
	`END-EXEC.`

`DELETE FROM MOV`
`   WHERE TYPE = 'HORROR' OR`
`        RATING = 'X';`
	`MOVE INP-TYPE    TO HVAR-TYPE.`
	`MOVE INP-RATING  TO HVAR-RATING.`
	
	`EXEC SQL`
	
	`END-EXEC.`

`DELETE FROM MOV`
`   WHERE QTY * PRICE < 10.00;`
	`MOVE INP-LIMIT-VAL TO HVAR-LIMIT`
	
	`EXEC SQL`
	
	`END-EXEC.`

Figure 16.   Interactive and embedded DELETE exercises.

2.8. INCLUDE

Recall from chapter 1 that one of the first steps in developing DB2 applications is to produce descriptions of your table's columns in COBOL copybook format. This is done by using the DB2I DCLGEN option. DCLGEN creates WORKING-STORAGE fields that can be copied into your program in either of two ways:

*   Manually — by using the ISPF editor;

*   Automatically during the precompile process — by using the INCLUDE command.

There are advantages to both, and I'm reasonably certain that your installation will have standards regarding when and how to obtain copybook definitions of your DB2 tables. If you use INCLUDE, here's how it works.

INCLUDE acts just like a COBOL COPY verb, or PANVALET INCLUDE statement. To INCLUDE COBOL field definitions, simply code INCLUDE anywhere in your program's WORKING-STORAGE SECTION.[3] As with all embedded SQL statements, INCLUDE must be typed between columns 12 and 72, begin with EXEC SQL, and end with END-EXEC.

You may remember an example of INCLUDE from chapter 1. We used it to obtain a copy of the SQLCA. When you want to copy in your DCLGEN statements, you code:

```
EXEC SQL INCLUDE      copybook END-EXEC.
```

---

[3]Ordinarily, you use INCLUDE to bring WORKING-STORAGE copybooks, but you may also use INCLUDE to pull in SQL or COBOL statements anywhere in your program.

where copybook is the PDS member name used to store the output from DCLGEN. You can obtain the PDS member name from the DBA who executed DCLGEN for the table your program's SQL statements reference, or simply make a note of the member name if you executed DCLGEN yourself.

The entire DCLGEN/INCLUDE process is illustrated for you in Figure 17.

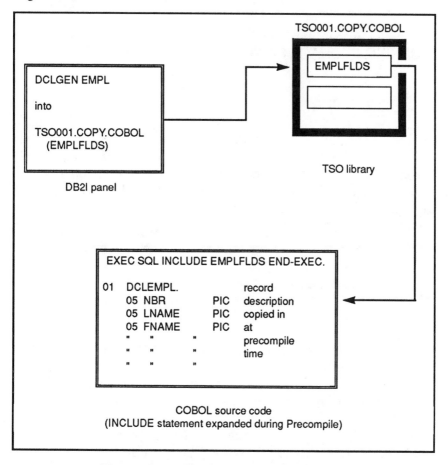

Figure 17. DCLGEN/INCLUDE process.

One item you will always INCLUDE in your SQL/COBOL programs is the SQLCA. This is a required set of WORKING-STORAGE fields used b, DB2 to communicate the success or failure of your SQL statement's execution. You will use the following statement to INCLUDE this data item in your program:

```
EXEC SQL    INCLUDE SQLCA   END-EXEC.
```

The SQLCA can be INCLUDED anywhere in your program's WORKING-STORAGE SECTION.

2.9.   WHENEVER

IBM has provided an error-handling mechanism that you can utilize in your program. It is activated by the WHENEVER statement. WHENEVER has several options which we will cover in more detail in chapter 5. For now, you will use WHENEVER to specify automatic error-handling on severe DB2 data access errors. You do this by coding the following:

```
EXEC SQL
      WHENEVER SQLERROR   GO   TO   error-handling-paragraph
END-EXEC.
```

at the beginning of the PROCEDURE DIVISION. You can actually place this statement anywhere "physically" before your first SQL statement, but I recommend standardizing on coding WHENEVER just after entry to your program.

WHENEVER inserts COBOL statements into your application program. Specifically, it adds IF-THEN-ELSE conditional logic to test for a value placed into SQLCODE by DB2. SQLCODE is a field in your program's SQLCA WORKING-STORAGE, which DB2 uses to communicate to your program the status (success or failure) of your SQL statement execution. If DB2 encounters an error while processing an SQL statement, the return code is a negative number. And if you've coded a WHENEVER statement like the one shown in the above example, program control will unconditionally branch to the error-handling paragraph specified as part of the WHENEVER statement.

WHENEVER is an embedded SQL statement and therefore must follow the same coding rules as all the other SQL statements:

WHENEVER:

- Must be typed between columns 12 and 72
- Begin with EXEC SQL
- End with END-EXEC.
- Follow a specific format

You will learn how to code various "specific formats" of the WHENEVER statement in chapter 5. Until then, place the following statement at the beginning of the Procedure Division in your programs:

```
EXEC SQL
      WHENEVER SQLERROR  GO  TO  999-ERROR-TRAP-RTN
END-EXEC.
```

This will cause your program to unconditionally branch to paragraph 999 if a severe SQL error is returned by DB2.

2.10.   SAMPLE PROGRAM I — SAMPLE01

The following pages show an example of a batch TSO program called SAMPLE01, which illustrates many of the SQL coding techniques covered in this chapter. You should "walk through" the program, carefully noting the following embedded SQL coding techniques:

•   INCLUDE SQLCA statement,

•   EMPL and PAY copybooks — externally copied into the program using the ISPF Editor,

•   The COBOL host program variables contained in the copybooks — definition and use,

•   WHENEVER SQLERROR statement,

•   The required COBOL MOVE statements to set up the SELECT statement

•   The SQL SINGLTON SELECT statement:
    — Coding format
    — host program variable usage (which fields refer to host program variables and which refer to DB2 table columns)
    — INTO clause,

•   The use of the DB2 data to produce the report line,

•   The error-handling paragraph (999)
    — Which WORKING-STORAGE fields were dumped.

This program should run if typed in correctly and preprocessed (we will cover program preprocessing in depth in chapter 3). You might wish to type it into a COBOL dataset on your TSO ID at this point. After reading chapter 3 you will be able to preprocess and execute it.

Again, remember to look at the tables illustrated in section 2.12 of this chapter.

```
 IDENTIFICATION DIVISION.
 PROGRAM-ID. SAMPLE01.
*REMARKS.    THIS PROGRAM READS IN EMPLOYEE NUMBERS FROM A
*TRANSACTION FILE, AND PRODUCES A REPORT LINE,
*ONE LINE FOR EACH EMPLOYEE.  THE TRANSACTION FILE HAS
*ONE FIELD IN IT, WHICH CONTAINS EMPLOYEE NUMBERS.
*THE TRANSACTION FILE IS CALLED EMPL-FILE-IN.
*THE PROGRAM USES THE EMPLOYEE DATABASE WHICH IS ILLUSTRATED
*IN APPENDIX B OF THIS BOOK
*
ENVIRONMENT DIVISION.
CONFIGURATION SECTION.
SOURCE-COMPUTER. IBM-370.
OBJECT-COMPUTER. IBM-370.
INPUT-OUTPUT SECTION.
FILE-CONTROL.
     SELECT EMPL-FILE-IN ASSIGN TO UT-S-EMPFILE.
DATA DIVISION.

FILE SECTION.

FD  EMPL-FILE-IN
RECORDING MODE IS F
BLOCK CONTAINS 0 RECORDS
RECORD CONTAINS 80 CHARACTERS
LABEL RECORDS ARE OMITTED
DATA RECORD IS EMPL-REC-IN.



01   EMPL-REC-IN.
         05 EMPL-NBR-IN   PIC X(02).
         05 FILLER        PIC X(78).

WORKING-STORAGE SECTION.
```

```
*  HOST PROGRAM VARIABLES — DATA ITEMS EXPLICITLY DEFINED
*  NOTE * THESE HOST VARIABLES WERE CREATED USING DCLGEN
*  I PULLED THEM INTO THE PROGRAM USING THE ISPF EDITOR
*  IF I WANTED TO INCLUDE THEM AT PRECOMPILE TIME, I WOULD
*  HAVE SPECIFIED THE FOLLOWING:
```

```
        EXEC SQL INCLUDE EMPL END-EXEC.
        EXEC SQL INCLUDE PAY END-EXEC.
```

```
DCLGEN TABLE(EMPL)
            LIBRARY(@TSOID.SPUFI.CNTL(DCLEMPL))
            APOST
. . . IS THE DCLGEN COMMAND THAT MADE THE FOLLOWING STATEMENTS
```

```
    EXEC SQL DECLARE EMPL TABLE
    (  NBR                    CHAR(2),
       LNAME                  CHAR(10),
       FNAME                  CHAR(6),
       DOB                    INTEGER,
       HIREDTE                INTEGER,
       PERF                   SMALLINT,
       JOB                    CHAR(4),
       DEPT                   CHAR(3),
       PROJ                   CHAR(2)
    )  END-EXEC.
```

```
COBOL DECLARATION FOR TABLE EMPL
```

```
01 DCLEMPL.
    10 NBR                  PIC  X(2).
    10 LNAME                PIC  X(10).
    10 FNAME                PIC  X(6).
    10 DOB                  PIC  S9(9)  USAGE COMP.
    10 HIREDTE              PIC  S9(9)  USAGE COMP.
    10 PER                  PIC  S9(4)  USAGE COMP.
    10 JOB                  PIC  X(4).
    10 DEPT                 PIC  X(3).
    10 PROJ                 PIC  X(2).
```

```
THE NUMBER OF COLUMNS DESCRIBED BY THIS DECLARATION IS 9
```

```
DCLGEN TABLE(PAY)
          LIBRARY(@TSOID.SPUFI.CNTL(DCLPAY))
          APOST
. . . IS THE DCLGEN COMMAND THAT MADE THE FOLLOWING STATEMENTS
```

```
   EXEC SQL DECLARE PAY TABLE
   (  NBR                    CHAR(2),
      HOURS                  DECIMAL(5,  2),
      RATE                   DECIMAL(5,  2),
      DED                    DECIMAL(5,  2),
      YTD                    DECIMAL(8,  2)
   ) END-EXEC.
```

```
COBOL DECLARATION FOR TABLE PAY
```

```
01 DCLPAY.
   10 NBR                    PIC  X(2).
   10 HOURS                  PIC  S999V99     USAGE  COMP-3.
   10 RATE                   PIC  S999V99     USAGE  COMP-3.
   10 DED                    PIC  S999V99     USAGE  COMP-3.
   10 YTD                    PIC  S999999V99  USAGE  COMP-3.
```

```
THE NUMBER OF COLUMNS DESCRIBED BY THIS DECLARATION IS 5
```

```
SQL COMMUNICATIONS AREA — DATA ITEMS PULLED IN VIA INCLUDE
```

Note: include of SQLCA
required fields

```
          EXEC SQL INCLUDE SQLCA END-EXEC.
```

```
*MISCELLANEOUS WORKING-STORAGE DATA ITEMS
```

```
01   WS-KTRS-SWITCHES.
     05 SW-EOF              PIC  X(01) VALUE 'N'.
        88 END-OF-FILE                 VALUE 'Y'.
     05 EMPL-FILE-IN-KTR PIC  S9(03) COMP-3  VALUE  +0.
     05 EMPL-ROW-KTR        PIC  S9(03) COMP-3  VALUE  +0.
     05 NBR-EMPL            PIC  X(02).
     05 SQLCODE-OUT         PIC  9(03) VALUE ZERO.
```

```
01   EMPL-FILE-MSG.
     05 FILLER            PIC  X(26)
        VALUE '* * * EMP FILE RECS IN -->'.
     05 EMPL-FILE-IN-STAT PIC  Z99.

01   EMPL-ROW-MSG.
     05 FILLER            PIC  X(24)
        VALUE  '* * * EMPL ROWS READ -->'.
     05 EMPL-ROW-STAT     PIC  Z99.

PROCEDURE DIVISION.
000-SETUP-ERROR-TRAP-RTN.
```

```
* THIS PORTION OF THE PROGRAM ACTIVATES THE SQL ERROR TRAPPING
* FACILITIES.  AT PRECOMPILE TIME, THE DB2 PRECOMPILER
* GENERATES COBOL INSTRUCTIONS TO INTERROGATE THE SQLCODE
* (RETURN CODE) FROM EACH CALL.  IF A SQLERROR CONDITION IS
* DETECTED (NEGATIVE RETURN CODE), EXECUTION WILL BRANCH TO THE
* 999-ERROR-TRAP-RTN TO DISPLAY AN APPROPRIATE ERROR MSG.
```

```
EXEC SQL
     WHENEVER SQLERROR  GO  TO  999-ERROR-TRAP-RTN
END-EXEC.
```

```
000-MAINLINE-RTN.
```

```
* THE MAINLINE CONTAINS THE DRIVER CODE TO PERFORM OUR DATA
* BASE ACCESS AND DISPLAY ROUTINES.

    OPEN INPUT EMPL-FILE-IN.

    PERFORM 600-READ-EMPL-FILE-IN THRU 600-EXIT.


    PERFORM 100-SELECT-RTN THRU 100-EXIT
        UNTIL END-OF-FILE OR SQLCODE LESS THAN 0.
```

```
    PERFORM 300-TERMINATE-RTN THRU 300-EXIT.

    MOVE ZERO TO RETURN-CODE.
    GOBACK.

000-EXIT.
    EXIT.


100-SELECT-RTN.


*  THIS STATEMENT IS KNOWN AS A SINGLETON SELECT, BECAUSE
*  IT RETURNS A SINGLE ROW FROM THE DATABASE
```

	Note:	move of search field from file to WS

```
            MOVE EMPL-NBR-IN TO NBR-EMPL.
```

```
    EXEC SQL
       SELECT
                      LNAME, FNAME, HOURS, RATE
               INTO
                      :LNAME, :FNAME, :HOURS, :RATE
       FROM
         EMPL,  PAY
       WHERE
         EMPL.NBR = PAY.NBR
         AND EMPL.NBR  =   :NBR-EMPL
    END-EXEC.
```

```
    IF SQLCODE = ZERO
       DISPLAY LNAME, FNAME, HOURS, RATE
       ADD +1 TO EMPL-ROW-KTR.

  PERFORM 600-READ-EMPL-FILE-IN THRU 600-EXIT.

100-EXIT.
    EXIT.
```

```
300-TERMINATE-RTN.                    `
    CLOSE EMPL-FILE-IN.

    MOVE EMPL-FILE-IN-KTR TO EMPL-FILE-IN-STAT.
    MOVE EMPL-ROW-KTR TO EMPL-ROW-STAT.

    DISPLAY EMPL-FILE-MSG.
    DISPLAY EMPL-ROW-MSG.

300-EXIT.
    EXIT.

600-READ-EMPL-FILE-IN.
    READ EMPL-FILE-IN
        AT END
            MOVE 'Y' TO SW-EOF
            GO TO 600-EXIT
    ADD +1 TO EMPL-FILE-IN-KTR.

600-EXIT.
    EXIT.

999-ERROR-TRAP-RTN.
    DISPLAY SQLCA.
    MOVE SQLCODE TO SQLCODE-OUT.
    DISPLAY SQLCODE-OUT.
999-EXIT.
    EXIT.
```

2.11.   WORKSHOP I — EASY COBOL/SQL PROGRAM

Now it's your turn to try coding the SQL statements for a complete
SQL/COBOL program. Shown below is a skeleton COBOL program called EZPROG. COBOL comments embedded in the program specify what actions you are to take to complete the
specified tasks, adding:

- SQL SELECT, UPDATE, and DELETE statements
- WHENEVER statement
- INCLUDE statement(s)

I have coded the error-handling paragraph for you. However, you must create the WHENEVER statement to branch to it upon receiving an SQL error condition from DB2. In the next chapter you will learn how to preprocess this program using JCL or the DB2I panels. For now, you can check your work with my solution given in appendix A.

Be sure to read all comments carefully.

```
IDENTIFICATION DIVISION.
PROGRAM-ID. EZPROG.
*REMARKS.  THIS PROGRAM REINFORCES THE CONCEPTS COVERED IN
*CHAPTER TWO OF THIS BOOK.
*YOU MUST SATISFY THE THREE REQUESTS LISTED IN THE
*PROCEDURE DIVISION USING EMBEDDED SQL STATEMENTS. THE
 PROGRAM
*LOGIC BASICALLY FALLS THROUGH THESE REQUESTS AND
 EXECUTES
*THEM SEQUENTIALLY.  YOU MAY USE LITERALS OR HOST VARIABLES.
*IF YOU CHOOSE TO USE HOST VARIABLES FOR REQUESTS 2 AND 3
 YOU
*WILL HAVE TO CREATE YOUR OWN IN THE WORKING-STORAGE
 SECTION.
*
*EZPROG USES THE VIDEO STORE DATABASE WHICH IS ILLUSTRATED
*IN APPENDIX B OF THIS BOOK
*
ENVIRONMENT DIVISION.
CONFIGURATION SECTION.
SOURCE-COMPUTER. IBM-370.
OBJECT-COMPUTER. IBM-370.
INPUT-OUTPUT SECTION.
DATA DIVISION.
```

```
FILE SECTION.

WORKING-STORAGE SECTION.


* HOST PROGRAM VARIABLES — DATA ITEMS EXPLICITLY DEFINED
* THESE COPYBOOKS WERE CREATED BY DCLGEN, AND COPIED INTO
* EZPROG MANUALLY.  IF YOU WANTED TO COPY THEM IN USING INCLUDE
* YOU WOULD CODE:
```

```
        EXEC SQL INCLUDE MOV END-EXEC.
        EXEC SQL INCLUDE CUST END-EXEC.
```

```
COBOL DECLARATION FOR TABLE MOV

01 DCLMOV.
   10 NBR              PIC S9(4)    USAGE COMP.
   10 TITLE-X          PIC X(20).
   10 TYPE-X           PIC X(6).
   10 RATING           PIC X(4).
   10 STAR             PIC X(10).
   10 QTY              PIC S9(4)  USAGE COMP.
   10 PRICE            PIC S999V99 USAGE COMP-3.

THE NUMBER OF COLUMNS DESCRIBED BY THIS DECLARATION IS 7
```

> Title and Type are reserved words in COBOL, so I had to rename them.

```
COBOL DECLARATION FOR TABLE CUST

01 DCLCUST.
   10 ID-X             PIC X(2).
   10 LNAME            PIC X(12).
   10 FNAME            PIC X(6).
   10 CITY             PIC X(15).
   10 ST               PIC X(2).

THE NUMBER OF COLUMNS DESCRIBED BY THIS DECLARATION IS 5
```

> Ditto for ID.

```
*  CODE THE INCLUDE STATEMENT HERE FOR THE SQL COMMUNICATIONS AREA
```

```
        EXEC SQL ??????  ?????  END-EXEC.
```

```
*  MISCELLANEOUS WORKING-STORAGE DATA ITEMS
   01   WS-KTRS-SWITCHES.
      05 SQLCODE-OUT   PIC 9(03)   VALUE 0.
```

```
 PROCEDURE DIVISION.
 000-SETUP-ERROR-TRAP-RTN.
```

```
*  THIS PORTION OF THE PROGRAM ACTIVATES THE SQL ERROR TRAPPING
*  FACILITIES.  AT PRE-COMPILE TIME, THE DB2 PRECOMPILER
*  GENERATES COBOL INSTRUCTIONS TO INTERROGATE THE SQLCODE
*  (RETURN CODE) FROM EACH CALL. IF A SQLERROR CONDITION IS
*  DETECTED (NEGATIVE RETURN CODE), EXECUTION WILL BRANCH TO THE
*  999-ERROR-TRAP-RTN TO DISPLAY AN APPROPRIATE ERROR MSG.
```

```
 EXEC SQL
     WHENEVER  ???????  ????  ?????????????????
 END-EXEC.
```

```
000-MAINLINE-RTN.
```

```
                     REQUEST 1
 CODE AN EMBEDDED SELECT STATEMENT TO RETURN THE
 MOVIE NUMBER, TITLE,  AND PRICE FOR 'TOOTSIE'
```

```
 MOVE SPACES TO DCLMOV.
 MOVE 'TOOTSIE' TO TITLE OF DCLMOV.
```

```
EXEC SQL
    SELECT    ????????????????????????????????
    INTO      ????????????????????????????????
    FROM      ????????????????????????????????
    WHERE     ????????????????????????????????
END-EXEC.
```

```
DISPLAY `****** REQUEST  1 ******'.
IF SQLCODE = ZERO
  DISPLAY DCLMOV.
DISPLAY SPACES.
```

```
                         REQUEST 2
CODE AN EMBEDDED SELECT STATEMENT TO RETURN THE
MOVIE QTY, PRICE AND TITLE FOR ALL COMEDIES COSTING
OVER $200 BUT LESS THAN $400   (USE BETWEEN).
```

```
MOVE SPACES TO DCLMOV.
MOVE 200    TO ??????.
MOVE 400    TO ??????.
```

```
EXEC SQL
    SELECT    ??????????????????????????????
    INTO      ??????????????????????????????
    FROM      ??????????????????????????????
    WHERE     ????????????? BETWEEN  ????? AND  ?????
END-EXEC.
```

```
DISPLAY `****** REQUEST  2 ******'.
IF SQLCODE = ZERO
  DISPLAY DCLMOV.
DISPLAY SPACES.
```

```
                          REQUEST 3
        CODE AN EMBEDDED SELECT STATEMENT TO RETURN
        ALL CUSTOMER INFORMATION FOR CUSTOMERS FROM HAWAII
        WYOMING AND VERMONT   ***(USE IN)***
        HARD CODE THE  IN  PORTION OF YOUR WHERE CLAUSE
        USING LITERALS VALUES — NOT HOST VARIABLES
```

MOVE SPACES TO DCLCUST.

```
EXEC SQL
    SELECT     ????????????????????????????????
    INTO       ????????????????????????????????
    FROM       ????????????????????????????????
    WHERE      ?????????  IN  ??????????????
END-EXEC.
```

    DISPLAY '****** REQUEST 3 ******'.
IF SQLCODE = ZERO
    DISPLAY DCLCUST.
DISPLAY SPACES.

DISPLAY '**** NORMAL END-OF-JOB ***'.
MOVE ZERO TO RETURN-CODE.
    GOBACK.

999-ERROR-TRAP-RTN.

ERROR TRAPPING ROUTINE FOR NEGATIVE SQLCODES

    DISPLAY '**** WE HAVE A SERIOUS PROBLEM HERE *****'.
    DISPLAY''999-ERROR-TRAP-RTN' '.
    MOVE SQLCODE TO SQLCODE-OUT.
    DISPLAY 'SQLCODE ==>' ' SQLCODE-OUT.
    DISPLAY SQLCA.
    DISPLAY SQLERRM.
    EXEC SQL ROLLBACK WORK END-EXEC.
        GOBACK.
999-EXIT.
    EXIT.

2.12. WORKSHOP II — SINGLETON SELECT PROGRAM

This program is a bit more difficult from an SQL processing complexity standpoint. Look over the flowchart in Figure 18 to make sure you understand the inputs and search arguments used in the SQL statement. There is only one SQL SELECT in the program, but it is rather complex, and you should try out your SQL solution using DB2I or QMF before you code it in your program. As in EZPROG, the specifications are given in the IDENTIFICATION DIVISION as comments. Helpful hints are also placed strategically throughout the rest of the program.

My solution can be found in Appendix B.

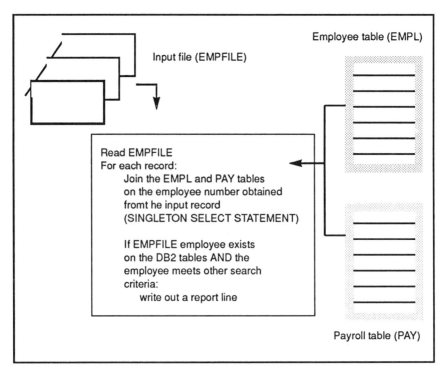

Figure 18. SINGLETON SQL statement inputs and search conditions.

```
IDENTIFICATION DIVISION.
PROGRAM-ID. SINGLTON.
*REMARKS.  THIS PROGRAM READS IN AN EMPLOYEE NUMBER FROM A
* FILE, SEARCHES A DB2 TABLE FOR THE EMPLOYEE ON THE
* FILE, JOINS THE EMPL AND PAY TABLES, AND PRODUCES
* A REPORT LINE FOR EMPLOYEES ON THE FILE, WHO:
* MAKE OVER $30,000, AND WHOSE PERF IS 1, 3 OR 5
* OR . . . . . . . . . .
* ARE IN THE MARKETING DEPARTMENT
*
ENVIRONMENT DIVISION.
CONFIGURATION SECTION.
SOURCE-COMPUTER. IBM-370.
OBJECT-COMPUTER. IBM-370.


INPUT-OUTPUT SECTION.
FILE-CONTROL.
      SELECT EMPL-FILE-IN ASSIGN TO UT-S-EMPFILE.
DATA DIVISION.


FILE SECTION.


FD  EMPL-FILE-IN
RECORDING MODE IS F
BLOCK CONTAINS 0 RECORDS
RECORD CONTAINS 80 CHARACTERS
LABEL RECORDS ARE OMITTED
DATA RECORD IS EMPL-REC-IN.


01 EMPL-REC-IN.
    05 EMPL-NBR-IN    PIC X(02).
    05 FILLER         PIC X(78).


WORKING-STORAGE SECTION.

*HOST PROGRAM VARIABLES — DATA ITEMS EXPLICITLY DEFINED
```

```
***  CODE INCLUDE STATEMENTS HERE TO COPY IN THE TABLE DECLARATIONS
***  FOR THE EMPL AND PAY TABLES — DESCRIPTIONS CAN BE FOUND IN
***  APPENDIX B.
***  THE INCLUDED COPYBOOKS WILL HAVE TO BE CREATED BY RUNNING
***  DCLGEN
```



```
┌────────────────────────────────────────────────────────────┐
│                                                            │
└────────────────────────────────────────────────────────────┘
```

```
┌────────────────────────────────────────────────────────────┐
│                                                            │
└────────────────────────────────────────────────────────────┘
```

```
***  CODE THE STATEMENT(S) HERE TO INCLUDE THE SQLCA
```

```
┌────────────────────────────────────────────────────────────┐
│                                                            │
└────────────────────────────────────────────────────────────┘
```

```
* MISCELLANEOUS WORKING-STORAGE DATA ITEMS


01 WS-KTRS-SWITCHES.
     05 SW-EOF          PIC X(01) VALUE 'N'.
        88 END-OF-FILE    VALUE 'Y'.
     05 EMPL-FILE-IN-KTR  PIC S9(03) COMP-3 VALUE +0.
        05 EMPL-ROW-KTR    PIC S9(03) COMP-3 VALUE +0.


01 OUTPUT-ROW.
     05 FILLER          PIC X(01) VALUE SPACES.
     05 NBR-RPTPIC X(02).
     05 FILLER          PIC X(04) VALUE SPACES.
     05 LNAME-RPT       PIC X(14).
     05 FILLER          PIC X(04) VALUE SPACES.
     05 FNAME-RPT       PIC X(08).
     05 FILLER          PIC X(04) VALUE SPACES.
     05 HOURS-RPT       PIC Z(02).99.
     05 FILLER          PIC X(04) VALUE SPACES.
     05 RATE-RPT        PIC Z(02).99.
```

```
01 EMPL-FILE-MSG.
      05 FILLER          PIC X(26)
         VALUE '* * * EMP FILE RECS IN ->'.
      05 EMPL-FILE-IN-STAT    PIC Z99.
      01 EMPL-REC-WS.
      05 EMPL-NBR-WS    PIC X(02).

01 EMPL-ROW-MSG.
      05 FILLER          PIC X(24)
         VALUE '* * * EMPL ROWS READ ->'.
      05 EMPL-ROW-STAT    PIC Z99.

* ERROR MSG AREA FOR CALLS TO DSNTIAR — WHICH DECODES YOUR SQL
* RETURN CODES (SQLCODE) FOR YOU.

01 ERROR-MSG.
      05 ERROR-LEN   PIC S9(04) COMP VALUE +960.
      05 ERROR-TEXT PIC X(120) OCCURS 8 TIMES
      INDEXED BY ERR-IDX.
01 ERROR-TEXT-LEN     PIC S9(09) COMP VALUE +120.

PROCEDURE DIVISION.

000-SETUP-ERROR-TRAP-RTN.

* THIS PORTION OF THE PROGRAM ACTIVATES THE SQL ERROR TRAPPING
* FACILITIES.  AT PRE-COMPILE TIME, THE D82 PRECOMPILER
* GENERATES COBOL INSTRUCTIONS TO INTERROGATE THE SQLCODE
* (RETURN CODE) FROM EACH CALL.  IF A SQLERROR CONDITION IS
* DETECTED (NEGATIVE RETURN CODE), EXECUTION WILL BRANCH TO
* 999-ERROR-TRAP-RTN WHICH WILL DISPLAY AN APPROPRIATE ERROR MSG.

* = = = = >   CODE YOUR ERROR TRAPPING STATEMENT(S) HERE
┌─────────────────────────────────────────────────────────────┐
│                                                             │
└─────────────────────────────────────────────────────────────┘

000-MAINLINE-RTN.

* THE MAINLINE CONTAINS THE DRIVER CODE TO PERFORM OUR DATA BASE
* ACCESS AND DISPLAY ROUTINES.
```

```
        OPEN INPUT EMPL-FILE-IN.

        PERFORM 100-READ-INFILE THRU 100-EXIT.

        PERFORM 200-DISPLAY-RPT THRU 200-EXIT
           UNTIL SQLCODE LESS THAN ZERO OR END-OF-FILE.

        PERFORM 300-TERMINATE-RTN THRU 300-EXIT.
        MOVE ZERO TO RETURN-CODE.
        GOBACK.

000-EXIT.
    EXIT.
100-READ-INFILE.

    READ  EMPL-FILE-IN
       AT END
    MOVE 'Y' TO SW-EOF
    GO TO 100-EXIT.

    ADD 1 TO EMPL-FILE-IN-KTR.


100-EXIT.
    EXIT.


200-DISPLAY-RPT.

* THIS PARAGRAPH SETS UP THE SQL PARAMETERS, PERFORMS THE
* PARAGRAPH TO MAKE THE CALL AND DISPLAYS THE RESULTS.
        PERFORM 250-CALL-DB2-RTN THRU 250-EXIT.

        IF SQLCODE = ZERO
        THEN
           MOVE NBR OF DCLEMPL TO NBR-RPT
           MOVE LNAME TO LNAME-RPT
           MOVE FNAME TO FNAME-RPT
           MOVE HOURS TO HOURS-RPT
           MOVE RATE TO RATE-RPT
```

```
            DISPLAY OUTPUT-ROW
            ADD +1 TO EMPL-ROW-KTR
        ELSE
            NEXT SENTENCE.

        PERFORM 100-READ-INFILE THRU 100-EXIT.

200-EXIT.
    EXIT.

250-CALL-DB2-RTN.

*  THIS PARAGRAPH SELECTS A ROW FROM THE EMPL AND PAY TABLES
*  JOINED ON EMPLOYEE NUMBER — WHICH IS OBTAINED FROM THE CURRENT
*  RECORD IN EMPL-FILE-IN.   SELECT CRITERIA INCLUDE:
*  — EMPLOYEE NUMBER FROM INPUT FILE USED AS SEARCH CONDITION
*  — (EARNINGS (YTD ON THE PAY TABLE) OVER $30,000 AND
*  PERFORMANCE EVALUATION = 1, 3, 5) OR
*  — (EMPLOYEE IS IN THE MARKETING DEPT)

        MOVE EMPL-NBR-IN    TO EMPL-NBR-WS.

*         CODE YOUR SINGLTON SELECT STATEMENT HERE            *
┌────────────────────────────────────────────────────────────┐
│                                                            │
│                                                            │
│                                                            │
│                                                            │
│                                                            │
└────────────────────────────────────────────────────────────┘


250-EXIT.
    EXIT.

300-TERMINATE-RTN.

        CLOSE EMPL-FILE-IN.
```

```
        MOVE EMPL-FILE-IN-KTR TO EMPL-FILE-IN-STAT.
        MOVE EMPL-ROW-KTR TO EMPL-ROW-STAT.

        DISPLAY EMPL-FILE-MSG.
        DISPLAY EMPL-ROW-MSG.

300-EXIT.
    EXIT.

999-ERROR-TRAP-RTN.

        ERROR TRAPPING ROUTINE FOR NEGATIVE SQLCODES


        DISPLAY '**** WE HAVE A SERIOUS PROBLEM HERE *****'.
        DISPLAY '999-ERROR-TRAP-RTN '.
        MULTIPLY SQLCODE BY -1 GIVING SQLCODE.
        DISPLAY 'SQLCODE ==> ' SQLCODE.
        DISPLAY SQLCA.
        DISPLAY SQLERRM.
        EXEC SQL ROLLBACK WORK END-EXEC.
        GOBACK.
999-EXIT.
    EXIT.
```

2.13.   EMPLOYEE AND VIDEO STORE DATABASE TABLES

VIDEO STORE DATABASE — PART 1 OF 2

BASE TABLE — MOV:

NBR	TITLE	TYPE	RATING	STAR	QTY	PRICE
1	GONE WITH THE WIND	DRAMA		GABLE	4	39.95
2	FRIDAY THE 13TH	HORROR	R	JASON	2	69.95
3	TOP GUN	DRAMA	PG	CRUISE	7	49.95
4	SPLASH	COMEDY	PG13	HANKS	3	29.95
5	101 DALMATIONS	COMEDY	G		3	59.95
6	BODY HEAT	DRAMA	R	TURNER	3	19.95
7	RISKY BUSINESS	COMEDY	R	CRUISE	2	44.55
8	COCOON	SCIFI	PG	AMECHE	2	
9	CROCODILE DUNDEE	COMEDY	PG13	HARRIS	2	69.95
10	TOOTSIE	COMEDY	PG	HOFFMAN	1	29.95

BASE TABLE — CUST:

ID	LNAME	FNAME	CITY	ST
01	DANGERFIELD	RODNEY	HARTFORD	CT
02	FIELD	SALLY	FRANKLIN	NY
03	NICHOLSON	JACK	HARTFORD	CT
04	MURRAY	FRED	BOZRAH	CT
05	MADDEN	JOHN	BRATTLEBORO	VT
06	WEST	MAE	PARK PLACE	CA
07	WOODWARD	JOANNE	GETTYSBURG	PA
08	ROGERS	ROY	HAPPY TRAILS	TX
09	RINGWALD	MOLLY	PINKSVILLE	CA
10	ROGERS	FRED	PARK PLACE	CA

VIDEO STORE DATABASE — PART 2 OF 2

BASE TABLE — I_M:

I_NBR	M_NBR
1	4
1	5
2	3
3	1
3	10
4	6
4	3
4	5
4	1
5	1
5	7
7	1
7	3
7	5
8	4
8	7
9	9
9	2
10	4
10	4
10	1
10	5
10	4

BASE TABLE — INV:

NBR	CUSTID	TOT	RENT	RETURN
1	01	9.55	87055	
2	02	13.55	87030	
3	02	21.01	87041	87042
4	01	11.25	87042	87072
5	03	12.55	87045	87051
6	02	9.75	87047	87051
7	04	10.35	86355	
8	04	12.55	87051	87053
9	05	10.35	87052	
10	02	7.55	87030	87060

EMPLOYEE DATABASE

BASE TABLE — EMPL:

NBR	LNAME	FNAME	DOB	HIREDTE	PERF	JOB	DEPT	PROJ
01	LOWE	ROB	53012	85012	4	PROG	FIN	01
02	SHIELDS	BROOKE	59131	87001	3	MAN	MKT	01
03	MOORE	ROGER	48111	86002	1	DIR	MKT	04
04	EASTWOOD	CLINT	41091	60120	3	PROG	FIN	03
05	MOSTEL	ZERO	21365	84211		PRES		
06	BURNS	GEORGE	11178	49001	2	SYS	FIN	01
07	O'NEAL	RYAN	42189	60121	3	DIR	ACC	05
08	MARVIN	LEE	32187	51876	2	VP	ACC	02
09	LANCASTER	BURT	41091	79092	1	AN	R&D	02
10	BLAIR	LINDA	54013	85012	1	PROG	MKT	

BASE TABLE — PAY:

NBR	HOURS	RATE	DED	YTD
01	8.89	43	128.78	11890.66
02	13.23	40	204.45	15840.78
03	6.11	49	94.76	11890.66
04	26.75	45	132.58	17605.66
05	67.82	37	394.69	79990.99
06	32.45	32	121.99	53421.23
07	26.75	49	101.56	32758.11
08	15.99	52	327.98	67870.01
09	43.59	24	0	28090.91
10	32.41	52	112.78	27000.01

2.14.   ANSWERS TO SELECTED EXERCISES
(in figures 13, 14, 15, and 16)

2.14.1   SELECT (part 1)

INTERACTIVE SQL	EMBEDDED SQL
| ```
SELECT NBR, TITLE, STAR
    FROM MOV
    WHERE TITLE = 'COCOON';
``` | ```
EXEC SQL
    SELECT NBR, TITLE, STAR
    INTO :NBR, :TITLE, :STAR
    FROM MOV
        WHERE TITLE = :TITLE
END-EXEC.
``` |
| ```
SELECT *
    FROM PROJ
        WHERE NAME = 'SYSTEM R';
``` | ```
EXEC SQL
    SELECT *
    INTO :NBR, :NAME, :DEPT,
        :MAJPROJ
        FROM PROJ
        WHERE NAME = :NAME
END-EXEC.
``` |
| ```
SELECT NBR
    FROM INV, CUST
        WHERE ID = CUSTID AND
        LNAME = 'WEST';
``` | ```
EXEC SQL
    SELECT NBR FROM INV, CUST
        WHERE ID = CUSTID AND
        LNAME = :LNAME


END-EXEC.
``` |
| ```
SELECT LNAME, HOURS, RATE,
        HOURS * RATE - DED
    FROM PAY,EMPL
    WHERE EMPL.NBR = PAY.NBR AND
    EMPL.NBR = 10;
``` | ```
EXEC SQL
    SELECT LNAME, HOURS, RATE,
        HOURS * RATE - DED
    INTO :LNAME, :HOURS, :RATE,
        :PAYCHECK FROM EMPL, PAY
    WHERE EMPL.NBR = PAY.NBR AND
            EMPL.NBR = :NBR-WS
END-EXEC.
``` |

2.14.1   SELECT (part 2)

INTERACTIVE SQL	EMBEDDED SQL
SELECT DEPT, AVG(YTD), MAX(YTD) FROM EMPL, PAY WHERE EMPL.NBR = PAY.NBR GROUP BY DEPT HAVING AVG(YTD) > 20000;	(see note #1) EXEC SQL SELECT DEPT, AVG(YTD), MAX(YTD) INTO :DEPT, :AVG-PAY, :MAX-PAY FROM EMPL, PAY WHERE WHERE EMPL.NBR = PAY.NBR GROUP BY DEPT HAVING AVG(YTD) > :MIN-VALUE
SELECT TITLE FROM MOV CORR_VAR WHERE NOT EXISTS (SELECT * FROM I_M WHERE M_NBR = CORR_VAR.NBR);	EXEC SQL SELECT TITLE INTO :TITLE FROM MOV CORR_VAR WHERE NOT EXISTS (SELECT * FROM I_M WHERE M_NBR = CORR_VAR.NBR) END-EXEC. (see note #2)

NOTE #1 — This statement should be coded using a symbolic cursor (see chapter 6), as there is a good chance that more than one row will be returned and a run-time error will result.

NOTE #2 — This rather philosophical query tests for movies that have not been rented (the fact that an entry exists for a movie number — M_NBR on the I_M table — signifies that the movie has been rented). It can be used as part of an outer-join, and is also useful in scrubbing tables for referential integrity problems.

2.14.2 INSERT

INTERACTIVE SQL	EMBEDDED SQL

INSERT INTO MOV
  VALUES
(23, 'BOTTOM GUN', 'PG13',
      'COMEDY', 'FRED GWYNNE',
      12, .41);
	EXEC SQL
	  INSERT INTO MOV VALUES
	    (:NBR,
	    :TITLE,
	    :RATING,
	     :TYPE,
	    :STAR,
	    :QTY,
	    :PRICE)
	END-EXEC.

INSERT INTO INV
  VALUES
(33, '12', 24.00, 89001, NULL)
	EXEC SQL
	    INSERT INTO INV VALUES
	    (:NBR,
	  :CUSTID,
	  :TOTAL,
	  :RENT,
	  NULL)
	END-EXEC.

INSERT INTO PAY
(NBR, HOURS, RATE, DED, YTD)
  VALUES
(31, 14, 23.99, 3300, 44000);
	EXEC SQL
	    INSERT INTO PAY
	    VALUES
	    (:NBR, :RATE,
	         :HOURS, :DED,
	     :YTD)
	END-EXEC.

2.14.3 UPDATE

INTERACTIVE SQL	EMBEDDED SQL

``
UPDATE MOV
   SET QTY = 8
      WHERE NBR = 9;
``
	``
	EXEC SQL
	   UPDATE MOV
	      SET
	         QTY = :QTY
	            WHERE NBR = :NBR
	END-EXEC.
	``

``
UPDATE MOV
   SET PRICE = PRICE * 1.15;
``
	``
	COMPUTE PRICE = PRICE * 1.15
	
	EXEC SQL
	      UPDATE MOV
	            SET PRICE = :PRICE
	END-EXEC.
	``

``
UPDATE MOV
   SET RATING = 'X',
      WHERE TYPE = 'HORROR';
``
	``
	MOVE INP-RATING TO HVAR-RATING.
	MOVE INP-TYPE TO HVAR-TYPE.
	
	EXEC SQL
	   UPDATE MOV
	         SET RATING = :HVAR-RATING
	      WHERE
	            TYPE = :HVAR-TYPE
	END-EXEC.
	``

2.14.4   DELETE

INTERACTIVE SQL	EMBEDDED SQL

`DELETE FROM MOV`
`   WHERE NBR = 9`
	`EXEC SQL`
	`   DELETE FROM MOV`
	`        WHERE NBR = :NBR`
	`END-EXEC.`

`DELETE FROM MOV`
`   WHERE TYPE = 'HORROR' OR`
`        RATING = 'X';`
	`MOVE INP-TYPE     TO HVAR-TYPE.`
	`MOVE INP-RATING   TO HVAR-RATING.`
	
	`EXEC SQL`
	`        DELETE FROM MOV WHERE`
	`   TYPE = :HVAR-TYPE OR`
	`   RATING = :HVAR-RATING`
	`END-EXEC.`

`DELETE FROM MOV`
`   WHERE QTY * PRICE < 10.00;`
	`MOVE INP-LIMIT-VAL TO HVAR-LIMIT`
	
	`EXEC SQL`
	`        DELETE FROM MOV`
	`        WHERE QTY * PRICE <`
	`                HVAR-LIMIT`
	`END-EXEC.`

Chapter 3

SQL/COBOL Program Preparation

After completing this chapter you will be able to describe the steps in preparing a COBOL program with embedded SQL statements for execution. You will also be able to discuss alternate methods of program preparation. Topics include:

3.1.   Program Preparation Overview
3.2.   Required Datasets
3.3.   Declaring WORKING-STORAGE Table Descriptions
        — DCLGEN
3.4.   Precompile Using JCL
3.5.   Precompile Using the DB2I Panels
3.6.   Compile/Link-Edit JCL
3.7.   Compile/Link-Edit Using the DB2I Panels
3.8.   BIND JCL
3.9.   BIND Using the DB2I Panels
3.10.   Running Your Program With JCL
3.11.   Running Your Program From the DB2I Panels
3.12.   Running Your Program From Within a CLIST
3.13.   DB2 Precompile/Bind Timestamp Problems
3.14.   Review Questions
3.15.   Answers to Selected Questions
3.16.   Workshop III

This chapter is meant to show you explicit details on how program preparation works using either JCL or the DB2I panels. Naturally, your own shop will have different libraries and dataset names from the ones I use in this chapter. There will also most likely be standards on how to preprocess a program (either using JCL or the DB2I panels). Consult your shop's standards and procedures guide or technical help desk before attempting to run the review exercises at the end of the chapter.

All examples in this chapter use OS/VS COBOL. If your shop will be using VS COBOL II, you will have to make several changes to the JCL in the examples. If you will be using the DB2I panels, you may also have to set up your session defaults differently for VS COBOL II.

3.1.   PROGRAM PREPARATION OVERVIEW

You've finished coding the workshop from the last chapter, and you just can't wait to run your program. Unfortunately, a few barriers remain, not the least of which is the program preparation task — multiple steps,[1] all of which must be accomplished successfully in order for you to run your program. Figure 19 shows the program preparation and run procedures in all their splendor. Let's review this "big picture" before we proceed to the details of each step.[2]

---

[1] IBM supplies a stored procedure (PROC) for program preparation called:

- DSNHCOB — for OS/VS COBOL
- DSNHCOB2 — for VS COBOL II

This PROC can help you put together the JCL for the steps of program preparation. For first-time DB2 users, this is as good a place as any to find canned JCL to get you started.

[2] These steps do not necessarily have to follow the order I have shown them in. Many shops will execute COMPILE/LINK after Precompile, then BIND as step 4.

Step 1. DCLGEN

DCLGEN creates COBOL copybook table descriptions for your program's WORKING-STORAGE host variables from DB2 table definitions stored in the DB2 System Catalog.

Step 2. PRECOMPILE

Precompile separates the SQL statements from non-SQL statements in your program, comments out the SQL statements in your COBOL source code, and replaces the original SQL with standard COBOL CALLs to a DB2 run-time interface program. Precompile also places the SQL statements from your program into a TSO library as a Data Base Request Module (DBRM). Finally, precompile produces a report (SYSPRINT) detailing the success or failure of the precompilation of your SQL statement's syntax.

Step 3. BIND

BIND compiles the SQL statements from the DBRM(s) you created in step 2. The output of this compile process is what is called an application plan — all the SQL for your application. This application plan is stored in the DB2 directory (a system database maintained by DB2) and is ready for your program to connect up with it at run time. Notice that I said BIND compiles "DBRM(s)" — plural. Some applications contain several levels of "called — calling" programs link-edited together. Any program, at any level in the application, could have embedded SQL statements in it. There

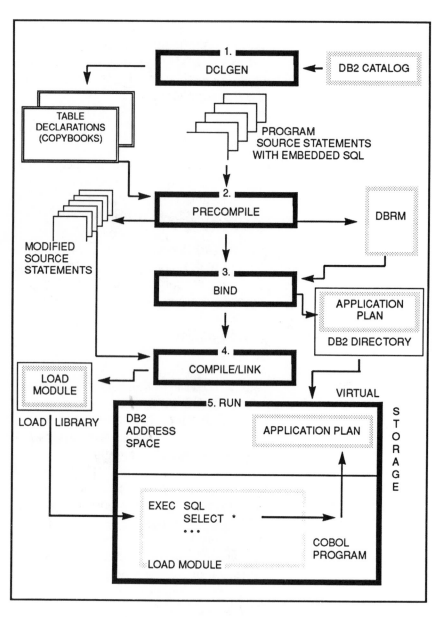

Figure 19.   Program preparation.

are several ways to BIND such modular applications. One option is to create a single large application plan named the same as the driver module, which contains the DBRMs of all the programs in the application. When you do this, you will BIND together several DBRMS in one BIND operation.

Step 4. COMPILE/LINK A standard COBOL compile follows your source code. You link-edit your program with the above-mentioned DB2 language interface module (DSNELI for TSO programs). The output of compile/link is an OS load module placed into an application load library.

Step 5. RUN At execute time, your JCL statements execute the TSO Terminal Monitor Program and pass it a series of commands and parameters. These commands instruct TSO to begin an attach process to DB2, load the application plan for your program, and fetch your program from the load library you link-edited it into. When your program issues its first SQL call statement (from the preprocess step above) DB2 connects your application plan with the correct SQL statement, executes the SQL statement, and returns a code to your program describing the success level of your SQL statement.

Sound complicated? Well it is at first. But if you take one step at a time it becomes quite easy to understand.

Before we go into each step, let's take a brief look at the datasets you will need to allocate and use in order to prepare and execute your SQL/COBOL program.

3.2   REQUIRED DATASETS

Figure 20 shows the required datasets needed for successful pre-process of a SQL/COBOL program. We'll take a brief look at each dataset and describe its purpose and definition.

3.2.1   COPYBOOK.COBOL

This dataset holds your DCLGEN table descriptions — your program's host variables. Because it contains COBOL WORKING-STORAGE fields, you usually create it as a COBOL PDS (a dataset with an extension of .COBOL). This way, valid COBOL numbers will be inserted by TSO in positions 1 — 6 of the records in the file.

You create one PDS member for each DB2 table in the file. The DCLGEN process builds these copybook members. DCLGEN is usually executed by applications programmers in the test environment and by DBA's in production — although your shop may have installation standards regarding who gets to DCLGEN what.

3.2.2   SOURCE.COBOL

You need a place to edit and store your COBOL source files. This will either be a standard ISPF COBOL library (again with an extension of .COBOL) or a Panvalet library. You develop your source programs using all the standard editing tools and techniques you use on any IBM application development effort (ISPF

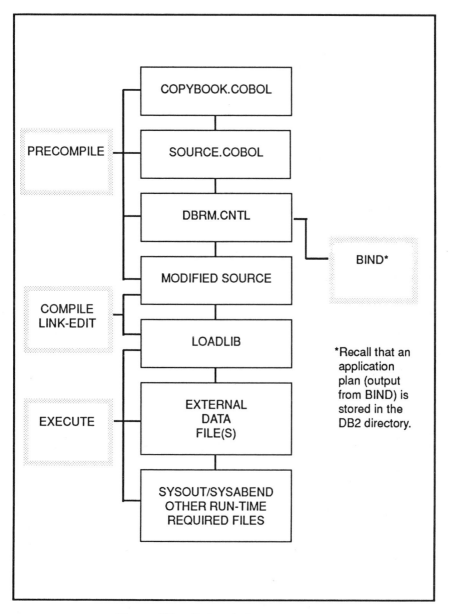

Figure 20. Datasets for preprocess.

Edit, External Copy, Split Screen, etc.). There is nothing sacred about how you work with, or store, your source code.

3.2.3   MODIFIED SOURCE

This dataset is usually a temporary file, which contains the modified source statements that are output from the precompile step. You really can't (and shouldn't) attempt to change your source statements after precompile. Often the dataset is a temporary workfile (&&DB2OUT in the JCL from our examples [Figure 23]). This dataset is passed from the precompile JCL step to the compile step and deleted at the end of the job.

3.2.4   DBRM.CNTL

You will need another TSO Partitioned Dataset to hold the DBRM that is output from precompile. This dataset is a standard TSO library:

```
DSORG=PO, LRECL=80, BLKSIZE=3200,
            RECFM = FB
```

Most shops will set up DBRM libraries well ahead of a development effort. If you don't have one, you can create a DBRMLIB using the normal ISPF 3.2 file allocation procedures. Give it an extension other than COBOL (.CNTL will do) so that no line numbers wind up in columns 1 — 6, and for heaven's sake, don't point back to your COBOL library with the DBRMLIB DD card in the precompile JCL (Figure 23 — //DBRMLIB). If you do, the precompiler will overwrite your COBOL program with your DBRM member at the end of the precompile step.

```
                              DCLGEN

===>  _

Enter table name for which declarations are required:
  1  SOURCE TABLE NAME       ===     MOV

Enter destination data set:        (Can be sequential or partitioned)
  2  DATA SET NAME           ===>   'DB2120.SRCLIB.COBOL(MOV)'
  3  DATA SET PASSWORD       ===>   (If password protected)


Enter options as desired:
  4  ACTION                  ===>   ADD   (ADD new or REPLACE old declara-
tion)
  5  COLUMN LABEL            ===>   (Enter YES for column label)
  6  STRUCTURE NAME ........===>                 (Optional)
  7  FIELD NAME PREFIX .....===>                 (Optional)
```

Figure 21. DCLGEN panel with entry for MOV table.

3.2.5   LOADLIB

You will need a standard OS load library to put your load module in when LINK-EDIT runs. You can use any load library to link into (even Panexec libraries), so again, if you don't have an existing load library specified for your development effort, you can create your own load library using ISPF panels in option 3.2. Note that the dataset attributes for a load library are usually device dependent. Your best bet in creating one using ISPF is to copy the statistics of an existing load library to find the LRECL, BLKSIZE, and dataset organization. Create your own SPACE allocations — and please don't swallow the disk pack. For the programs in this book, 10 Primary tracks, 10 Secondary tracks, and 3 directory blocks will be more than sufficient.

```
DCLGEN TABLE(PAY)
           LIBRARY(DB2120.SRCLIB.COBOL(PAY))
           APOST
. . . IS THE DCLGEN COMMAND THAT MADE THE FOLLOWING STATEMENTS

    EXEC SQL DECLARE PAY TABLE
    (  NBR                      CHAR(2),
       HOURS                    DECIMAL(5,   2),
       RATE                     DECIMAL(5,   2),
       DED                      DECIMAL(5,   2),
       YTD                      DECIMAL(8,   2)
    )  END-EXEC.

COBOL DECLARATION FOR TABLE PAY

01 DCPAY.
    10 NBR                      PIC  X(2).
    10 HOURS                    PIC  S999V99   USAGE   COMP-3.
    10 RATE                     PIC  S999V99   USAGE   COMP-3.
    10 DED                      PIC  S999V99   USAGE   COMP-3.
    10 YTD                      PIC  S999999V99 USAGE   COMP-3.

THE NUMBER OF COLUMNS DESCRIBED BY THIS DECLARATION IS 5
```

Figure 22. Sample DCLGEN output — host program variables.

3.2.6   EXTERNAL DATA FILES and Other Run-Time Required Files

If your program uses external files in its processing, you will naturally have to supply DD cards for these files. You will also have to supply a SYSDBOUT or SYSABEND card, as well as the standard SYSOUT cards for program displays.

3.3   DECLARING WORKING-STORAGE TABLE DESCRIPTIONS — DCLGEN

As you learned in section 3.2, the DCLGEN operation builds COBOL copybook field descriptions of your DB2 tables. These

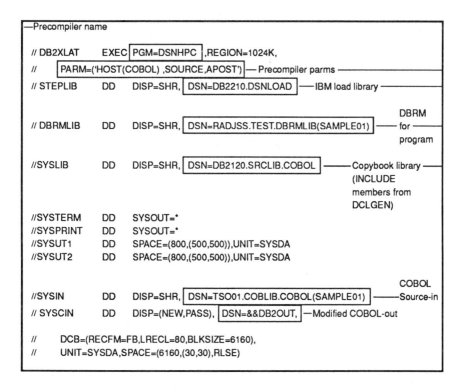

Figure 23. DB2, COBOL precompile step (JCL).

copybook fields are used as your program's host variables (data access input/output areas and SQL WHERE condition search argument variables). Creating program host variables using DCLGEN is a widely used procedure. It guarantees COBOL field/DB2 column accuracy, and prevents human error (manual typing problems). It is also very easy to do.

As you can see from Figure 21, all you do is fill in the DCLGEN panel (option 2 from the DB2I Main Menu) with your table name and the name of the PDS you want to specify as the receiving file for your copybook statements. You press ENTER, and DB2I creates a file of:

- WORKING-STORAGE fields

- DECLARE TABLE statement

using the table/column definitions stored in the System Catalog. The target PDS member your DCLGEN output goes into should be a TSO library with a COBOL extension (.COBOL). This will guarantee that the file has the prerequisite COBOL line numbers in columns 1-6.

After you have completed a DCLGEN for a table, you can bring the copybook file into your COBOL program in one of two ways:

1. Add the following lines to your program's WORKING-STORAGE:

```
EXEC SQL
      INCLUDE <membername>
END-EXEC.
```

where membername is the name you gave as your target PDS library member on the DCLGEN panel. During program preparation, the precompiler will extract the file from your copybook library and insert the statements into your COBOL program.

2. You can simply copy the file into your program using external copy from within EDIT on your program.

Figure 22 shows an example of the copybook file that DCLGEN creates. If you are not going to physically copy the DCLGEN file into your program (if you use the INCLUDE option), it is important that you view the file during the program development and coding process. You can use ISPF Split Screen (usually PF2) while you are editing your source code, or you can simply print out a hard-copy listing to reference.

The TABLE DECLARE statement on top of the COBOL WORK-ING-STORAGE fields acts as program documentation and can be used by the DB2 precompiler to verify your program's SQL statement syntax more completely. If you leave out, or comment out, the DECLARE TABLE statement, the precompiler may not be able to flag certain errors in your SQL statements. These errors *will* be caught during BIND, but you will have wasted a COMPILE and LINK/EDIT run in the interim. It is my recommendation that you always leave the DECLARE TABLE statements in your program.

Now we'll take a look at two different methods of preprocessing your programs: through JCL and by using the DB2I panels:

3.4   PRECOMPILE USING JCL

A sample JCL deck for precompiling an OS/VS COBOL program is shown in Figure 23. Note the important DD cards:

•	STEPLIB	This DD card must point to (among other installation specific PDSs) the library that holds the IBM supplied, DB2 executable modules. It is usually called something like DSN210.DB2.DSNLOAD — where DSN210 refers to DB2 version 2.1 (so if your shop is running DB2 1.3, the high-level qualifier would be something like DSN130, etc.). You may have some trouble finding this library name at your shop and may need to seek out a technical support person or two. I have seen some really clever names (disguises) for this library in my travels. Don't give up on finding it though, because you can't do without the modules it contains.

- SYSLIB   This DD card points to your copybook PDS. You should have no trouble locating this library name — you may (in fact) have created it yourself.
- SYSCIN   This DD card points to your COBOL source code.
- SYSPRINT   This DD card will contain precompiler error messages and other information of interest.

3.5   PRECOMPILE USING THE DB2I PANELS[3]

The DB2I Precompile panel is shown in Figure 24. If you read the previous section, you recognize most of the panel entries as the "important" DD cards, with the exception of the DB2 library. DB2I gets this dataset from your ISPF logon PROC. You must fill out all of the entries I have entered in the example.

3.6   COMPILE/LINK-EDIT JCL

A sample JCL deck for compiling and link-editing an OS/VS COBOL program is shown in Figure 27. As you can see, there is very little out of the ordinary to be found in these steps. The only significant items of interest are in the Link-Edit step. They include:

---

[3]If you are going to use the DB2I panels shown in Figures 24-26 to prepare your program, you may have to access the DB2I Defaults panel and modify some of the application language default parameters. The DB2I Defaults (Figure 26) panel contains entries for things like Compile and Link-Edit options, apostrophes vs. quote options, etc. These defaults are established during DB2 installation and can easily be tailored to your requirements. You will also have to fill in the DB2 Program Preparation panel (shown in Figure 25). This panel is a general processing setup panel. The options are self-explanatory.

```
                              PRECOMPILE
===>  _

Enter precompiler data sets:
  1   INPUT DATA SET ...........===>  'TSO01.COBLIB.COBOL(SAMPLE01)'
  2   INCLUDE LIBRARY ..........===>  'DB2120.SRCLIB.COBOL'
'
  3   DSNAME QUALIFIER .........===>  TEMP    (for building data set names)
  4   DBRM DATA SET ............===>  'RADJSS.TEST.DBRMLIB(SAMPLE01)'

Enter processing options as desired:
  5   WHERE TO COMPILE .........===>  FOREGROUND
  6   OTHER OPTIONS ............===>

PRESS:    ENTER to process       END to exit    HELP for more information
```

Figure 24. DB2I panel to precompile a COBOL program.

```
                         DB2 PROGRAM PREPARATION
===>  _

Enter the following:
  1   INPUT DATA SET NAME ......===>  'TSO01.COBLIB.COBOL(SAMPLE01)'
  2   DATA SET NAME QUALIFIER ..===>  TEMP          (for building dataset names)
  3   PREPARATION ENVIRONMENT ...===>  FOREGROUND   (FOREGROUND, BACKGROUND,
                                                     EDITJCL)
  4   RUN-TIME ENVIRONMENT .....===>  TSO           (TSO, CICS, IMS)
  5   STOP IF RETURN CODE >= ...===>  8 (Lowest terminating return code)
  6   OTHER OPTIONS ............===>

Select functions:           Display panel?      Perform function?
  7   CHANGE DEFAULTS ..........===>  Y    (Y/N)   . . . . . . . . . . . . .
  8   PL/I MACRO PHASE .........===>  N    (Y/N)   ===> N   (Y/N)
  9   PRECOMPILE ...............===>  Y    (Y/N)   ===> Y   (Y/N)
 10   CICS COMMAND TRANSLATION...............===> N    (Y/N)
 11   BIND ....................===>  Y    (Y/N)   ===> Y   (Y/N)
 12   COMPILE OR ASSEMBLE ......===>  Y    (Y/N)   ===> Y   (Y/N)
 13   LINK ....................===>  N    (Y/N)   ===> Y   (Y/N)
 14   RUN .....................===>  N    (Y/N)   ===> Y   (Y/N)

PRESS:    ENTER to process       END to exit     HELP for more information
```

Figure 25. The DB2 Program Preparation panel.

```
                          DB2I DEFAULTS
===>  _

Change defaults as desired:
  1  DB2 NAME ..................===>  DSN        (Subsystem identifier)
  2  DB2 CONNECTION RETRIES ...===>  0          (How many retries for DB2
                                                 connection)
  3  APPLICATION LANGUAGE .....===>  COBOL      (COBOL, COB2, FORT, ASM,
                                                 ASMH, PLI)
  4  LINES/PAGE OF LISTING ....===>  60         (A NUMBER FROM 5 TO 999)
  5  MESSAGE LEVEL ............===>  I          (Information, Warning, Error,
     ........................              Severe)
  6  COBOL STRING DELIMITER ...===>  DEFAULT    (DEFAULT, ' or "')
  7  SQL STRING DELIMITER .....===>  DEFAULT    (DEFAULT, ' or "')
  8  DECIMAL POINT ............===>  .          (. or ,)

  9  DB2I JOB STATEMENT: ......===>  (Optional if your site has a SUBMIT exit)
     ===>
     ===>
     ===>
     ===>


PRESS:    ENTER to process        END to exit    HELP for more information
```

Figure 26.   DB2I Defaults Panel.

- The SYSLIB DD card from the IBM supplied DB2 load modules;

- The INCLUDE statement for the DB2 run-time host language interface module. There are several interface modules. You must choose the one designated for your executing environment:

  — DSNELI for TSO programs
  — DFSLI000 for IMS DC programs
  — DSNCLI for CICS programs.

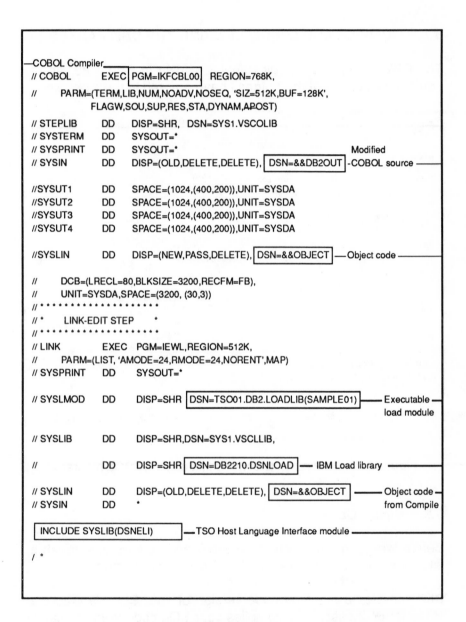

```
—COBOL Compiler—
// COBOL        EXEC PGM=IKFCBL00,  REGION=768K,
//       PARM=(TERM,LIB,NUM,NOADV,NOSEQ, 'SIZ=512K,BUF=128K',
              FLAGW,SOU,SUP,RES,STA,DYNAM,APOST)
// STEPLIB      DD   DISP=SHR,  DSN=SYS1.VSCOLIB
// SYSTERM      DD   SYSOUT=*
// SYSPRINT     DD   SYSOUT=*                                    Modified
// SYSIN        DD   DISP=(OLD,DELETE,DELETE), DSN=&&DB2OUT -COBOL source —

//SYSUT1       DD   SPACE=(1024,(400,200)),UNIT=SYSDA
//SYSUT2       DD   SPACE=(1024,(400,200)),UNIT=SYSDA
//SYSUT3       DD   SPACE=(1024,(400,200)),UNIT=SYSDA
//SYSUT4       DD   SPACE=(1024,(400,200)),UNIT=SYSDA

//SYSLIN       DD   DISP=(NEW,PASS,DELETE), DSN=&&OBJECT —Object code —

//       DCB=(LRECL=80,BLKSIZE=3200,RECFM=FB),
//       UNIT=SYSDA,SPACE=(3200, (30,3))
// * * * * * * * * * * * * * * * * * * *
// *    LINK-EDIT STEP    *
// * * * * * * * * * * * * * * * * * * *
// LINK         EXEC PGM=IEWL,REGION=512K,
//       PARM=(LIST, 'AMODE=24,RMODE=24,NORENT',MAP)
// SYSPRINT     DD   SYSOUT=*

// SYSLMOD      DD   DISP=SHR DSN=TSO01.DB2.LOADLIB(SAMPLE01) — Executable —
                                                               load module

// SYSLIB       DD   DISP=SHR,DSN=SYS1.VSCLLIB,

//              DD   DISP=SHR DSN=DB2210.DSNLOAD — IBM Load library —

// SYSLIN       DD   DISP=(OLD,DELETE,DELETE), DSN=&&OBJECT —— Object code —
// SYSIN        DD   *                                          from Compile

   INCLUDE SYSLIB(DSNELI)      —TSO Host Language Interface module —

/ *
```

Figure 27.   JCL deck to compile/link-edit a COBOL program.

3.7.   COMPILE AND LINK-EDIT USING THE DB2I PANELS

The DB2I Compile/Link-Edit Panel is shown in Figure 28. Again, you must fill out all of the entries I have entered in the example.

```
              PROGRAM PREPARATION:   COMPILE, LINK, AND RUN
===>  _

Enter compiler or assembler options:
   1   INCLUDE LIBRARY ..........===>
   2   INCLUDE LIBRARY ..........===>
   3   OPTIONS ..................===>    TEMP

Enter linkage editor options:
   4   INCLUDE LIBRARY ..........===>    'DB2210.DSMLOAD'
   5   INCLUDE LIBRARY ..........===>
   6   INCLUDE LIBRARY ..........===>
   7   LOAD LIBRARY .............===>    'TSO01.DB2.LOADLIB(SAMPLE01)'
   8   OPTIONS ..................===>

Enter run options:
   9   PARAMETERS ...............===>
  10   SYSIN DATASET ............===>
  11   SYSPRINT DS ..............===>


PRESS:    ENTER to process      END to exit       HELP for more information
```

Figure 28.   DB2I panel to compile/link-edit a COBOL program.

3.8.   BIND JCL

Before we go into the details on BIND and how to accomplish it, let's discuss just what exactly "BIND" is and what it does.

BIND creates a machine code version of your SQL data access statements. It essentially compiles your SQL code from the native format the statements exist in, in the DBRMs, to an executable structure that IBM calls an application plan. In creating an application plan, BIND goes through several steps. BIND:

- Verifies your SQL statement syntax
    - SQL statement format
    - DB2 data object spelling, etc.

- Verifies that the BINDing ID has the necessary authorization on the access requests against the DB2 objects in the plan. In other words, the ID of the person who attempts to BIND the plan must be authorized to access the DB2 data in the manner the program requests.

- Selects an optimized access path to the data. In doing this BIND considers:
    - Available Indexes
    - Table sizes
    - Data access request intent and scope (what you are doing with the table(s) and how much of a table you might access)
    - Efficiency of using available indexes to perform each specific data access
    - Distribution of column values throughout the table

- Builds the application plan — a control structure that establishes a relationship between your application program and the DB2 data it accesses.

Except for IMS/VS applications, you can name your application plan anything you want within the legal naming conventions:

- 8 character maximum.
- The plan name must be unique within the DB2 subsystem.
- The plan name must start with an alphabetic character.

However, it is my suggestion that you standardize by naming application programs and plans the same. This is a requirement for IMS/VS programs and will aid in DB2 application plan administration at the system level in any environment (TSO, CICSor IMS).

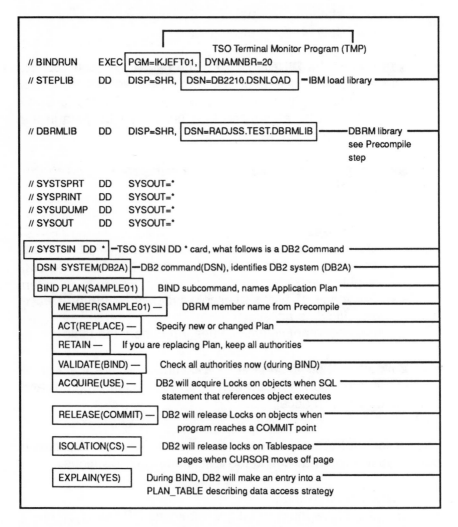

Figure 29. JCL deck to BIND a DBRM and create an application plan.

Besides the separate authorizations your ID must have on the DB2 objects used by your program, your ID must also have the authority to BIND the application plan name you use, or you must have the resource authority to add application plans to DB2. This level of resource authority is called BINDADD. You will have to check with your DBA or DB2 systems administrator before you attempt to BIND the applications in the workshop for this course. Strict guidelines describing installation procedures are usually in place, and you will have to adhere to them to be successful in BINDing your programs. Now take a look at Figure 29, the JCL to BIND a plan, and some of the BIND options.

Note that the program you are executing is IKJEFT01. This is the name of the TSO Terminal Monitor Program (TMP). You pass the TMP a DSN command in the DD * card. The DSN command invokes the TSO/DB2 command processor and allows you to pass DB2 a BIND command to compile your DBRMs into an application plan. In the BIND command you specify the DBRM-LIB, the application plan name. You also specify a set of BIND parameters which have to do with run-time DB2 table locking, validity checking, and authorization checking. These parameters could be the source of a full chapter on DB2 performance and tuning, and I will go into some of them in depth in chapter 7. For now the rule of thumb will be to specify:

Isolation level   ==> CS
Resource acquisition   ==> USE
Resource release   ==> COMMIT

for online programs, or applications which require concurrent table access, and:

Isolation level   ==> RR
Resource acquisition   ==> ALLOCATE
Resource release   ==> DEALLOCATE

for batch programs, or applications which are experiencing dead-lock or contention problems.

The DB2 subsystem name is DB2A. You can have multiple copies of DB2 on the same MVS machine (one DB2 for developing and testing applications, another for staging to and from production, and a production DB2 subsystem, etc.). You must name the DB2 you want to BIND your application plan in. You specify this on the SYSTEM subcommand of the DSN command.

Note the hyphen (-) used in the DSN command as a continuation character.

The EXPLAIN subcommand of BIND is used to obtain a descrip-tion of the access path chosen by the DB2 Optimizer (part of the BIND step) for your SQL request. The options are EXPLAIN (NO) — don't make an entry in the PLAN TABLE[4], and EXPLAIN (YES) — make entries in the PLAN TABLE. The EXPLAIN process will be described in detail in chapter 7. Until then, you will probably want to use EXPLAIN (NO). To use EXPLAIN (YES), you must own a PLAN TABLE (you must have created one on your ID) or the BIND step will fail.

To see the BIND defaults and other options available, study the DB2I BIND panel shown in Figure 30.

3.9   BIND USING THE DB2I PANELS

The DB2I BIND panel is shown in Figure 30. Note that there are entries for all the pertinent BIND parameters discussed in the above JCL example. As a matter of fact, this particular panel is so

---

[4]The statements to build a PLAN_TABLE are listed in Chapter 7, section 7.

easy to use that many installations which require JCL for precompile, compile/link, and execute allow (or require) you to use the
BIND panel to create your application plan.

3.10.   RUNNING YOUR PROGRAM WITH JCL

Once you have successfully precompiled, compiled, and link-edited, and run BIND on your SQL/COBOL program, you are ready to

```
                             BIND
===>  _

Enter DBRM dataset name(s).
  1  LIBRARY(s) ...............===>  'RADJSS.TEST.DBRMLIB'
  2  MEMBER(s) ................===>  SAMPLE01
  3  PASSWORD(s) .............===>

  4  MORE DBRMs ..............===>  NO          (YES to list more DBRMs)


Enter options as desired:
  5  PLAN NAME ...............===>  SAMPLE01    (Required to create a plan)
  6  ACTION ON PLAN ..........===>  REPLACE     (REPLACE or ADD)
  7  RETAIN EXECUTION
     AUTHORITY ...............===>  YES         (YES to retain user list)
  8  ISOLATION LEVEL .........===>  CS          (RR or CS)
  9  PLAN VALIDATION TIME .....===>  RUN         (RUN or BIND)
 10  RESOURCE ACQUISITION
     TIME ....................===>  USE         (USE or ALLOCATE)
 11  RESOURCE RELEASE TIME ....===>  COMMIT      (COMMIT or DEALLOCATE)
 12  EXPLAIN PATH SELECTION ...===>  YES         (NO or YES)



PRESS:    ENTER to process      END to exit   HELP for more information
```

Figure 30.   DB2I panel to BIND a DBRM and create an application
plan.

execute (test) it. Figure 31 illustrates the sequence of events that happen when you execute a TSO batch program that accesses DB2 data. Note that as in the BIND step, you EXECute IKJEFT01 (the TSO Terminal Monitor Program, TMP). TMP acts as the program supervisor in charge of all resources except DB2 data. When you execute IKJEFT01 you pass it a DSN command (RUN) which:

•   Invokes the TSO/DB2 command processor, allowing you to issue the RUN command for your DB2 program.

•   Establishes a "THREAD" — a set of control blocks which provide the means to use DB2 resources (Task Control Blocks for DB2 programs).

•   Begins the process of connecting your program to your program's application plan

•   Loads a copy of your program from your load library into virtual storage and passes control to the entry point in your procedure division. At the first SQL statement executed in your program, control is passed to DB2 (via a CALL to the Host Language Interface module you Link-Edited to). This CALL was created by the precompiler. The addresses of your WORKING-STORAGE host variables, the SQLCA, and SQL statement identifiers are passed to DB2 in the CALL. The SQL statement identifiers (a date/timestamp and an assigned unique number for each SQL statement) allow DB2 to locate the executable SQL structure (now in your application plan) and match it with the correct CALL statement substituted for that SQL statement at precompile time.

Figure 32 shows the necessary JCL to execute a TSO batch program. You may need extra DD cards for your program's external

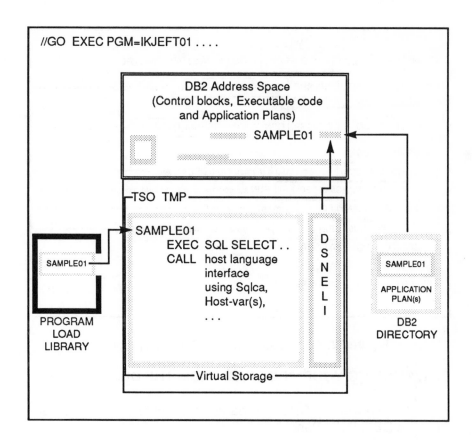

Figure 31.   TSO batch program execution.

files as required by your processing. Note that you do not need DD cards for DB2 tables you reference in your SQL statements (recall that your program needs no environment or Data Division entries for DB2 tables either). One note on the JCL in Figure 32. The DB2 subsystem (DB2A) must be the same DB2 you specified during BIND. In other words, you must BIND your application plans on the same DB2 system you intend to run on.

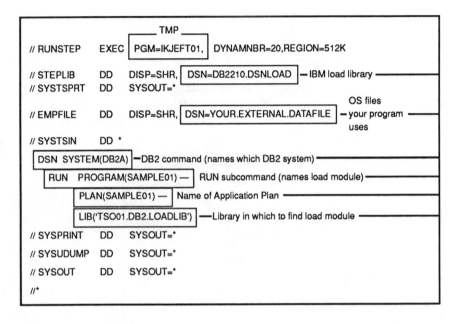

Figure 32.   JCL deck to run a TSO batch program.

3.11. RUNNING YOUR PROGRAM FROM THE DB2I PANELS

Figure 33 shows the DB2I run panel to execute a TSO program from the DB2I RUN Panel.[5]

Prior to running your program this way, you must allocate any OS (external files) to your TSO session using TSO ALLOC commands — one ALLOC command for each external file name in the "SELECT-ASSIGN" clause in the Environment Division. You would typically issue this command from ISPF option 6 — TSO Command Processor panel. A sample ALLOC command is shown at the top of the next page.

---

[5]Programs run from the panel will execute in foreground mode.

```
===> ALLOC FI(EMPFILE) DA('YOUR.EXTERNAL.DATAFILE')
```

TSO Allocate command

COBOL external file (EMPFILE) allocated to YOUR.EXTERNAL.DATAFILE
Equivalent to JCL — //EMPFILE DD DSN=YOUR.EXTERNAL.DATAFILE . . .

3.12   RUNNING YOUR PROGRAM FROM WITHIN A CLIST

As an alternative to either running your program in batch mode
using JCL or running it in foreground mode using the DB2I panels, you can also execute your TSO SQL/COBOL program using

```
                              RUN
===> _

Enter the name of the program you want to run
   1  DATA SET NAME ............===>  'TSO01.DB2.LOADLIB (SAMPLE01)'
   2  PASSWORD .................===>             (Required if dataset is
                                                 password protected)


Enter the following as desired:
   3  PARAMETERS ...............===>
   4  PLAN NAME ................===>    SAMPLE01   (Required if different
                                                  from program name)'
   5  WHERE TO RUN .............===>    FOREGROUND (FOREGROUND, BACKGROUND,
                                                  or EDITJCL)




NOTE:  Information for running command processors is on the HELP panel.
PRESS:    ENTER to process      END to exit    HELP for more information
```

Figure 33.   DB2I panel to execute a TSO program in the foreground.

a CLIST.[6] CLISTS are extremely flexible and can be useful in simulating an interactive environment for your end users.

The following is an example of a CLIST designed to execute SAMPLE01. The DB2 subsystem name is specified as DB2A.

```
PROC 0
      DSN SYSTEM(DB2A)
      IF LASTCC = 0 THEN
            DO
                  DATA
                        RUN  PROGRAM(SAMPLE01) -
                             PLAN(SAMPLE01) -
                             LIB('TSO01.DB2.LOADLIB')
                        END
                  ENDDATA
            END
      EXIT
```

Executing a program from within a TSO CLIST

Most of the DB2 specific commands and subcommands are the same as those found in the JCL and DB2I panel.

3.13. DB2 PRECOMPILE/BIND TIMESTAMP PROBLEMS

As the precompiler modifies your COBOL program, it creates a WORKING-STORAGE data structure for each SQL statement. This data structure contains, among other things, a unique numeric identifier for the SQL statement, the type of SQL statement (SELECT, INSERT, UPDATE, DELETE, etc.), and a system-generated date/timestamp value. The same date/timestamp value is tacked onto your program's DBRM (DBRMs contain a copy of all the SQL statements in your program).

---

[6]CLIST — TSO Command procedure language.

When you BIND your DBRM, this date/timestamp is inserted into a column of the DB2 System Catalog table SYSIBM.SYSDBRM, which describes various aspects of your application plan. At execute time, the date/timestamp value from your program's WORK-ING-STORAGE data structure is compared to the date/timestamp value stored in the SYSIBM.SYSDBRM. If the two are not identical, your program receives a negative SQL return code, which will shut down your application plan — ending your run.

DB2 goes through this procedure to ensure that the version of your SQL/COBOL source code is "in synch" with the executable SQL in the application plan — in other words, that you haven't changed your source, precompiled, compiled, and link-edited *without* REBINDing your plan.

What this means to you is that when you do maintenance on an SQL/COBOL program, you should go through all the steps in the program preparation process.[7]

3.14. REVIEW QUESTIONS

1. List the steps in preparing a Non-SQL COBOL program:

   * _____

   * _____

   * _____

---

[7]Technically, you don't have to precompile and bind if you
your COBOL logic, but I strongly recommend spending the fe
utes on the machine to keep all versions of your source and
synch.

2. List the steps in preparing a COBOL program containing embedded SQL statements:

*
_____

*
_____

*
_____

*
_____

*
_____

*
_____

3. List the datasets you need for the various steps of the program development process (obtain correct file names from your installation standards manual or technical support personnel):

*
_____

*
_____

*
_____

*
_____

*
_____

*
_____

4. Fill in the blanks in the JCL job steps in figures 34, 35, 36, and 37, to precompile, compile and link-edit, BIND, and run a program called FLUBBER. The IBM supplied load modules are in DB2130.DSNLOAD, and your DB2 test subsystem is called DB2T. You make up the rest of the data names. FLUB-

BER requires two external output files to execute, STU-FOUT1 and STUFOUT2. STUFOUT1 and STUFOUT2 have already been allocated.

Bind Hints: FLUBBER is a TSO program that runs in a batch system. The system has been experiencing deadlock and contention problems. You do not have a PLAN TABLE. The FLUBBER application plan name is a new plan name (this is your first BIND of the FLUBBER PLAN).

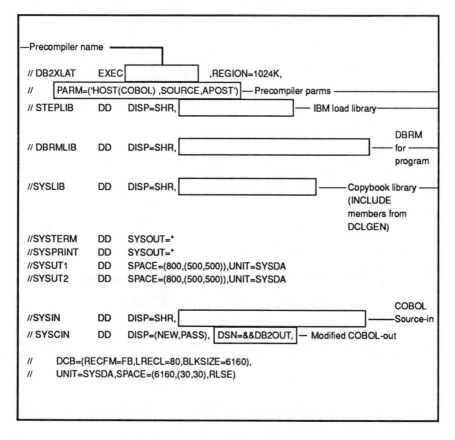

Figure 34. Precompile.

```
┌──COBOL Compiler──┐
  // COBOL     EXEC┌─────────────┐  ,  REGION=768K,
  //       PARM=(TERM,LIB,NUM,NOADV,NOSEQ, 'SIZ=512K,BUF=128K',
                FLAGW,SOU,SUP,RES,STA,DYNAM,APOST)
  // STEPLIB   DD    DISP=SHR,  DSN=SYS1.VSCOLIB
  // SYSTERM   DD    SYSOUT=*
  // SYSPRINT  DD    SYSOUT=*                              Modified
  // SYSIN     DD    DISP=(OLD,DELETE,DELETE), │DSN=&&DB2OUT,│ -COBOL source ──

  //SYSUT1     DD    SPACE=(1024,(400,200)),UNIT=SYSDA
  //SYSUT2     DD    SPACE=(1024,(400,200)),UNIT=SYSDA
  //SYSUT3     DD    SPACE=(1024,(400,200)),UNIT=SYSDA
  //SYSUT4     DD    SPACE=(1024,(400,200)),UNIT=SYSDA

  //SYSLIN     DD    DISP=(NEW,PASS,DELETE), │DSN=&&OBJECT,│ ── Object code──

  //         DCB=(LRECL=80,BLKSIZE=3200,RECFM=FB),
  //         UNIT=SYSDA,SPACE=(3200, (30,3))
  // * * * * * * * * * * * * * * * * * * *
  // *    LINK-EDIT STEP    *
  // * * * * * * * * * * * * * * * * * * *
  // LINK      EXEC  PGM=IEWL,REGION=512K,
  //       PARM=(LIST, 'AMODE=24,RMODE=24,NORENT',MAP)
  // SYSPRINT  DD    SYSOUT=*

  // SYSLMOD   DD    DISP=SHR┌──────────────────────┐── Executable ──
                                                      load module

  // SYSLIB    DD    DISP=SHR,DSN=SYS1.VSCLLIB,

  //          DD    DISP=SHR┌──────────────┐─ IBM Load library ──

  // SYSLIN    DD    DISP=(OLD,DELETE,DELETE), │DSN=&&OBJECT│ ── Object code──
  // SYSIN     DD    *                                          from Compile

  │ INCLUDE SYSLIB(    )│ ─TSO Host Language Interface module ──

  / *
```

Figure 35.   Compile/Link-Edit.

3.15. ANSWERS TO SELECTED QUESTIONS

1. COMPILE
   LINK/EDIT
   RUN

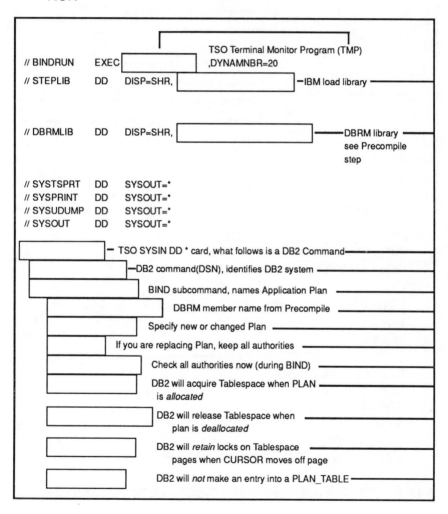

Figure 36. Bind.

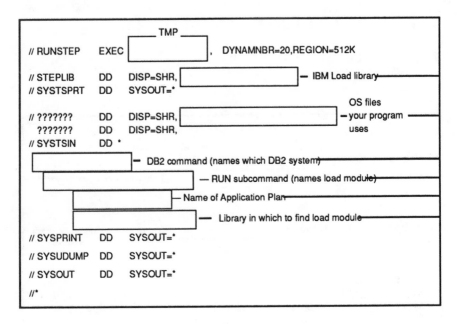

Figure 37.   Run.

2.   DCLGEN
     PRECOMPILE
     COMPILE
     LINK-EDIT
     BIND
     RUN

3.   COPYBOOK.COBOL
     SOURCE.COBOL
     DBRMLIB.CNTL
     APPL.LOADLIB
     EXTERN.DATA
     SYSOUT/SYSDBOUT/SYSPRINT etc.

3.15.1   Filled in Job Steps (see Figure 38, 39, 40, and 41)

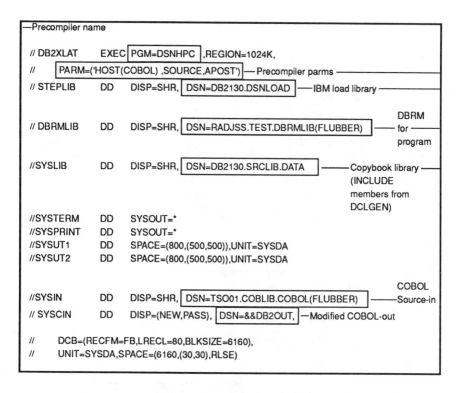

```
—Precompiler name

// DB2XLAT      EXEC  PGM=DSNHPC  ,REGION=1024K,
//          PARM=('HOST(COBOL) ,SOURCE,APOST')  — Precompiler parms ————
// STEPLIB      DD    DISP=SHR,  DSN=DB2130.DSNLOAD  ——IBM load library ————

                                                                    DBRM
// DBRMLIB      DD    DISP=SHR,  DSN=RADJSS.TEST.DBRMLIB(FLUBBER)    —— for ——
                                                                    program

//SYSLIB       DD    DISP=SHR,  DSN=DB2130.SRCLIB.DATA    ———— Copybook library ———
                                                           (INCLUDE
                                                           members from
                                                           DCLGEN)
//SYSTERM      DD    SYSOUT=*
//SYSPRINT     DD    SYSOUT=*
//SYSUT1       DD    SPACE=(800,(500,500)),UNIT=SYSDA
//SYSUT2       DD    SPACE=(800,(500,500)),UNIT=SYSDA

                                                                    COBOL
//SYSIN        DD    DISP=SHR,  DSN=TSO01.COBLIB.COBOL(FLUBBER)    ——Source-in
// SYSCIN      DD    DISP=(NEW,PASS),  DSN=&&DB2OUT,  —Modified COBOL-out

//        DCB=(RECFM=FB,LRECL=80,BLKSIZE=6160),
//        UNIT=SYSDA,SPACE=(6160,(30,30),RLSE)
```

Figure 38. Precompile.

3.16.   WORKSHOP III

In chapter 2, you wrote several programs. Now it is time to try them out by preparing and executing them. You will probably have to visit someone at your installation and obtain a copy of the JCL procedure to do this. Modify the procedure according to the instruction given by the person at your shop. Below you will find a short checklist of what you will need to accomplish:

• Allocate all the necessary files (see above review questions).

```
—COBOL Compiler
  // COBOL       EXEC  PGM=IKFCBL00   REGION=768K,
  //      PARM=(TERM,LIB,NUM,NOADV,NOSEQ, 'SIZ=512K,BUF=128K',
              FLAGW,SOU,SUP,RES,STA,DYNAM,APOST)
  // STEPLIB     DD    DISP=SHR,  DSN=SYS1.VSCOLIB
  // SYSTERM     DD    SYSOUT=*
  // SYSPRINT    DD    SYSOUT=*                                          Modified
  // SYSIN       DD    DISP=(OLD,DELETE,DELETE),  DSN=&&DB2OUT  -COBOL source ——

  //SYSUT1      DD    SPACE=(1024,(400,200)),UNIT=SYSDA
  //SYSUT2      DD    SPACE=(1024,(400,200)),UNIT=SYSDA
  //SYSUT3      DD    SPACE=(1024,(400,200)),UNIT=SYSDA
  //SYSUT4      DD    SPACE=(1024,(400,200)),UNIT=SYSDA

  //SYSLIN      DD    DISP=(NEW,PASS,DELETE),  DSN=&&OBJECT  —Object code ——

  //      DCB=(LRECL=80,BLKSIZE=3200,RECFM=FB),
  //      UNIT=SYSDA,SPACE=(3200, (30,3))
  // * * * * * * * * * * * * * * * * * * * *
  // *    LINK-EDIT STEP    *
  // * * * * * * * * * * * * * * * * * * * *
  // LINK        EXEC  PGM=IEWL,REGION=512K,
  //      PARM=(LIST, 'AMODE=24,RMODE=24,NORENT',MAP)
  // SYSPRINT    DD    SYSOUT=*

  // SYSLMOD     DD    DISP=SHR  DSN=TSO01.DB2.LOADLIB(FLUBBER)  —— Executable ——
                                                                  load module

  // SYSLIB      DD    DISP=SHR,DSN=SYS1.VSCLLIB,

  //             DD    DISP=SHR  DSN=DB2130.DSNLOAD — IBM Load library ——

  // SYSLIN      DD    DISP=(OLD,DELETE,DELETE),  DSN=&&OBJECT  —— Object code —
  // SYSIN       DD    *                                          from Compile

     INCLUDE SYSLIB(DSNELI)     —TSO Host Language Interface module ——

  / *
```

Figure 39.   Compile/Link-Edit.

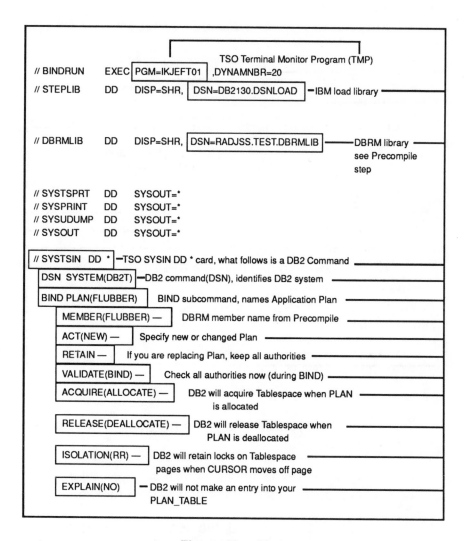

Figure 40. Bind.

• Generate the CUST and MOV tables for EZPROG and the EMPL and PAY tables for SINGLTON and SAMPLE01 in DB2. Appendix B contains the CREATE TABLE and INSERT statements to build these tables.

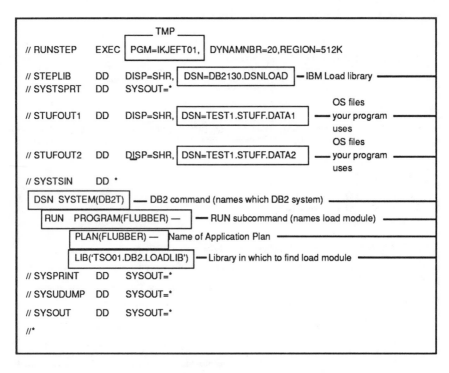

Figure 41.   Run.

- Test out the SQL statements in the programs — use either SPUFI or QMF.

- Obtain authorization to create or use an application plan. See your database administrator or help desk for this.

- Obtain and modify, or create, the JCL necessary to preprocess and run the program (or use the DB2I panels). Again, see your database administrator or help desk for this.

If you typed in SAMPLE01, you might want to preprocess it first, as it should run successfully (barring any typos). You will need an external file (LRECL=80, FB, BLKSIZE=80) for EMPFILE. You

can create this on TSO. It should contain a few records with numbers 01 through 10 in positions 1 and 2 of the records.

There are no solutions for this workshop in the book. Every shop
maintains its own unique approach to program preparation, so
you will have to contact your DB2 database administrator or systems administrator for assistance in completing this workshop.
The information in this chapter has given you enough of a background so that you can probably modify existing JCL or use the
DB2I panels with little assistance.

Chapter 4

Using Host
Variables

After completing this chapter you will be able to describe in detail the use of the various types of COBOL host variables. You will also be able to create your own host variables and understand the use of Null indicators, host structures, and variable assignment. Topics include:

4.1.   Host Variable Review
4.2.   Coding Requirements
4.3.   Host Variable Assignment Compatibilities
4.4.   Allowable Data Declarations of Host Variables
4.5.   Host Structures
4.6.   Null Indicator Variables
4.7.   Null Indicator Structures
4.8.   Host Variable Considerations
4.9.   Host Variable Exercises
4.10.   Exercise Solutions

4.1.   HOST VARIABLE REVIEW

Recall from chapters 1 and 2, that you define input/output areas for DB2 data in your program's WORKING-STORAGE or LINK-AGE SECTION. This is illustrated in Figure 42:

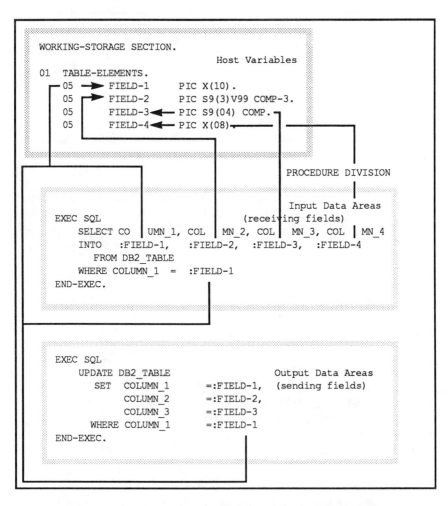

Figure 42. WORKING-STORAGE host variables referenced in SQL statements.

As Figure 42 illustrates, host variables are used for either input/output data areas (when used in the SELECT or SET clause) or search fields (when used in the WHERE clause). Host variables can also be used in two other ways in application programs:

1.   As SELECTed literal values in the SELECT clause:

```
SELECT NBR, QTY, QTY * :PRICE-INCREASE, :PRICE-INCREASE
    FROM MOV;
```

2.   As output fields in other SQL clauses:

```
UPDATE MOV SET QTY = :NEW-QUANTITY
    INSERT INTO MOV VALUES (:INPUT-NBR, :INPUT-TITLE . . . . .
```

And, as we've seen, you can obtain host variable definitions in one of two ways:

1.   Create them yourself manually.

2.   Use the field definitions generated by DCLGEN.

Most of the time you will want to use the field definitions generated by DCLGEN. These definitions match your DB2 table-column definitions perfectly and save much coding effort.

However, under certain circumstances you will need to create your own host variables. This chapter will help you learn how to do this.

4.2.   CODING REQUIREMENTS

The rules for coding COBOL host variables, shown in Figure 43, are straightforward and simple:

- COBOL host variables are coded in the WORKING-STORAGE and/or LINKAGE SECTIONs of your application program.

- Any valid COBOL variable name can be used in an SQL statement as a host variable (this means you use hyphens instead of under-scores).

- You cannot use several of the standard COBOL clauses such as JUSTIFIED or BLANK WHEN ZERO when coding a host variable.

- There is only one situation where you can use the OCCURS clause. It is when you are coding Null indicator structures (covered later in this chapter).

- You should precede your COBOL host variable with a colon when it is used within an SQL statement (EXEC SQL . . . END-EXEC). Do not precede your COBOL host variable with a colon when it is used outside of an SQL statement. Actually, DB2 allows you some free-dom in preceding host variables with colons, and there is a list of "when you need/when do you not need" colons in the "DB2 Application Programming Guide." It has been my experience that you should standardize on always preceding your host variables with a colon in an SQL statement. First of all, this avoids your having to remember the dozen or so rules surrounding "when you need/when do you not need" colons. Further, some real confusion in coding can ensue when you don't set apart your host variables from similar or like named DB2 columns. The bottom line is, since there is no penal-ty for preceding host variables with colons in an SQL statement, always do so.

Figure 43.   Coding rules for host variables

4.3.   HOST VARIABLE ASSIGNMENT COMPATIBILITIES

DB2 column values are assigned to host variables during the SELECT operation. DB2 column values are updated (SET) during the execution of INSERT and UPDATE operations. To avoid run-time errors and other potential problems (such as truncation or precompile errors), always try to match your DB2 columns with their exact COBOL host variable's representation. The easiest way to do this, of course, is to use the DCLGEN definitions whenever possible. A chart of valid representations (definitions) is shown in section 4.4 of this chapter.

In some cases, however, it may not be possible to be able to predict the exact field size or specification being passed from your program to DB2 or vice versa. In these cases the rules in Figure 44 apply.

•   Datatypes are generally only compatible with like datatypes:
    — Character columns with PIC X fields.
    — Numeric columns with PIC S9 fields.
    — Date/Time/Timestamp columns with PIC X fields.

•   DB2 will perform conversions on data within like datatypes:
    — Character columns will be padded with spaces or truncated.
    — Numeric columns will be padded with zeros, lose fractions, or be truncated.

•   Null values:
    — Cannot be assigned to DB2 columns that are defined as NOT NULL.
    — Cannot be assigned to host variables that do not have an associated null indicator variable — we will be covering null indicator variables in section 4.6 of this chapter.

•   Violations of the rules concerning NULL values can result in run-time failures of your program.

•   If DB2 converts and truncates character or numeric data, the result of the operation is a run-time WARNING flag set in the SQLCA SQLWARN fields (see chapter 5)

Figure 44.   Datatype compatibilities and conversions.

There are a few other rules concerning character, string, and date/time data assignment and conversion that may be of some interest. These are stated in the *DB2 Application Programming Guide.*

Now let's take a look at the valid COBOL declarations for host variables.

4.4. ALLOWABLE DATA DECLARATIONS OF HOST VARIABLES

DB2 is very particular about the data definitions for fields used as host variables. You will most likely receive a precompiler error message reading:

UNDEFINED OR UNUSABLE HOST VARIABLE

if your COBOL definitions are not consistent with the ones shown in the chart in Figure 45.

You may abbreviate certain WORKING-STORAGE clauses when coding DB2 host variables:

Allowable Abbreviation	Original Clause
PIC	PICTURE or PICTURE IS
COMP	COMPUTATIONAL or USAGE IS COMPUTATIONAL
USAGE	USAGE IS
S9(4)	S9999
X(3)	XXX

	DB2 DATA TYPE		DESCRIPTION	INTERNAL LENGTH	NUMERIC RANGE	COBOL EQUIVALENCE
N U M E R I C	INTEGER (INT)		WHOLE NUMBER (LARGE INTEGER)	4 BYTES (PRECISION 31 BITS)	-2147483648 to +2147483647	01 NUM PIC S9(9) COMP.
	SMALLINT		WHOLE NUMBER (SMALL INTEGER)	2 BYTES (PRECISION 15 BITS)	-32768 to +32767	01 NUM PIC S9(4) COMP.
	FLOAT (n)	REAL	SINGLE PRECISION FLOATING 1<n ≤ 21)	4 BYTES FLOATING (32 BITS)	5.4E -79 to 7.2E +75	01 NUM COMP-2
		DOUBLE PRECISION	DOUBLE PRECISION FLOATING (22 <n ≤ 53)	8 BYTES FLOATING (64 BITS)	5.4E -79 TO 7.2E +75	
	DECIMAL (P, Q) (DEC)		DECIMAL NUMBER (P = precision) (Q = scale)	((P/2) + 1) BYTES MAX(P) = 15 DIGITS	-999999999999999 +999999999999999	01 NUM PIC S9(P)V9(2) COMP-3
C H A R A C T E R	CHARACTER (n) (CHAR)		FIXED LENGTH CHARACTER STRING	n BYTES	n MAXIMUM 254 CHARACTERS	01 STR PIC X(n)
	VARCHAR (n)		VARYING LENGTH CHARACTER STRING	2 to m + 2 BYTES	m + MAXIMUM RECORD LENGTH (APPROX. 4K) (INCLUDED IN DEFINITION)	01 STR 49 STRL PIC S9(4) COMP. 49 STRD PIC X(m)
	LONG VARCHAR		VARYING LENGTH CHARACTER STRING (MAX. PAGE)		>254 APPROX. 4K (CALCULATED BY DB2)	
D A T E - T I M E	DATE		Date	4 BYTES (a three part value)	year-month-day 0001 - 01 - 01	FORMAT DEFINED AT DB2 INSTALLATION (STRING FORMAT AT LEAST 8) EX: 12/25/1988
	TIME		Time	3 BYTES (a three part value)	hours-minutes-seconds 00.00.00 to 24.00.00	FORMAT DEFINED AT DB2 INSTALLATION (STRING FORMAT AT LEAST 4) EX: 13.20.24
	TIMESTAMP		Time Stamp	10 BYTES (a seven part value)	year-month-day hour-minute-second-msec 0001-01-01.00.00.000000 9999-12-31-24.00.00.000000	(STRING FORMAT AT LEAST 16) EX: 1989-01-18-12.10.00.000000
G R A P H I C	GRAPHIC (n)		FIXED LENGTH STRING OF DOUBLE BYTE CHARACTERS	2n BYTES	n MAXIMUM 127 DOUBLE BYTE CHARACTERS	01 STRG1 PIC G(n) DISPLAY-1.
	VARGRAPHIC (m)		VARYING LENGTH STRING OF DOUBLE BYTE CHARACTERS	2 to 2 m + 2 BYTES	m < MAXIMUM RECORD LENGTH (APPROX. 2K) (INCLUDED IN DEFINITION)	01 STRG2. 49 STRG2L PIC S9(n) COMP 49 STRG20 G(nC) DISPLAY-1
	LONG VARGRAPHIC		VARYING LENGTH STRING OF DOUBLE BYTE CHARACTERS (MAX. PAGE)		> 127 APPROX. 2K (CALCULATED BY DB2)	

Figure 41. Valid SQL/COBOL host variable definitions.

A few important notes concerning the chart in Figure 45.

- For host variable definitions not within a host structure[1] (individual host variables), use COBOL level number 01 or 77. For host variable definitions within a host structure, use level numbers 02 through 48.

- Using a FILLER item within a host structure makes the structure invalid.

- Variable character fields are defined with a group level specifier and two 49 level specifiers:

A length specifier: 49 FIELD-LTH PIC S9(04) COMP.

The character field which
contains the actual DB2 data: 49 FIELD-DATA PIC X(n).
n represents the largest value that can fit in the column (from the column definition VARCHAR(n).

```
10   VARCHAR-FLD.—
     49 FLD-LENGTH:  PIC S9(04) COMP.
     49 FLD-DATA:      PIC X(40).
```

When you use variable character fields to insert data into a DB2 table, only the number of characters indicated by the length specifier are inserted.

When a variable character field is used as the receiving field in an SQL SELECT statement, only the actual number of characters in the DB2 data are transferred into the data portion. The length specifier contains this number.

---

[1] Host structures are defined in section 4.5 of this chapter.

4.5. HOST STRUCTURES

A host structure is a COBOL group level data structure, representing all fields SELECTed in a results table row. It is defined as an 01 level data item in WORKING-STORAGE and can be used in an SQL statement in place of elementary level (individual) field references. Figure 46 is an example.

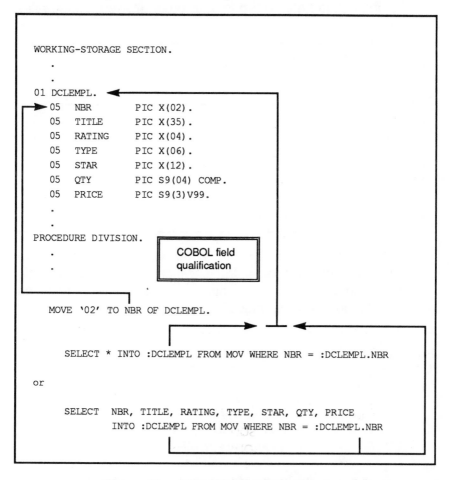

Figure 46. Example using host structure.

Figure 42 illustrates a few points of interest:

• You SELECT into the host structure simply by referring to the entire 01 GROUP LEVEL data name prefixed by a colon.

• *Within your SQL statements*: When you reference elementary field items of a host structure that have duplicate data names defined elsewhere in your program, you must qualify the field as follows:

Structure-name.Field-name (DCLEMPL.NBR)

Example:

```
EXEC SQL
   SELECT EMPL.NBR, LNAME, HOURS
      INTO :DCLEMPL.NBR, :LNAME, :HOURS
   FROM EMPL, PAY WHERE EMPL.NBR = PAY.NBR AND
      EMPL.NBR = :DCLEMPL.NBR
END-EXEC.
```

• *Within your SQL statements*: When you reference elementary field items of a host structure that *do not* have duplicate data names defined elsewhere in your program, you can refer to them by their unqualified name:

Example:

```
EXEC SQL
   SELECT LNAME, HOURS, DEPT
      INTO :LNAME, :HOURS, :DEPT
   FROM EMPL, PAY WHERE EMPL.NBR = PAY.NBR AND
      DEPT IN ('MKT', 'ACC', 'FIN', 'R&D')
END-EXEC.
```

- *Outside of your SQL statements*: When you reference elementary field items of a host structure that have duplicate data names defined elsewhere in your program, you must qualify them with the COBOL "FIELD OF STRUCTURE" qualification:

```
MOVE EMPL-NBR-IN TO NBR OF DCLEMPL.

                         Field of Structure
```

And, of course, when you reference distinct field item names outside of an SQL statement in COBOL, you do not need any additional qualification.

Because structures seem so much easier to code than individual fields, you may be wondering why I didn't introduce them sooner. The reason I didn't is that using host structures ties your program to existing table definitions and destroys application/data independence. What this means is that if the table definition changes, your program's SQL must change with it — *whether or not the table changes actually affect your data access processing.* This means more (and in most cases needless) COBOL program maintenance.

The other reason for avoiding the use of host structures is performance. Access only the data elements you *need* for your program's processing specification. If you are reading in entire DB2 table rows using SELECT * and don't need all of the columns in the row, you may be incurring far more internal DB2 I/O and internal CPU processing than necessary for your specific access need. This is particularly true when the SQL statement requires sorting. To write efficient SQL/COBOL programs unlearn the old "READ and WRITE records" mentality and learn to code your SQL statements to access data at the field element level.

4.6. NULL INDICATOR VARIABLES

A null indicator variable (or indicator variable) is a WORKING-STORAGE field you associate with a host variable that allows DB2 to indicate the assignment of a null value to that field during the execution of a SELECT statement. You define indicator variables as elementary level data items with a picture clause of PIC S9(04) COMP in WORKING-STORAGE. You associate an indicator variable with a host variable by coding the indicator variable (preceded by a colon) immediately after the host variable in your SQL statement. This is illustrated in Figure 47.

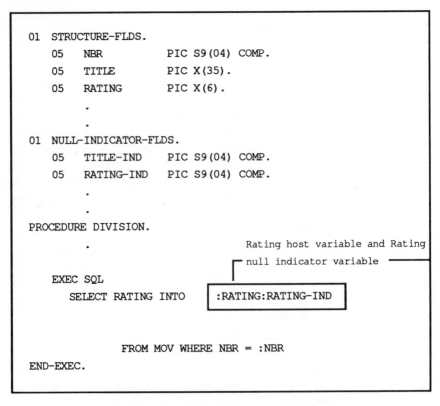

Figure 47. Null indicator variables.

Indicator variables "indicate" several possible exceptional conditions:

- If the column you are retrieving is null, DB2 puts a negative value in the indicator variable (recall that if you retrieve a null column into a host variable without an indicator variable your application plans will shut down at run-time).

- If the value for the column is null because of a numeric or arithmetic conversion error, DB2 sets the indicator variable to -2.

- If a character column has been truncated, DB2 puts a positive integer in the indicator variable equal to the original length of the string.

You can also use indicator variables to insert or set null values on DB2 tables.

Up to now, you have only seen one way to INSERT or UPDATE a DB2 table with a null value. That is by using the keyword NULL physically coded in your SQL statement:

```
UPDATE MOV SET QTY = NULL WHERE TITLE = :INPUT-TITLE

INSERT INTO MOV VALUES (:INPUT-NBR, :INPUT-TITLE, NULL . . . . etc.
```

This is probably unacceptable for most "real-life" applications, because your program would only "find out" *during execution* whether or not to insert or update a column with a NULL value. A typical scenario would be:

- Your program reads an input file or screen.

- Based on the input value(s) obtained during execution, you place either a null or a real value in the DB2 table.

For this reason, most of the time you will not be able to "hard code" a NULL into your embedded SQL statements.

The solution to this problem is to use null indicators. During INSERT or UPDATE execution, DB2 checks the indicator variable (if one exists) for each host variable field. If the indicator variable contains a negative number, DB2 places a null value in the column. You can use this process to conditionally update table values with nulls.

Specify the logic as shown in Figure 48.

```
        05    RATING         PIC X(6).
        05    RATING-IND     PIC S9(04) COMP.


    PROCEDURE DIVISION.

    read input file or screen
    move and check values in fields
    If rating = spaces (or some value signifying null insertion)
        move -1     to rating-ind.
    else
        move zero to rating-ind.

    EXEC SQL UPDATE MOV SET RATING = RATING:RATING-IND WHERE . . . .
```

Figure 48.   Logic to handle NULL insertion variably.

4.7.   NULL INDICATOR STRUCTURES

If you choose to use host structures in your SQL statements, you have to use what are called null indicator structures to handle DB2 null value assignment during execution. Null indicator structures are one-level COBOL tables (one OCCURS clause) which contain the necessary elementary fields to accept negative values

from DB2 for potential null columns. As always, they are defined
in WORKING-STORAGE as shown in Figure 49.

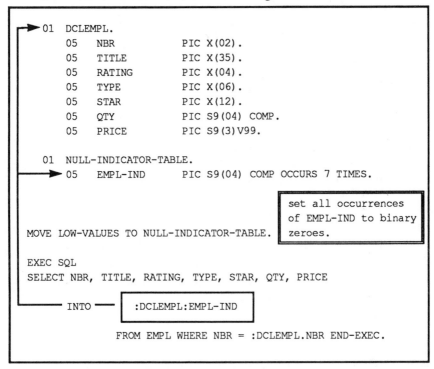

```
01  DCLEMPL.
      05   NBR          PIC X(02).
      05   TITLE        PIC X(35).
      05   RATING       PIC X(04).
      05   TYPE         PIC X(06).
      05   STAR         PIC X(12).
      05   QTY          PIC S9(04) COMP.
      05   PRICE        PIC S9(3)V99.

   01  NULL-INDICATOR-TABLE.
      05   EMPL-IND     PIC S9(04) COMP OCCURS 7 TIMES.

                                                set all occurrences
                                                of EMPL-IND to binary
   MOVE LOW-VALUES TO NULL-INDICATOR-TABLE.     zeroes.

   EXEC SQL
   SELECT NBR, TITLE, RATING, TYPE, STAR, QTY, PRICE
          INTO       :DCLEMPL:EMPL-IND

              FROM EMPL WHERE NBR = :DCLEMPL.NBR END-EXEC.
```

Figure 49.   Example using null indicator structure.

Figure 49 shows how to define and use a null indicator structure
with a host structure in a Singleton SELECT statement. In the
example, EMPL-IND is an array containing seven fields, each of
which can be tested for a negative value. There is a positional
correspondence between the nth selected column and the nth
occurrence in the indicator structure array. If, for example, EMPL-
IND(5) contains a negative value, the corresponding host variable
in the host structure (STAR) contains a null value. Of course, this
can make for some rather interesting COBOL edit and value testing logic routines.

Before we leave the topic of nulls and null indicator variables, one more question needs to be addressed. The question is:

When do I need to use null indicator variables in my SQL statements?

The answer is:

> For SELECT:
>
> > Every potentially null column (column *not* defined as NOT NULL or NOT NULL WITH DEFAULT) that you SELECT must have an associated null indicator.
>
> For UPDATE and INSERT:
>
> > Every column you wish to INSERT or UPDATE that should be null due to data input values must have an associated null indicator and you can use the logic routine described in Figure 48 to accomplish this.

4.8.   HOST VARIABLE CONSIDERATIONS

There are a few final considerations you should know about before you try the review exercises for this chapter.

4.8.1.   Called/Calling Programs and Host Variables

If a called program issues SQL statements that use host variables passed to it by the calling program, the called program must first reset a DB2 flag called the SQL-INIT-FLAG. This flag is used by DB2 to initialize your host variables at the first executable SQL statement. To reset the flag, issue the following statement —

before the first SQL statement in your program's PROCEDURE
DIVISION:

```
MOVE ZEROS TO SQL-INIT-FLAG.
```

4.8.2.   Overflow Problems

You can get column overflow as a result of conversion problems
(retrieving an INTEGER column into a PIC S9(04) host variable),
or calculations or arithmetic expressions in SQL statements.
When this happens, DB2 sets on some switches in the SQLCA,
which we will be covering in depth in the next chapter.

4.8.3.   Truncation Problems

Retrieving an 80 character CHAR column value into a PIC X(65)
truncates the rightmost 15 characters. Again, warnings are set in
the SQLCA.

The important point to remember is to refer to the chart in figure
44 to find the correct DB2 column/host variable declaration. This
will avoid many of the problems discussed in this chapter.

4.9.   HOST VARIABLE EXERCISES

1.   Given the following DB2 table description, code a host struc-
     ture and the necessary host variables for all columns in the
     table. Include null indicator variables where appropriate.

```
DEFINE TABLE POTPOURRI
(FIX_CHAR              CHAR (125) NOT NULL              ,
 VAR_CHAR             VARCHAR (17)  NOT NULL WITH DEFAULT  ,
 SMALL_INT           SMALLINT                            ,
 BIG_INT             INTEGER                             ,
 DATE_COL               DATE        NOT NULL             ,
 TIME_COL               TIME                             ,
 DECIMAL_COL         DEC(9,2)      )  IN DATABASE SQLSAYLES ;
```

```
01 _____

   05 _____

   05 _____

      49 _____

      49 _____

   05 _____

   05 _____

   05 _____

   05 _____

   05 _____
```

2.   Code a Singleton SELECT of all columns into the host vari-
     ables you defined in question 1.

```
EXEC SQL
  SELECT      _____
     INTO     _____
     FROM     _____
     WHERE FIX_CHAR = _____ END-EXEC.
```

3. Code a Singleton SELECT * into the host structure you defined in question 1. (Hint: How will you handle potential null values in the results rows?). Also code COBOL IF-THEN-ELSE logic to test for the presence of nulls in the host structure after the SELECT statement is executed.

```
EXEC SQL
    SELECT _____
      INTO _____
      FROM _____
WHERE FIX_CHAR = _____ END-EXEC.


(code IF-THEN-ELSE logic here)
```

4. Code host variables for the following SELECT statement:

```
SELECT AVG(QTY * 1.1), MAX(QTY), 'QUANTITY FIELDS'
       FROM MOV;
```

```
01 _____

   05 _____

   05 _____

   05    _____
```

4.10.   EXERCISE SOLUTIONS

1.

```
01  DCLPOTPOURRI.
    05   FIX-CHAR              PIC X(125).
    05   VAR-CHAR
        49  VAR-CHAR-LTH       PIC S9(04) COMP.
        49  VAR-CHAR-DATA      PIC X(17).
    05   SMALL-INT             PIC S9(04) COMP.
    05   BIG-INT               PIC S9(09) COMP.
    05   DATE-COL              PIC X(10).
    05   TIME-COL              PIC X(08).
    05   DECIMAL-COL           PIC S9(7)V99 COMP-3.


01  NULL-FIELDS.
    05   SMALL-NULL            PIC S9(04) COMP.
    05   BIG-NULL              PIC S9(04) COMP.
    05   TIME-NULL             PIC S9(04) COMP.
    05   DEC-NULL              PIC S9(04) COMP.
```

2.

```
EXEC SQL SELECT FIX_CHAR, VAR_CHAR, SMALL_INT,
BIG_INT, DATE_COL,
   TIME_COL, DECIMAL_COL      INTO

   :FIX-CHAR:VAR-CHAR,     :SMALL-INT:SMALL-NULL,
   :BIG-INT:BIG-NULL,      :DATE-COL,
   :TIME-COL:TIME-NULL,:DECIMAL-COL:DEC-NULL
       FROM POTPOURRI
WHERE FIX-CHAR = :FIX-CHAR END-EXEC.
```

3.

```
    WORKING-STORAGE fields required:
01  IND-TABLE.
    05   IND-ARRAY    PIC S9(04) COMP OCCURS 4 TIMES.
       .
       .
EXEC SQL

   SELECT * INTO :DCLPOTPOURRI:IND-ARRAY
   FROM POTPOURRI
   WHERE FIX CHAR = :FIX-CHAR                    END-EXEC.

IF  IND-ARRAY(1) IS LESS THAN ZERO
THEN
    MOVE 'something or other' TO SMALL-INT.

IF  IND-ARRAY(2) IS LESS THAN ZERO
THEN
    MOVE 'something or other' TO BIG-INT.

IF  IND-ARRAY(3) IS LESS THAN ZERO
THEN
    MOVE 'something or other' TO TIME-COL.

IF  IND-ARRAY(4) IS LESS THAN ZERO
THEN
    MOVE 'something or other' TO DECIMAL-COL.
```

4.

```
01  FIELDS-WS.
    05   QTY-AVG      PIC S9(5)V99 COMP-3.
    05   QTY-MAX      PIC S9(4) COMP.
    05   LIT          PIC X(15).
```

Chapter 5

Handling SQL Return Codes

After completing this chapter you will be able to describe the different fields in the SQLCA and be able to use these fields in problem diagnosis. You will also learn how to code the appropriate WHENEVER statements to generate automated error-handling logic. Topics include:

5.1. Handling Run-Time Errors and Exceptional Conditions
5.2. The SQLCA Fields and Their Use
5.3. The WHENEVER Statement
5.4. WHENEVER Considerations
5.5. DSNTIAR — The SQL Return Code Module
5.6. Review Questions
5.7. Exercise Solutions
5.8. Workshop — III

5.1. HANDLING RUN-TIME ERRORS AND EXCEPTIONAL CONDITIONS

It would be just terrific if the programs we executed never ABENDed or encountered conditions we hadn't planned for during development. But you and I know that this is seldom, if ever, the

case. More than likely, given the complexity of today's logic specifications and the sheer amount of data in production files,
"encountering the unexpected" is the rule rather than the exception. And if you have been programming long enough, it's a safe
bet that you've incorporated various "defensive programming"
strategies into your coding style to trap run-time errors or exceptional situations and handle them gracefully. One favorite spot in
COBOL application programs to encounter problems is during the
Database access request.

Different database systems offer different types and levels of support for handling run-time problems. Most of DB2's support
centers around the fields in the SQL Communications Area
(SQLCA). It is necessary for you to handle the various run-time
errors or exceptional situations by testing the values in the
SQLCA fields and taking appropriate actions. The ways and
means of doing this are the subject of this chapter.

5.1.1.   DB2 and the SQLCA

When DB2 processes an SQL statement in your program,it places
a value (a return code) in the SQLCODE field of the SQLCA. The
value in the SQLCODE field indicates the success or failure of
your statement's execution. There are three possible situations:

1.   DB2 encounters a severe error while processing your statement. The return code value in SQLCODE is negative. No
data is returned to your program.

2.   DB2 encounters an exceptional condition, but can continue
processing your statement. The return code value in SQL-
CODE is positive. In this case, data is returned to your program.

3.   DB2 processes your statement without incident. The return
code value in SQLCODE is zero. Data is returned to your
program.

DB2 also updates other fields in the SQLCA with information
regarding the status of your SQL statement's execution. Of primary importance are the SQLWARN fields, a set of warning flags
which are set to "W" to signify various exception conditions.
These exception situations occur when a zero or positive SQL-
CODE is returned to your program *and* the result is in some ways
suspicious. For instance, if a value was truncated as a result of
conversion during execution, SQLCODE is 0. However, one of the
previously mentioned SQL warning flags (SQLWARN1) contains a
"W" to indicate truncation.

A great deal of information about error and exception conditions is
available in the SQLCA, and there are two ways to evaluate the
important fields of this structure:

•   Automated Error handling using WHENEVER — As we have
seen in previous chapters, WHENEVER automatically generates IF-THEN-ELSE logic which tests for certain classes of
return codes and then branches to specified paragraphs
within your program if the test is true.

•   Programmer-defined logic — In place of WHENEVER, you
may code your own customized error-handling routines after
SQL statements. Programmer-defined routines have the
advantage of being able to use certain COBOL logic constructs that WHENEVER currently does not.

You will learn how to build error-handling routines using both
WHENEVER and programmer-defined logic in this chapter. But
before you do this, let's analyze the SQLCA and see what we
have to work with.

5.2.   THE SQLCA FIELDS AND THEIR USE

Recall from Chapter 1 that you must INCLUDE a copy of the DB2 SQLCA SQL Communications Area in your program's WORKING-STORAGE by coding:

```
EXEC SQL INCLUDE SQLCA END-EXEC.
```

At precompile time the above code is commented out and replaced by the COBOL 01 LEVEL data item, shown in Figure 50:

```
01  SQLCA
    05   SQLCAID          PIC X(8).
    05   SQLCABC          PIC S9(9) COMPUTATIONAL.
    05   SQLCODE          PIC S9(9) COMPUTATIONAL.
    05   SQLERRM.
         49  SQLERRML     PIC S9(4) COMPUTATIONAL.
         49  SQLERRMC     PIC X(70).
    05   SQLERRP          PIC X(8).
    05   SQLERRD OCCURS 6 TIMES.
                          PIC S9(9) COMPUTATIONAL.
    05   SQLWARN.
         10  SQLWARN0     PIC X(1).
         10  SQLWARN1     PIC X(1).
         10  SQLWARN2     PIC X(1).
         10  SQLWARN3     PIC X(1).
         10  SQLWARN4     PIC X(1).
         10  SQLWARN5     PIC X(1).
         10  SQLWARN6     PIC X(1).
         10  SQLWARN7     PIC X(1).
    05   SQLEXT           PIC X(8).
```

Figure 50.   SQLCA fields.

Some of the fields in the SQLCA are critical, some are of interest only in certain situations, and others are, for the most part, unimportant. Let's find out which are which.

5.2.1. SQLCAID

This field is basically a storage identifier, useful in finding the SQLCA in dumps and ABEND print-outs. It contains the value "SQLCA."

5.2.2. SQLCABC

The SQLCABC contains the length of the SQLCA. Its current value is 136.

5.2.3. SQLCODE

As we have been discussing, the SQLCODE contains a DB2 return code value. There are several hundred possible return codes. You will find many of the important "application oriented" problem return codes in appendix D. In general:

• A zero in the SQLCODE means successful execution,

• A negative value in the SQLCODE means unsuccessful execution,

• A positive value in the SQLCODE means successful execution, but with an exception condition.

For a complete listing of the possible DB2 return codes, consult the IBM *DB2 Messages and Codes* Manual.

5.2.4.   SQLERRM (SQLERRML and SQLERRMC)

This varying length field contains hexadecimal information on error conditions. The information contained in this field can be used by systems programmers and technical support personnel to debug difficult or complex error situations — situations where the return code value in the SQLCODE is not sufficient to determine the cause of the error.

5.2.5.   SQLERRP

This field provides additional internal diagnostic information, such as the name of the DB2 run-time module in which the error occurred. This information is typically *not* useful in problem determination by application programmers. It is meant for systems programmers, database administrators and other interested parties to investigate.

5.2.6.   SQLERRD

A COBOL array (table) of six values:

* SQLERRD(1) Contains a Relational Data System[1] error code.
* SQLERRD(2) Contains a Data Manager[2] error code.
* SQLERRD(3) Contains the number of DB2 table rows affected by INSERT, UPDATE or DELETE SQL statements.
* SQLERRD(4) Contains floating point values that roughly indicate the relative estimate of resources required for the statement.

[1,2,3]Relational Data System, Data Manager, and Buffer Manager are internal DB2 executable modules.

- SQLERRD(5) Contains the position or column of a syntax error for a dynamic SQL statement.
- SQLERRD(6) Contains a Buffer Manager[3] error code.

Of the six array values in SQLERRD, the most useful is SQLERRD(3), which can be employed for internal/external file balancing, as well as in debugging problem situations.

5.2.7.   SQLWARN Flags

A list of eight flags, describing exception conditions that occurred during SQL statement execution.

- SQLWARN0   Lead-in flag. SQLWARN0 contains a "W" if an exception condition occurred, otherwise it contains a blank.
- SQLWARN1   Truncation flag. SQLWARN1 contains a "W" if a character column was truncated when assigned to a host variable.
- SQLWARN2   Null elimination flag. SQLWARN2 contains a "W" if fields containing null values were eliminated from the argument of a function such as AVG, COUNT, etc.
- SQLWARN3   Host structure mismatch flag. SQLWARN3 contains a "W" if the number of table columns in a SELECT * statement is greater than the number of fields in a host structure. This warning occurs when a DB2 table is altered, columns are added, and application programs using SELECT * into host structures are not maintained to reflect the changes.
- SQLWARN4   Unconditional update flag. SQLWARN4 contains a "W" if an UPDATE or DELETE statement does not include a WHERE clause (you will update every row of the table).

- SQLWARN5   SQL/DS conversion flag. SQLWARN5 contains a "W" if an attempt was made to execute an SQL statement unique to SQL/DS.
- SQLWARN6   Date/Timestamp conversion flag. SQLWARN6 contains a "W" if DB2 had to adjust the day portion of a date/timestamp value to correct an invalid date (i.e., you added one MONTH to the date August 31 which would give you September 31. Since there is no September 31, the date will become September 30, and SQLWARN6 will be set to "W").
- SQLWARN7   Not currently used.

5.2.8.   SQLEXT

Not currently used.

As you can see, many of the SQLWARN fields can be important aids in debugging exception conditions. My suggestion is to inspect SQLWARN0 after each call, and if it contains a "W," perform a routine to test SQLWARN1 through SQLWARN6 for further problem determination (I suppose you could skip checking SQL-WARN5 unless you've recently converted from SQL/DS to DB2). A COBOL routine to manually inspect the SQLWARN fields is coded in Figure 51.

5.3.   THE WHENEVER STATEMENT

The WHENEVER statement generates logic to branch to specific areas of your application program if an error, exception condition, or warning exists as a result of executing an SQL statement. We have been using WHENEVER in our sample programs to branch to 999-SQLERROR-RTN if an SQLERROR occurred. Understand that what WHENEVER does is to add the following "IF"

```
CHECK-SQLWARN-RTN.SQL

    IF SQLWARN0 NOT EQUAL 'W'
    THEN
        GO TO CHECK-SQLWARN-EXIT.

    IF SQLWARN1 = 'W'
    THEN
        PERFORM 999-TRUNCATE-RTN.

    IF SQLWARN2 = 'W'
    THEN
        PERFORM 999-NULL-CHECK-RTN.

    IF SQLWARN3 = 'W'
    THEN
        PERFORM 999-TOO-MANY-FLDS-RTN.

    IF SQLWARN4 = 'W'
    THEN
        PERFORM 999-ROLLBACK-RTN.

    IF SQLWARN6 = 'W'
    THEN
        PERFORM 999-DATE-CONVERT-RTN.

CHECK-SQLWARN-EXIT.
    EXIT.
```

Figure 51.   SQLWARN handling routine.

statement to your COBOL program immediately following each executable SQL statement:

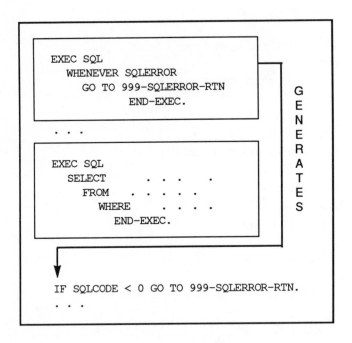

```
        EXEC SQL
            WHENEVER SQLERROR
                GO TO 999-SQLERROR-RTN
                    END-EXEC.

        . . .

        EXEC SQL
            SELECT     . . . .    .
                FROM   . . . . .
                    WHERE   . . . .
                        END-EXEC.


        IF SQLCODE < 0 GO TO 999-SQLERROR-RTN.
        . . .
```

The format for the WHENEVER statement is:

```
EXEC SQL
            WHENEVER <general-condition> <unconditional-action>
END-EXEC.
```

where "general-condition" allows you to specify one of three levels of error exception circumstances, and "unconditional-action" allows you to specify one of two actions.

5.3.1.   GENERAL-CONDITION

There are three types of general-condition WHENEVER can process:

- SQLWARNING   A SQLWARNING condition occurs when SQLWARN0 is set to "W," or SQLCODE contains a positive value other than +100.
- SQLERROR   A SQLERROR condition occurs when SQLCODE contains a negative value.
- NOT FOUND   A NOT FOUND condition (SQLCODE = +100) occurs when DB2 cannot find a row to satisfy your WHERE clause's search condition, or when there are no more rows in a results table to fetch (retrieve into your program using a symbolic cursor).

5.3.2.   UNCONDITIONAL-ACTION

There are only two actions WHENEVER can take as a result of execution:

- CONTINUE   CONTINUE causes your program to execute the Next Sequential Instruction following the SQL statement.
- GOTO   GOTO unconditionally branches to a paragraph or section in your program.

Note: For some reason, the current version of the DB2 precompiler allows you to code "GOTO" as well as "GO TO." However, the IBM DATABASE 2 Version 2 Application Programming Guide *specifies it as "GO TO." To be safe (say if IBM pulls the plug on "GOTO" in a future release) code it as two separate words.*

Let's take a look at some examples, in Figure 52, using combinations of "general-conditions" and "unconditional-actions."

```
EXEC SQL
     WHENEVER SQLERROR GO TO 999-ERROR-TRAP-RTN
END-EXEC.
     ** If SQLCODE < 0, program control is transferred
        unconditionally to paragraph 999-
```

```
EXEC SQL
     WHENEVER SQLERROR CONTINUE
END-EXEC.
     ** If SQLCODE < 0, program control falls through
        to the Next Sequential Instruction*
```

```
EXEC SQL
     WHENEVER SQLEWARNING GO TO 888-EXCEPTION-EVALUATE-RTN
END-EXEC.
     ** If SQLCODE > 0, but not equal to +100
        program control is transferred
        unconditionally to paragraph 888-
```

```
EXEC SQL
     WHENEVER SQLWARNING CONTINUE
END-EXEC.
     ** If SQLCODE > 0, but not equal to +100
        program control falls through to the
        Next Sequential Instruction
```

```
EXEC SQL
     WHENEVER NOT FOUND GO TO 777-NOMATCH-ON-SEARCH-RTN
END-EXEC.
     ** If SQLCODE = +100, program control is transferred
        unconditionally to paragraph 777-
```

```
EXEC SQL
     WHENEVER NOT FOUND CONTINUE
END-EXEC.
     ** If SQLCODE = +100, program control falls through
        to the Next Sequential Instruction
```

Figure 52. Combinations of WHENEVER conditions.

• Next Sequential Instruction The COBOL instruction that physically follows the current COBOL instruction in your listing.

WHENEVER affects all SQL statements that "physically" follow it, until the end of your program code or the next WHENEVER statement is encountered. This means that at different places in your program, you can specify different actions based on error or exception conditions. This can get somewhat confusing, particularly if your program contains many PERFORM or GOTO branches. Which WHENEVER logic is in effect depends on the previous physical WHENEVER statement(s), not the logical path you may be PERFORMING or branching within. My recommendation is that if you use WHENEVER to handle error and exception conditions, only use one set of WHENEVER statements (one for each general-condition you wish to handle with WHENEVER) per program.

The only exception to this rule of thumb might be within the actual error-trapping paragraphs WHENEVER takes you to. If within a 999-ERROR-TRAPPING-RTN paragraph you want to issue manual SQL ROLLBACK commands regardless of the outcome of previous SQL statement execution, you might specify:

```
EXEC SQL WHENEVER SQLERROR CONTINUE END-EXEC.
```

This will allow you to execute multiple ROLLBACK statements in case of SQL error situations.

5.4. WHENEVER CONSIDERATIONS

Before we discuss the pluses and minuses of using the WHENEVER statement to handle error and exception conditions, you should probably hunt down your shop's documentation on using WHENEVER. It can probably be found in something like a *DB2 Standards and Procedures Manual,* which can be obtained from your local DB2 database administrator or DB2 system administrator. You will probably find the issue concerning whether or not to use, or how to use, WHENEVER, has been resolved in your installation, and you should follow the coding standards set forth.

5.4.1.   WHENEVER Pluses

WHENEVER *automates* the SQL error and exception-handling processing in your program. You may never have to code a single IF-THEN-ELSE to evaluate the results of your SQL statement execution. This is done uniformly by the precompiler, and there is no possibility of human error. The precompiler will never forget to check the SQLCODE after an SQL statement.

WHENEVER can also *standardize* the SQL error- and exception-handling processing at your installation. Each program can copy or INCLUDE the error-trapping paragraph code necessary to work with WHENEVER. This too can raise your productivity level.

5.4.2.   WHENEVER Minuses

WHENEVER does not allow conditional branching, PERFORM, or CALL statements. This means that (except for the rather useless CONTINUE option) program control will never return to the Next Sequential Instruction following the SQL statement that caused the branch to the error or exception paragraph. This is a serious deficiency, particularly for exception condition handling — SQLWARNINGs and NOT FOUNDs. Most of the time you will *not* want to break out of a PERFORM UNTIL chain after an exception condition. Using WHENEVER statements like:

```
         EXEC SQL WHENEVER SQLWARNING GO
            TO EXCEPTION-PARA END-EXEC.
```

makes this very difficult to accomplish. You could potentially set switches and use various other programming techniques (carry paragraph names in fields, etc.) to get around the problem, but it is not a trivial effort. Of course, for severe SQL problems (negative SQLCODE values — SQLERRORs) your application plan will shut down[4] and you will want to end your program regardless.

My suggestion is to use WHENEVER SQLERROR as a standard method for handling negative SQLCODEs, and to implement programmer defined exception handling routines for all other conditions.

5.5. DSNTIAR.   THE SQL RETURN CODE MODULE

IBM supplies a handy dump program called DSNTIAR with DB2. DSNTIAR will translate the SQLCODE into readable (usable) English and can be used in installation standard error- and exception-handling routines to display problem information on Dumps, or job SYSOUT reports. It is fairly easy to use and requires only a few standard inputs and outputs:

You must code certain fields in your WORKING-STORAGE SECTION:

---

[4]Except in one or two rare circumstances involving CICS programs and certain deadlock situations.

```
01  SQLCA.
        . . .
01  ERROR-MSG.
        05    ERROR-LEN      PIC S9(04) COMP VALUE +960.
        05    ERROR-TEXT     PIC X(120) OCCURS 8 TIMES
                    INDEXED BY ERR-IDX.
01  ERROR-TEXT-LEN      PIC S9(09) COMP VALUE +120.
```

You CALL DSNTIAR in the following way:

```
CALL 'DSNTIAR' USING
                    SQLCA,
                    ERROR-MSG,
                    ERROR-TEXT-LEN.
```

After DSNTIAR has placed the translated message for your SQL-CODE in the WORKING-STORAGE table (shown above as ERROR-MSG), you can display it, write it to an ABEND file, etc.

Remember to INCLUDE DSNTIAR at Link-Edit time if you are going to use it.

5.6. REVIEW QUESTIONS

For the first four questions code WHENEVER statements to handle the error or exception conditions specified.

1.   If a negative return code value is assigned for any call, branch unconditionally to the paragraph: XXX-DUMP-RTN.

2.   If a +100 return code value is assigned for any call, branch unconditionally to the paragraph: EMPL-NOT-FOUND-ON-TABLE.

3.   If a positive return code (but not a +100) is assigned, or if any of the SQL warning flags are set to "W," branch unconditionally to the paragraph: HMM-LETS-CHECK-INTO-THIS.

4.   If a positive return code (but not a +100) is assigned, or any of the SQL warning flags are set to "W," continue processing with the Next Sequential Instruction.

For questions 5 through 8, code custom IF-THEN-ELSE logic to handle the error or exception conditions specified.

5.   If a negative SQLCODE is returned for this SQL statement, branch unconditionally to the paragraph: XXX-DUMP-RTN.

6.   If a +100 SQLCODE is returned for this SQL statement, branch to the paragraph: EMPL-NOT-FOUND-ON-TABLE, and return to the Next Sequential Instruction.

7.   If a positive return code (but not a +100) is assigned, or if any of the SQL warning flags are set to "W" for this SQL statement, call the installation module: WARNCHKR, with the following information:

   • The address of the SQLCA
   • The name of the program
   • The name of the paragraph
   • The type of SQL statement that resulted in the warning.

8.   If a positive return code (but not a +100) is assigned, or if any of the SQL warning flags are set to "W," continue processing with the Next Sequential Instruction.

5.7.   EXERCISE SOLUTIONS

5.7.1.   USING WHENEVER

1.   EXEC SQL WHENEVER SQLERROR GOTO XXX-DUMP-RTN END-EXEC.

2.   EXEC SQL WHENEVER NOT FOUND GOTO EMPL-NOT-FOUND-ON-TABLE END-EXEC.

3.   EXEC SQL WHENEVER SQLWARNING GOTO HMM-LETS-CHECK-INTO-THIS END-EXEC.

4.   EXEC SQL WHENEVER SQLWARNING CONTINUE END-EXEC.

5.7.2.   CUSTOM CODE

5.   IF SQLCODE < ZERO
        GOTO XXX-DUMP-RTN.

6.   IF SQLCODE = +100
        PERFORM EMPL-NOT-FOUND-ON-TABLE.

7.   (COBOL If and Move statements to initialize SQL statement)

     IF (SQLCODE > ZERO AND SQLCODE NOT EQUAL +100) OR
        SQLWARN0 = 'W'
           CALL 'WARNCHKR' USING
                SQLCA,
                'MODULE',
                'PARA-NAME',
                SQL-WHICH-STATEMENT-WS.

8.   IF (SQLCODE > ZERO AND SQLCODE NOT EQUAL +100) OR
        SQLWARN0 = 'W'
     THEN
        NEXT SENTENCE.

5.8. WORKSHOP IV

Time for another program. Shown below is a skeleton COBOL program called VARIOUS, so named because it doesn't really do anything from a business data processing perspective, but it does illustrate various points and techniques you've been learning in the past two chapters. COBOL comments embedded in the program code specify what actions you are to take to complete the program, adding:

- INCLUDE statements
- WHENEVER statements, or custom error-handling logic
- SQL SELECT, UPDATE, and DELETE statements

You must design and code your own error- and exception-handling paragraphs. As you may guess, there are three areas to address:

> You *must* code an error-handling paragraph for negative SQL return codes (you may use DSNTIAR for this, or simply dump various WORKING-STORAGE fields as we've done up to now.

> I leave it up to you as to whether or not you wish to verify the SQL warnings. You will find individual checks for specific situations already in place in the Procedure Division. However, you may or may not want to have one central paragraph that handles SQLWARNING type return codes. Also, how you access this paragraph is up to you.

> I leave it up to you as to whether or not you want to address NOT FOUND conditions with a centralized paragraph at all.

When you are finished coding your program, I suggest you check them against my solution in appendix A. Then, modify the JCL you used to preprocess your program(s) from chapter 3, changing the:

- PROGRAM NAME
- PLAN NAME
- DBRM NAME

and reexecute the JCL to test your (our) results. You do not need any external files for this program.

Note that we are using a new table in this workshop. It is called CELEBRITY_RACE, and the values in it are listed below.

ENTRANT	CAR	DRIVER	PRICE	MILEAGE	PURCHASE	QUAL_TIM
1	LINCOLN	MARIO SPAGHETTI	3400.88	5400	1987-01-01	01.14.39
2	SEAHAWK	MRS. PAUL	1940.25	2100	1984-05-29	07.23.51
3	300 ZX	PAUL NEWMAN	189.99	12788	1988-05-22	00.54.33
4	LAND ROVER	MAGGIE THATCHER	———	15400	1985-12-25	11.55.24
5	———	MILLARD FILLMORE	1999.99	———	1983-10-31	08.33.56

BASE TABLE — CELEBRITY_RACE

```
IDENTIFICATION DIVISION.
 PROGRAM-ID. VARIOUS.
*REMARKS. THIS PROGRAM USES SEVERAL DIFFERENT DATATYPES AND
*    PROGRAMMING TECHNIQUES TO REINFORCE THE LESSONS ON
*    HOST PROGRAM VARIABLES AND ERROR-HANDLING ROUTINES
*    COVERED DURING CHAPTERS FOUR AND FIVE.
*
ENVIRONMENT DIVISION.
CONFIGURATION SECTION.
SOURCE-COMPUTER. IBM-370.
OBJECT-COMPUTER. IBM-370.
DATA DIVISION.
WORKING-STORAGE SECTION.

*HOST PROGRAM VARIABLES - DATA ITEMS EXPLICITLY DEFINED

     EXEC SQL INCLUDE CELEBRIT END-EXEC.
     EXEC SQL INCLUDE SQLCA END-EXEC.
```

```
01  MISC-DATA-ITEMS.
    05    SMALL-FIELD       PIC X(02).
    05    LONG-FIELD        PIC X(22).
    05    AVG-MILEAGE       PIC ??????
    05    SQLCODE-OUT       PIC 9(03).
    05    NUL-FIELD         PIC ??????
    05    NUL-FIELD-1       PIC ??????
    05    NUL-STRUCT.
       10    NUL            PIC S9(04) COMP OCCURS 8 TIMES.
```

```
PROCEDURE DIVISION.
*
000-SETUP-ERROR-TRAP-RTN.
*****************************************************************
*        CODE THE CORRECT ERROR-TRAPPING ROUTINES TO:         *
*                                                             *
*    BRANCH TO 999-ERROR-TRAP-RTN ON A NEGATIVE SQLCODE       *
*    CONTINUE PROCESSING UPON FINDING A POSITIVE SQLCODE      *
*    CONTINUE PROCESSING UPON END OF DATA                     *
*                                                             *
*****************************************************************
```

```
EXEC SQL
    WHENEVER SQLERROR ?????????????????????????????
END-EXEC.
```

```
EXEC SQL WHENEVER SQLWARNING ???????????????????
```

```
EXEC SQL WHENEVER NOT FOUND ????????????????????
```

```
*
 000-MAINLINE-RTN.
*
     DISPLAY 'BEGINNING OF PROGRAM — VARIOUS'.
     DISPLAY SPACES.
*
     PERFORM 200-TEST-RTN THRU 200-EXIT.
*
     MOVE ZERO TO RETURN-CODE.
     GOBACK.
*
 000-EXIT.
     EXIT.
200-TEST-RTN.
*
 ******************************************************************
 ***   CODE AND EXECUTE THE FOLLOWING DATABASE REQUESTS      ***
 ***                                                         ***
 ***   (AFTER EACH CALL, DISPLAY THE REQUEST NUMBER,         ***
 ***   THE ROW RETURNED (IF APPROPRIATE) AND THE SQLCODE     ***
 ******************************************************************
*
 ******************************************************************
 *1)   UPDATE THE CELEBRITY RACE TABLE:                          *
 *     SET THE PURCHASE EQUAL TO THE CURRENT DATE — AND          *
 *     THE QUALIFYING TIME EQUAL TO 71 SECONDS ***be careful   ****
 *     DB2 is very picky about valid times ***, FOR ALL ROWS IN  *
 *     THE TABLE. AFTER THE CALL, DISPLAY SQLERRD(3) TO VERIFY   *
 *     THE NBR OF ROWS UPDATED BY THE CALL.                      *
 ******************************************************************
```

```
     EXEC SQL UPDATE




     END-EXEC.
```

```
        DISPLAY '*** REQUEST 1 ***, SQLCODE'.
        MOVE SQLCODE TO SQLCODE-OUT.
        DISPLAY SQLCODE-OUT.
        DISPLAY '*** NBR ROWS UPDATED = ' SQLERRD(3).

*
****************************************************************
*2)   CALCULATE THE AVG(MILEAGE) FOR THE MERCEDES BENZ        *
*     YOU WILL NEED A NULL-INDICATOR FOR YOUR HOST            *
*     VARIABLE — WHY?                                         *
****************************************************************
```

```
        EXEC SQL




        END-EXEC.
```

```
        DISPLAY '*** REQUEST 2 ***'.
        DISPLAY '*** NULL-VALUE ===> ' NULL-FIELD.
        DISPLAY '*** SQLCODE AND AVG-MILEAGE'.
        MOVE SQLCODE TO SQLCODE-OUT.
        DISPLAY SQLCODE-OUT.
        DISPLAY AVG-MILEAGE.

*
****************************************************************
*3)   CALCULATE THE AVERAGE ENTRANT CAR MILEAGE FOR          *
*     ALL CARS.                                              *
*     AFTER THE CALL DISPLAY THE SQLWARNINGS TO CHECK        *
*     FOR NULL                                               *
*     VALUES IN THE ROWS.                                    *
****************************************************************
```

```
    EXEC SQL




    END-EXEC.
```

```
*
    DISPLAY '*** REQUEST 3 ***'.
    DISPLAY '*** AVERAGE ===> ' AVG-MILEAGE.
    DISPLAY '*** SQLCODE ***'.
    MOVE SQLCODE TO SQLCODE-OUT.
    DISPLAY SQLCODE-OUT.
*
    DISPLAY '*** WARNINGS ***, SQLWARN0, SQLWARN2 '.
    DISPLAY SQLWARN0.
    DISPLAY SQLWARN2.
*

****************************************************************
* 4)  SELECT DRIVER INTO SMALL-FIELD FOR DRIVER 'MARIO         *
*     SPAGHETTI'                                               *
*     CHECK AND DISPLAY SQLWARN(S) AFTER THE CALL              *
****************************************************************
*
*    MOVE 'MARIO SPAGHETTI' TO LONG-FIELD.
```

```
  EXEC SQL SELECT DRIVER

     WHERE DRIVER = :LONG-FIELD

  END-EXEC.
```

```
        DISPLAY `*** REQUEST 4 ***'.
        DISPLAY `*** SMALL-FIELD ===> ` SMALL-FIELD.
        DISPLAY `*** SQLCODE ***'.
        MOVE SQLCODE TO SQLCODE-OUT.
        DISPLAY SQLCODE-OUT.
        DISPLAY `*** WARNINGS ***, SQLWARN0, SQLWARN2 `.
        DISPLAY SQLWARN0.
        DISPLAY SQLWARN1.
*
 *************************************************************
* 5A) INSERT A ROW INTO CELEBRITY RACE. IF SQLCODE = ZERO      *
*     ISSUE A COMMIT WORK STATEMENT.                          *
* 5B) RETRIEVE AND DISPLAY THE ROW YOU JUST INSERTED          *
 *************************************************************
*
        MOVE 11                    TO ENTRANT, DRIVER-LEN.
        MOVE `LEE IACOCCA'         TO DRIVER-TEXT.
        MOVE `ARIES K'             TO CAR.
        MOVE 1                     TO MILEAGE.
        MOVE 7900                  TO PRICE.
        MOVE `1988-10-01'          TO PURCHASE.
        MOVE `00.01.00'            TO QUAL-TIM.
```

```
 EXEC SQL                                          5a.
    INSERT INTO ?????????????
    (:
     :
     :
     :
     :
     :
     :                 )
 END-EXEC.
```

```
        DISPLAY `*** REQUEST 5A ***'.
        DISPLAY `*** SQLCODE ***'.
        MOVE SQLCODE TO SQLCODE-OUT.
        DISPLAY SQLCODE-OUT.
```

```
                                                              5b.
   IF ???????? > 4
   EXEC SQL ??????????? END-EXEC.
```

```
   EXEC SQL

   END-EXEC.
```

```
      DISPLAY '*** REQUEST 5B ***'.
      DISPLAY '*** TABLE-ROW ===> ' DCLCELEBRITY-RACE.
      DISPLAY '*** SQLCODE ***'.
      MOVE SQLCODE TO SQLCODE-OUT.
      DISPLAY SQLCODE-OUT.


*****************************************************************
* 6)   DELETE ALL ROWS FROM CELEBRITY RACE — WHERE             *
*      PURCHASE = THE CURRENT DATE.                            *
*       **** DISPLAY SQLWARNINGS AND SQLERRD(3) ****           *
*      IF SQLERRD(3) INDICATES THAT YOU HAVE ERASED OVER FOUR  *
*      ROWS IN THE TABLE, ISSUE THE ROLLBACK WORK COMMAND.     *
*****************************************************************
```

```
      EXEC SQL
         ??????? ??????? ??????????
      END-EXEC.
```

```
      DISPLAY SPACES.
      DISPLAY '*** REQUEST 6 ***'.
      DISPLAY '*** SQLCODE ***'.
      MOVE SQLCODE TO SQLCODE-OUT.
      DISPLAY SQLCODE-OUT.
*
      DISPLAY '*** NBR ROWS DELETED = ' SQLERRD(3).
```

```
     IF SQLCODE = 0
         EXEC SQL ?????????? ???????? END-EXEC.
```

*

```
     DISPLAY '*** SQLCODE AFTER ROLLBACK ***'.
     MOVE SQLCODE TO SQLCODE-OUT.
     DISPLAY SQLCODE-OUT.
200-EXIT.
     EXIT.
```

```
     *** Code your Error and Exception handling routines here ***
```

Chapter 6

DB2 CURSOR Operations

After completing this chapter you will be able to define and use symbolic CURSORs to retrieve multiple rows selected as a result of SQL statement execution. You will also learn how to limit DB2's update scope to a single row using CURSORs. Topics include:

6.1.   Why CURSORs?
6.2.   What Is a CURSOR?
6.3.   Defining a CURSOR for Retrieval
6.4.   OPENing a CURSOR
6.5.   Retrieving Rows (FETCH) With CURSOR
6.6.   CLOSEing a CURSOR
6.7.   Using a CURSOR in Retrieval Operations
6.8.   Updating a Table Using a Symbolic Cursor
6.9.   Defining a CURSOR for DELETE
6.10.   Using Multiple CURSORs
6.11.   Review Questions
6.12.   Solutions
6.13.   Workshop V
6.14.   Workshop VI
6.15.   Workshop VII
6.16.   Workshop Tables

6.1. WHY CURSORS?

Back in the fifties when Admiral Grace Hopper and her cohorts were putting together symbolic programming languages like COBOL and FORTRAN, file access was hardwired into the language at the record level. There were very few crystal balls in existence then, and no one foresaw the time when one data access statement could retrieve or update multiple records. They had their hands full just trying to keep moths (bugs) out of the computer tubes long enough to run compiles.

By the time Dr. E. F. Codd postulated the viability of relational databases and set-level data access/manipulation through mathematical language operators (the early 1970s), COBOL (which had been around for almost 20 years), was very much set in its ways regarding the unit of I/O data transfer. This unit was (and still is) the record — singular. There is no mechanism in OS/VS COBOL (or COBOL II for that matter) to handle set-level I/O operations. This is no problem for UPDATE and DELETE operations as these are processed by DB2. Multiple row SELECT operations, however, must be handled by COBOL and these pose a major league dilemma.

6.1.1. Singleton SELECT versus Symbolic Cursor Processing

As we've seen in our SQL/COBOL programs, Singleton SELECT statements can only act on a single row (record) at a time. Yet many (probably most) of your SQL statements create results tables containing multiple records. So the designers of the SQL host language interface had to come up with a scheme allowing programs to work (in some way) with multiple rows retrieved as a result of an SQL statement execution. Enter the Symbolic Cursor.

6.2.   WHAT IS A CURSOR?

As we have discussed very briefly in chapters 1 and 2, there is a DB2 object (IBM calls it a "structure") called a symbolic cursor. CURSORs are used like pointers to move through rows of a multiple row results table built by the execution of an SQL SELECT statement. This is illustrated in Figure 53:

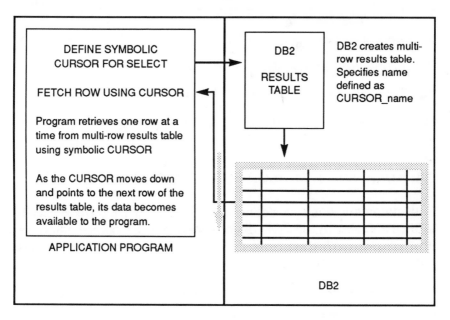

Figure 53. Symbolic Cursor used like movable pointer through results table.

As Figure 53 shows, CURSORS symbolically define (name) a temporary results table. The rows of the results table are made available to the program one at a time for retrieval. CURSORs process results tables from top to bottom (first row to last row). And they must be used in application programs in place of Singleton SELECTs if your SQL statement execution results in more than one row. CURSORs also allow you to issue UPDATE or DELETE statements that affect only one row. This can be a useful technique in handling some types of application processing requirements.

There are four separate statements involved with using symbolic CURSORs in application programs:

1.   Define (DECLARE) the CURSOR.

2.   Activate (OPEN) the CURSOR.

3.   Retrieve a row (FETCH) using the CURSOR.

4.   Deactivate (CLOSE) the CURSOR.

Let's see how to define CURSORs for retrieval.

6.3.   DEFINING A CURSOR FOR RETRIEVAL

The statement used to define a CURSOR is DECLARE CUR-SOR. DECLARE CURSOR defines the symbolic cursor name for an SQL SELECT statement. It is very simple to use and follows the format specified in Figure 54:

```
EXEC SQL
      DECLARE <cursor_name> CURSOR FOR
          <SELECT statement>
END-EXEC.
```

Where:

*   <cursor_name> must be a valid DB2 object data name (up to 18 characters, beginning with an alphabetic character and using underscores (_) not hyphens (-).

- <SELECT statement> is any valid SQL SELECT statement in native SQL format — that is, not Singleton SELECT INTO format.

Let's take a look at a couple of DECLARE CURSOR examples.

You can DECLARE a CURSOR anywhere within the Procedure Division or Working-Storage Section of your program. If Working-Storage seems a strange place to be issuing SQL SELECT statements, don't be confused. Remember that declaring a cursor

```
EXEC SQL
    DECLARE QTY_BY_TYPE CURSOR FOR
        SELECT TYPE, AVG(QTY) FROM MOV
            GROUP BY TYPE
END-EXEC.
```

```
EXEC SQL
    DECLARE SEL_ALL_DRAMA CURSOR FOR
        SELECT * FROM MOV
            WHERE TYPE = 'DRAMA'
END-EXEC.
```

```
EXEC SQL
    DECLARE JOIN_EM CURSOR FOR
        SELECT LNAME, INV.NBR, RENT
            FROM CUST, INV
                WHERE CUST.ID = INV.CUSTID
END-EXEC.
```

Figure 54.   Symbolic cursor examples.

does not execute the SELECT statement for that cursor, it simply defines the cursor name and associates the name with an SQL select statement.

Execution of the statement begins when you OPEN the cursor.

6.4.   OPENING A CURSOR

There's really not much to the OPEN cursor statement. An example is shown below:

```
EXEC SQL OPEN <cursor_name> END-EXEC.
```

OPEN statement example

All that is required is that you spell the cursor_name correctly, and that the cursor_name you specify be defined in your program. A few points to keep in mind, however:

- You must open a cursor before you attempt to retrieve rows from it (FETCH) or CLOSE it — kind of brings you back to the old OS file processing days, remembering to open your files before you read from or write to them.
- You may not open a cursor twice without having closed it between successive OPENs (deja vu with OS files again).
- All search fields in your statements are evaluated by DB2 at OPEN time. This means that whatever values you want DB2 to search on or use as SELECTed literals must be initialized prior to executing OPEN — not DECLARE CURSOR.

This last point is important and bears repeating. It is OPEN that is the first executable SQL statement of the four statements involved in using a CURSOR. Upon OPEN, DB2 reads your search field values, executes the SQL statement defined for the CURSOR you specify, and builds your results table. This is illustrated for you in Figure 55.

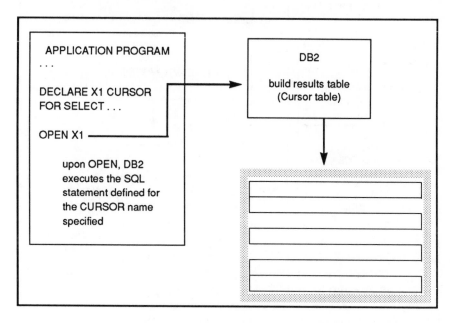

Figure 55.   OPEN statement execution.

OPEN does not assign any results table rows to your host program variables. For that we need the FETCH statement.

6.5.   RETRIEVING ROWS (FETCH) WITH CURSOR

FETCH is used to retrieve one row at a time from the results table built by OPEN. Fetch returns the rows into your program's host variables. When all of the rows of a results table have been FETCHed, DB2 places a +100 value into SQLCODE. The FETCH operation is illustrated in Figure 56.

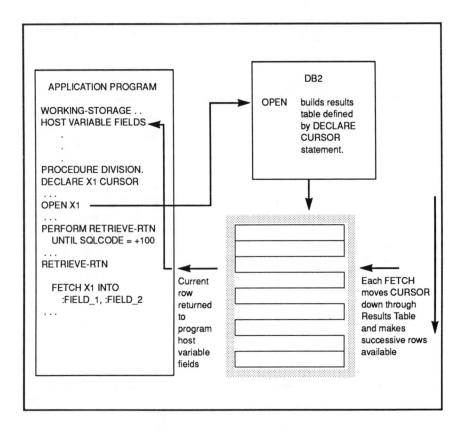

Figure 56.   FETCH statement execution.

The format for the FETCH statement is shown below:

```
EXEC SQL FETCH <cursor_name> INTO <fld_1, fld_2, fld_n> END-EXEC.
```

FETCH statement format.

As you can see from the above example, the FETCH operation is very similar to traditional OS file read processing:

- You FETCH a DECLAREd and OPENed cursor (<cursor_name>) into a set of host variable fields (just like you READ a defined and OPENed external file into WORK-ING-STORAGE).
- You would typically put the FETCH statement inside a program loop — a paragraph that is PERFORMed UNTIL. UNTIL when? Until either you obtain the information you need from FETCHed rows, or there are no more rows left to FETCH from the results table.
- Your CURSOR travels from the first to the last row or the results table built by OPEN execution on your SELECT statement. At the end of the table, your program receives a +100 SQLCODE, and no more rows are available. If you want to reprocess any rows in the results table, you must CLOSE the cursor and reopen it.
- Your cursor cannot travel upwards in the results table.
- There is a positional correspondence between the SELECTed column names in your DECLARE CURSOR statement and the FETCHed INTO host variable fields in your FETCH statement — they must match on a one-for-one basis:

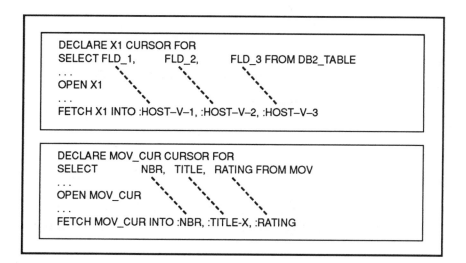

```
DECLARE X1 CURSOR FOR
SELECT FLD_1,      FLD_2,       FLD_3 FROM DB2_TABLE
. . .
OPEN X1
. . .
FETCH X1 INTO :HOST–V–1, :HOST–V–2, :HOST–V–3
```

```
DECLARE MOV_CUR CURSOR FOR
SELECT          NBR,  TITLE,  RATING FROM MOV
. . .
OPEN MOV_CUR
. . .
FETCH MOV_CUR INTO :NBR, :TITLE-X, :RATING
```

This last point is very important and a potential problem area (landmine) in SQL/COBOL programming. You may get a precompile error if you mix and match the wrong datatypes by coding DECLAREd and FETCHed columns out of order. This would alert you to the problem. But if you mix up columns with compatible datatypes, you might not get a precompile error. This would lead to either run-time ABENDs or, worse, garbage ending up on the Database.

6.6.   CLOSEing A CURSOR

After you have finished retrieving the rows from your results table, you CLOSE the CURSOR you have been processing with. CLOSE has a very simple format, which is shown below:

```
EXEC SQL CLOSE <cursor_name> END-EXEC.
```

CLOSE cursor format

where cursor_name is a previously DECLAREd and OPENed CURSOR.

CLOSE:

*   Releases the resources acquired during CURSOR processing;
*   Allows you to reuse (reOPEN) the CURSOR again if needed;
*   Is not required, DB2 will close all open cursors at program end.

6.7.   USING A CURSOR IN RETRIEVAL OPERATIONS

Let's review the four steps used in processing with a symbolic cursor, shown in Figure 57.:

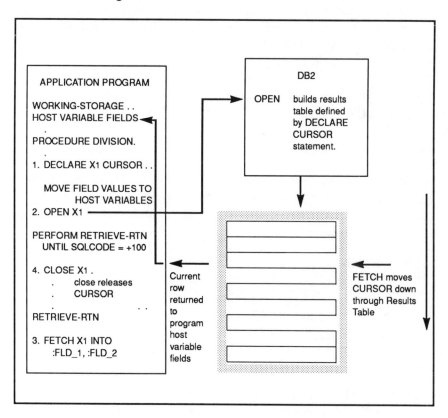

Figure 57.   Symbolic CURSOR processing.

As described in Figure 57, the normal course of events in processing DB2 tables using symbolic cursors is as follows:

1.   Define the CURSOR SELECT with the DECLARE CURSOR statement. This can be done anywhere in the WORKING-

STORAGE SECTION (remember that OPEN is the first run-time executable SQL statement in using a cursor) or the PROCEDURE DIVISION.

2.   Move your search argument values to host variables refer-enced in the WHERE clause of the DECLAREd SELECT statement and OPEN the cursor.

3.   Perform a routine to FETCH rows into your host variables until you fulfill your processing's access requests or reach the end of the results table (SQLCODE = +100).

4.   CLOSE the cursor.

To finish your review on symbolic cursor retrieval operations, study the annotated sample program listing that follows. Note carefully the use of the cursor processing techniques presented so far in this chapter.

```
 IDENTIFICATION DIVISION.
 PROGRAM-ID. SAMPLE02
*REMARKS.  THIS PROGRAM USES A CURSOR TO READ THROUGH
*    ALL THE ROWS OF TWO JOINED TABLES.
 ENVIRONMENT DIVISION.
 CONFIGURATION SECTION.
 SOURCE-COMPUTER. IBM-370.
 OBJECT-COMPUTER. IBM-370.
 DATA DIVISION.
 WORKING-STORAGE SECTION.
*HOST PROGRAM VARIABLES — DATA ITEMS EXPLICITLY DEFINED


*****************************************************************
*DCLGEN TABLE(EMPL)                                             *
*         LIBRARY(TSTJSS.SPUFI.CNTL(DCLEMPL))                   *
*         APOST                                                 *
*    IS THE DCLGEN COMMAND THAT MADE THE FOLLOWING STATEMENTS   *
*****************************************************************
```

```
        EXEC SQL DECLARE EMPL TABLE
        ( NBR                CHAR(2),
          LNAME              CHAR(10),
          FNAME              CHAR(6),
          DOB                INTEGER,
          HIREDTE            INTEGER,
          PERF               SMALLINT,
          JOB                CHAR(4),
          DEPT               CHAR(3),
          PROJ               CHAR(2)
              )  END-EXEC.

*****************************************************************
* COBOL DECLARATION FOR TABLE EMPL                             *
*****************************************************************
01   DCLEMPL.
     10   NBR        PIC X(2).
     10   LNAME      PIC X(10).
     10   FNAME      PIC X(6).
     10   DOB        PIC S9(9) USAGE COMP.
     10   HIREDTE    PIC S9(9) USAGE COMP.
     10   PERF       PIC S9(4) USAGE COMP.
     10   JOB        PIC X(4).
     10   DEPT       PIC X(3).
     10   PROJ       PIC X(2).
*****************************************************************
* THE NUMBER OF COLUMNS DESCRIBED BY THIS DECLARATION IS 9 *
*****************************************************************


*****************************************************************
*DCLGEN TABLE(PAY)                                             *
*LIBRARY(TSTJSS.SPUFI.CNTL(DCLPAY))                            *
*APOST                                                         *
*. . .     IS THE DCLGEN COMMAND THAT MADE THE FOLLOWING STATEMENTS*
*****************************************************************

        EXEC SQL DECLARE PAY TABLE
        ( NBR                CHAR(2),
          HOURS              DECIMAL(5, 2),
          RATE               DECIMAL(5, 2),
          DED                DECIMAL(5, 2),
```

```
              YTD              DECIMAL(8, 2)
                  )   END-EXEC.
      ****************************************************************
      *  COBOL DECLARATION FOR TABLE PAY                            *
      ****************************************************************

      01    DCL  PAY.
            10   NBR          PIC X(2).
            10   HOURS        PIC S999V99 USAGE COMP-3.
            10   RATE         PIC S999V99 USAGE COMP-3.
            10   DED          PIC S999V99 USAGE COMP-3.
            10   YTD          PIC S999999V99 USAGE COMP-3.


      ****************************************************************
      *  THE NUMBER OF COLUMNS DESCRIBED BY THIS DECLARATION IS 5   *
      ****************************************************************

      *MISCELLANEOUS WORKING-STORAGE DATA ITEMS

      01    WS-KTRS-SWITCHES.
            05   EMPL-ROW-KTR  PIC S9(03) COMP-3 VALUE +0.

      01    OUTPUT-ROW.
            05   FILLER       PIC X(01) VALUE SPACES.
            05   NBR-RPT      PIC X(02).
            05   FILLER       PIC X(04) VALUE SPACES.
            05   LNAME-RPT    PIC X(14).
            05   FILLER       PIC X(04) VALUE SPACES.
            05   FNAME-RPT    PIC X(08).
            05   FILLER       PIC X(04) VALUE SPACES.
            05   HOURS-RPT    PIC Z(02)V99.
            05   FILLER       PIC X(04) VALUE SPACES.
            05   RATE-RPT     PIC Z(02)V99.

      *ERROR MSG AREA FOR CALLS TO DSNTIAR — WHICH DECODES YOUR
      *SQL RETURN CODES (SQLCODE) FOR YOU.

      01    ERROR-MSG.
            05   ERROR-LEN    PIC S9(04) COMP VALUE +960.
            05   ERROR-TEXT   PIC X(120) OCCURS 8 TIMES
                      INDEXED BY ERR-IDX.
```

```
01   ERROR-TEXT-LEN      PIC S9(09) COMP VALUE +120.

EXEC SQL INCLUDE SQLCA END-EXEC.

PROCEDURE DIVISION.

000-SETUP-ERROR-TRAP-RTN.

*THIS PORTION OF THE PROGRAM ACTIVATES THE SQL ERROR TRAPPING
*FACILITIES. AT PRECOMPILE TIME, THE DB2 PRE-COMPILER
*GENERATES COBOL INSTRUCTIONS TO INTERROGATE THE SQLCODE
* (RETURN CODE) FROM EACH CALL. IF A SQLERROR CONDITION IS
*DETECTED (NEGATIVE RETURN CODE), EXECUTION WILL BRANCH TO THE
*999-ERROR-TRAP-RTN TO DISPLAY AN APPROPRIATE ERROR MSG.

     EXEC SQL WHENEVER SQLERROR GO TO 999-ERROR-TRAP-RTN
          END-EXEC.

000-MAINLINE-RTN.

*THE MAINLINE CONTAINS THE DRIVER CODE TO PERFORM OUR DATA
*BASE ACCESS AND DISPLAY ROUTINES.

     PERFORM 100-DECLARE-CURSOR-RTN THRU 100-EXIT.

     PERFORM 150-OPEN-CURSOR-RTN THRU 150-EXIT.

     PERFORM 200-FETCH-RTN THRU 200-EXIT
     UNTIL SQLCODE NOT = ZERO

     PERFORM 300-CLOSE-CURSOR-RTN THRU 300-EXIT.

     MOVE ZERO TO RETURN-CODE.
     GOBACK.

000-EXIT.
     EXIT.
```

> Processing rtn:
> - open cursor
> - fetch rows
>   until no more
>   rows (+100)

100-DECLARE-CURSOR-RTN.

*THIS STATEMENT DEFINES THE CURSOR (G1) AND ASSOCIATES IT
*WITH THE SELECT STATEMENT

```
1.      EXEC SQL
            DECLARE G1 CURSOR FOR
                SELECT
                    EMPL.NBR,
                    LNAME,              Note:   retrieval cursor (G1)
                    FNAME,                      no into clause like
                    HOURS,                      singleton select
                    RATE                        statement
                FROM
                    EMPL, PAY
                WHERE
                    EMPL.NBR = PAY.NBR
            END-EXEC.
```

100-EXIT.
    EXIT.

150-OPEN-CURSOR-RTN.

*THIS STATEMENT ACTIVATES THE CURSOR — EXECUTES THE SQL
*SELECT STATEMENT.

```
2.      EXEC SQL
            OPEN G1 END-EXEC.
```

150-EXIT.
    EXIT.

200-FETCH-RTN.

*THIS PARAGRAPH SETS UP THE SQL PARAMETERS, PERFORMS THE
*PARAGRAPH TO FETCH THE ROW, AND DISPLAYS THE RESULTS.

```
PERFORM 250-FETCH-A-ROW THRU 250-EXIT.
IF SQLCODE = ZERO
THEN
        MOVE            NBR OF DCLEMPL
                                TO NBR-RPT
        MOVE        LNAME   TO LNAME-RPT
        MOVE        FNAME   TO FNAME-RPT
        MOVE        HOURS   TO HOURS-RPT
        MOVE        RATE    TO RATE-RPT
        DISPLAY OUTPUT-ROW
ELSE
        NEXT SENTENCE.

200-EXIT.
    EXIT.


250-FETCH-A-ROW.

*THIS PARAGRAPH FETCHES A ROW FROM THE EMPL AND PAY TABLES
*AND MOVES SPECIFIC DATA FIELDS INTO THE NBR, LNAME, FNAME
*HOURS AND RATE FIELDS.
```

```
3.      EXEC SQL
        FETCH G1
                INTO
                    :DCLEMPL.NBR,
                    :LNAME,
                    :FNAME,
                    :HOURS,
                    :RATE
        END-EXEC.
```

fetch statement:
note correspondence between
host variable field positions,
and original select column
position

```
250-EXIT.
    EXIT.

300-CLOSE-CURSOR-RTN.

*THIS STATEMENT CLOSES THE "ACTIVE SET"
```

```
4.      EXEC SQL
            CLOSE G1 END-EXEC.
```

```
300-EXIT.
    EXIT.

999-ERROR-TRAP-RTN.
    CALL 'DSNTIAR' USING SQLCA, ERROR-MSG, ERROR-TEXT-LEN
    IF RETURN-CODE = ZERO
    THEN
        PERFORM 999-ERROR-PRINT-RTN THRU 999-EXIT
        VARYING ERR-IDX FROM 1 BY 1
        UNTIL ERR-IDX > 8
    ELSE
        DISPLAY 'PROBLEM IN CALL TO DSNTIAR', SQLCA,
            RETURN-CODE.

999-ERROR-PRINT-RTN.
    DISPLAY ERROR-TEXT (ERR-IDX).
999-EXIT.
    EXIT.
```

6.8.   UPDATING A TABLE USING A SYMBOLIC CURSOR

6.8.1.   Global UPDATE Processing

Many swords in life have two edges. While one side can work for you, the other side (particularly if you're not careful) can work against you. So it goes with updating in set-oriented languages. Because one statement can potentially update many (or even all) rows of a table, set-oriented languages provide processing power that can greatly simplify many data update requirements. Accordingly, because one statement can potentially update many (or even all) rows of a table, set-oriented languages can propagate garbage throughout a table far more easily than traditional record-at-a-time processing languages. Also, set-level updating may not be adequate to solve certain application requirements involving complex editing and file manipulation.

6.8.2.   Localized UPDATE Processing

To solve some of the problems associated with set-level updating, you can use the UPDATE WHERE CURRENT OF statement. UPDATE WHERE CURRENT OF limits the scope of DB2 updates to one row at a time, specifically the row your cursor is positioned on (the last row FETCHed into your program). UPDATE WHERE CURRENT OF has a very simple format:

```
EXEC SQL UPDATE <col_1, col_n> WHERE CURRENT OF <cursor_name>
END-EXEC.
```

UPDATE WHERE CURRENT OF:

*   Allows you to retrieve a row and do some further investigation on the values in the row (perhaps CALL a module or do some edits that are more complex than allowed for in SQL syntax) — then UPDATE or not UPDATE the row.
*   Limits the scope of the UPDATE operation to only those column values selected in the "current row" (the row last FETCHed).
*   Is usually coded after the FETCH statement, but within the same processing unit (paragraph or PERFORMed paragraphs).
*   Requires a special form of the DECLARE CURSOR statement, shown below:

```
EXEC SQL DECLARE <cursor_name> CURSOR FOR
    SELECT COL_1, COL_2, COL_n
        FROM DB2_TABLE
            WHERE CONDITION

        FOR UPDATE OF COL_1, COL_3, COL_N

END-EXEC.
```

DECLARE CURSOR statement — FOR UPDATE OF

As you can see from the above diagram, our retrieval-only DECLARE CURSOR statement has been amended and now contains the following clause:

```
FOR UPDATE OF COL_1, COL_3, COL_n
```

This clause allows you to use the UPDATE WHERE CURRENT OF statement after FETCH to update single rows of a DB2 table. Specifically:

• You must DECLARE any column(s) you intend to UPDATE. Put another way, you may not UPDATE a column with UPDATE WHERE CURRENT OF that is not specified in the FOR UPDATE OF clause in your DECLARE CURSOR statement.

6.8.3.   When Can't You Update Using a Cursor?

Certain types of SELECT statements are by nature "read-only;" that is, you may not DECLARE CURSORS . . . FOR UPDATE OF these statements. Such read-only SELECT statements include:

• SELECT statements that join tables,
• SELECT statements that contain:
  — Built-in functions
  — Literals in the SELECT clause
  — GROUP BY
  — Arithmetic expressions in the SELECT clause
  — Subselects that reference different tables
  — DISTINCT
  — ORDER BY
  — UNION;

• SELECT statements that reference views which contain any of the above.

In fact, only SELECT statements which SELECT row/column sub-sets of a single table are candidates for UPDATE WHERE CUR-RENT OF processing.

Figure 58 presents a logical view of the UPDATE WHERE CUR-RENT OF techniques covered so far.

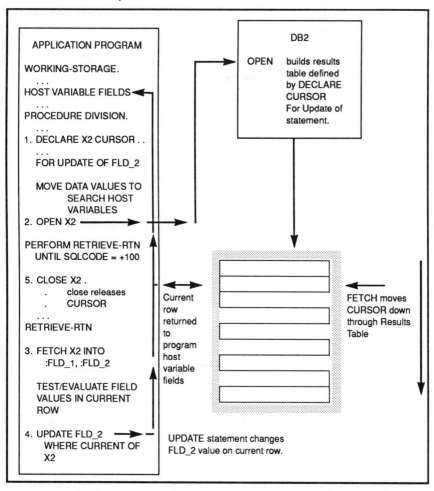

Figure 58.   Symbolic CURSOR processing — FOR UPDATE.

6.9.   DEFINING A CURSOR FOR DELETE

6.9.1.   Localized DELETE Processing

As you know, the standard SQL DELETE statement has the same power and scope as UPDATE. DELETE's effect is to remove any and all rows from a table that satisfy the WHERE condition in the statement. This can be none, one, many, or all table rows. You can probably imagine that the same considerations exist for using DELETE as for UPDATE. Luckily, we can use the SQL DELETE WHERE CURRENT OF statement to limit row deletion to the current table row. It is coded almost exactly like UPDATE WHERE CURRENT OF:

```
EXEC SQL DELETE FROM <table_n> WHERE CURRENT OF <cursor_name>
END-EXEC.
```

DELETE WHERE CURRENT OF:

- Allows you to retrieve a row and do some further investigation on the values in the row before deciding whether or not to delete the row.
- Limits the scope of the DELETE operation to only the "current row" (the row last FETCHed).
- Is usually coded after the FETCH statement, but within the same processing unit (paragraph or PERFORMed paragraphs).
- Requires a special form of the DECLARE CURSOR statement shown below:

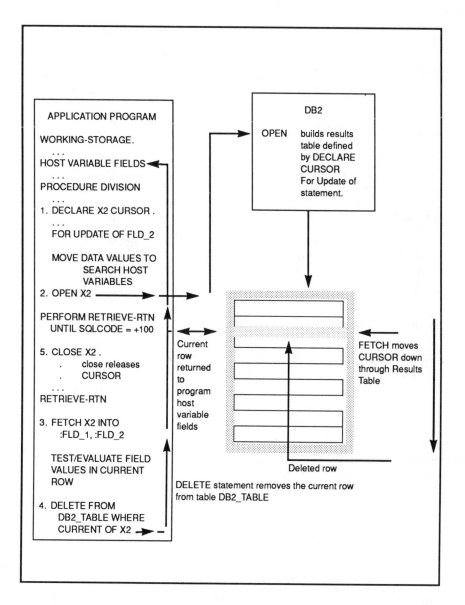

Figure 59. Symbolic CURSOR processing — localized DELETE processing.

```
EXEC SQL DECLARE <cursor_name> CURSOR FOR
   SELECT COL_1, COL_2, COL_n
      FROM DB2_TABLE
         WHERE CONDITION
   FOR UPDATE OF COL_1
END-EXEC.
```

DECLARE CURSOR statement — FOR UPDATE OF.

As you can see, the DECLARE CURSOR statement for DELETE WHERE CURRENT OF is the same as UPDATE WHERE CURRENT OF. If you want to use cursor delete processing, you will need to DECLARE your cursor FOR UPDATE OF at least one column.

A logical view of cursor delete processing is shown in Figure 59:

Before you try your hand at coding the programs at the end of the chapter that use UPDATE and DELETE WHERE CURRENT OF statements, study program SAMPLE03 listed for you below.

```
IDENTIFICATION DIVISION.
 PROGRAM-ID. SAMPLE03.
*REMARKS.    THIS PROGRAM UPDATES EMPLOYEE PERFORMANCE AND RATE
*     COLUMNS BASED ON VALUES STORED IN A WORKING-STORAGE
*     TABLE (COBOL TABLE). THE LOGIC IN THE PROGRAM IS BASED ON
*     SEARCH OF THE WORKING-STORAGE TABLE, AS WELL AS A SEQUENTIAL
*     SCAN OF A DB2 TABLE.
ENVIRONMENT DIVISION.
 CONFIGURATION SECTION.
 SOURCE-COMPUTER. IBM-370.
 OBJECT-COMPUTER. IBM-370.
 DATA DIVISION.
 WORKING-STORAGE SECTION.
```

```
*HOST PROGRAM VARIABLES - DATA ITEMS EXPLICITLY DEFINED
*****************************************************************
*DCLGEN TABLE(EMPL)                                             *
*    LIBRARY(TSTJSS.SPUFI.CNTL(DCLEMPL))                        *
*    APOST IS THE DCLGEN COMMAND THAT MADE THE FOLLOWING        *
*    STATEMENTS                                                 *
*****************************************************************
     EXEC SQL DECLARE @TSOID.EMPL TABLE
          (NBR              CHAR(2),
           LNAME            CHAR(10),
           FNAME            CHAR(6),
           DOB              INTEGER,
           HIREDTE          INTEGER,
           PERF             SMALLINT,
           JOB              CHAR(4),
           DEPT             CHAR(3),
           PROJ             CHAR(2)
          ) END-EXEC.
*****************************************************************
* COBOL DECLARATION FOR TABLE EMPL                              *
*****************************************************************
01   DCLEMPL.
     10    NBR          PIC X(2).
     10    LNAME        PIC X(10).
     10    FNAME        PIC X(6).
     10    DOB          PIC S9(9) USAGE COMP.
     10    HIREDTE      PIC S9(9) USAGE COMP.
     10    PERF         PIC S9(4) USAGE COMP.
     10    JOB          PIC X(4).
     10    DEPT         PIC X(3).
     10    PROJ         PIC X(2).
*****************************************************************
* THE NUMBER OF COLUMNS DESCRIBED BY THIS DECLARATION IS 9      *
*****************************************************************



*SQL COMMUNICATIONS AREA - DATA ITEMS PULLED IN VIA INCLUDE

     EXEC SQL INCLUDE SQLCA END-EXEC.
```

```
*MISCELLANEOUS WORKING-STORAGE DATA ITEMS
01    EMPL-TABLE-VALUES.
      05    EMPL-VALUES  PIC X(12) VALUE '012083022'.
      05    EMPL-ROW-WS REDEFINES EMPL-VALUES OCCURS 3 TIMES
                  INDEXED BY EMPL-IDX.
      10 EMPL-NBR-WS    PIC X(02).
      10 EMPL-PERF-WS   PIC 9(01).
```

> Note: this COBOL table provides new values for the PERF column on the DB2 table.

```
01    HIT-FLAG-WS       PIC X(01).
      88 TABLE-HIT   VALUE 'Y'.


01    MISC-FIELDS.
      05 NULL-IND        PIC S9(04) COMP.

*ERROR MSG AREA FOR CALLS TO DSNTIAR — WHICH DECODES YOUR
*SQL RETURN CODES (SQLCODE) FOR YOU.

01    ERROR-MSG.
      05    ERROR-LEN   PIC S99(04) COMP VALUE +960.
      05    ERROR-TEXT  PIC X(120) OCCURS 8 TIMES
         INDEXED BY ERR-IDX.
01    ERROR-TEXT-LEN    PIC S9(09) COMP VALUE +120.

PROCEDURE DIVISION.

000-SETUP-ERROR-TRAP-RTN.


*THIS PORTION OF THE PROGRAM ACTIVATES THE SQL ERROR TRAPPING
*FACILITIES. AT PRECOMPILE TIME, THE DB2 PRECOMPILER
*GENERATES COBOL INSTRUCTIONS TO INTERROGATE THE SQLCODE
* (RETURN CODE) FROM EACH CALL. IF A SQLERROR CONDITION IS
*DETECTED (NEGATIVE RETURN CODE), EXECUTION WILL BRANCH TO THE
*999-ERROR-TRAP-RTN TO DISPLAY AN APPROPRIATE ERROR MSG.

      EXEC SQL WHENEVER SQLERROR GO TO 999-ERROR-TRAP-RTN
         END-EXEC.


000-MAINLINE-RTN.

*THE MAINLINE CONTAINS THE DRIVER CODE TO PERFORM OUR DATA
*BASE ACCESS AND DISPLAY ROUTINES.
```

```
        PERFORM 100-DECLARE-CURSOR-RTN THRU 100-EXIT.

        PERFORM 200-DISPLAY-RPT THRU 200-EXIT
             UNTIL SQLCODE = +100.

        PERFORM 300-TERMINATE-RTN THRU 300-EXIT.

        MOVE ZERO TO RETURN-CODE.
        GOBACK.

    000-EXIT.
        EXIT.

     100-DECLARE-CURSOR-RTN.
```

```
    1.      EXEC SQL
                DECLARE G1 CURSOR FOR
                    SELECT
                        NBR,                     Note:   update cursor (G1)
                        PERF                             qualified table name
                    FROM                                 update perf column
                        EMPL
                    FOR UPDATE OF PERF
                END-EXEC.
```

```
* THIS STATEMENT OPENS THE G1 CURSOR
```

```
    2.      EXEC SQL
                OPEN G1 END-EXEC.
```

```
     100-EXIT.
        EXIT.

     200-DISPLAY-RPT.
```

```
* THIS PARAGRAPH SETS UP THE SQL PARAMETERS, PERFORMS THE
* PARAGRAPH TO MAKE THE CALL AND DISPLAYS THE RESULTS. NOTE
* THE USE OF SQLCODE RETURN VALUES IN THE PROCESSING.
```

```
PERFORM 275-FETCH-ROW-RTN THRU 275-EXIT.

IF SQLCODE = ZERO
THEN
        PERFORM 280-TABLE-SEARCH-RTN THRU 280-EXIT
        IF TABLE-HIT
        THEN
                PERFORM 290-UPDATE-ROW-RTN THRU 290-EXIT
                MOVE      NBR          TO NBR-RPT
                MOVE  PERF TO PERF-RPT
                DISPLAY OUTPUT-ROW
                ADD +1 TO ROW-KTR
        ELSE
                NEXT SENTENCE
ELSE
        NEXT SENTENCE.

 200-EXIT.
      EXIT.


 275-FETCH-ROW-RTN.
```

```
report
writing
routine
```

```
*THIS PARAGRAPH FETCHES A ROW FROM THE EMPL AND PAY TABLES
*AND MOVES SPECIFIC DATA FIELDS INTO THE NBR AND PERF FIELDS.

        MOVE ZERO TO NULL-IND.
```

```
3.        EXEC SQL
              FETCH G1
              INTO
                :NBR,
                :PERF:NULL-IND
          END-EXEC.
```

Note: standard fetch
statement null
indicator. Positional
column order is still
significant.

```
 275-EXIT.
      EXIT.


 280-TABLE-SEARCH-RTN.
*THIS PARAGRAPH SEARCHES A WORKING-STORAGE TABLE TO FIND THE
```

```
*EMPLOYEE NBR. IF FOUND, IT MOVES THE PERF TO THE HOST PROGRAM
*VARIABLE PERF FIELD.
```

```
        MOVE 'N' TO HIT-FLAG-WS
        SET EMPL-IDX TO 1.
```

> this search routine determines
> eligibility for update and report-
> ing. Note the use of a COBOL
> sequential search.

```
        SEARCH EMPL-ROW-WS
            AT END GO TO 280-EXIT
                WHEN NBR = EMPL-NBR-WS(EMPL-IDX)
                    MOVE EMPL-PERF-WS(EMPL-IDX) TO PERF
                    MOVE 'Y' TO HIT-FLAG-WS.

    280-EXIT.
        EXIT.


    290-UPDATE-ROW-RTN.
```

```
*THIS PARAGRAPH UPDATES A ROW FROM THE EMPL TABLE BY MOVING THE
*NEW PERF TO THE DB2 TABLE ROW.
```

```
        IF NULL-IND < 0
            MOVE ZERO TO PERF.
```

> Note: negative null-indicator
>   logic

```
    4.      EXEC SQL
                UPDATE EMPL
                    SET PERF = :PERF
                    WHERE CURRENT OF G1
            END-EXEC.
```

> update where current of: sets
> perf = generated perf from
> working-storage

```
    290-EXIT.
        EXIT.

    300-TERMINATE-RTN.
```

```
    5.      EXEC SQL CLOSE G1 END-EXEC.
```

```
        MOVE ROW-KTR TO ROW-STAT.
        DISPLAY ROW-MSG UPON CONSOLE.

  300-EXIT.
      EXIT.

  999-ERROR-TRAP-RTN.
        CALL 'DSNTIAR' USING SQLCA, ERROR-MSG, ERROR-TEXT-LEN.
        IF RETURN-CODE = ZERO
        THEN
              PERFORM 999-ERROR-PRINT-RTN THRU 999-EXIT
                    VARYING ERR-IDX FROM 1 BY 1
                    UNTIL ERR-IDX > 8
        ELSE
                    DISPLAY 'PROBLEM WITH DSNTIAR', SQLCA,
                    RETURN-CODE.

  999-ERROR-PRINT-RTN.

        DISPLAY ERROR-TEXT (ERR-IDX); UPON CONSOLE.

  999-EXIT.
      EXIT.
```

6.10. USING MULTIPLE CURSORS

There is no (theoretical) limit to the number of cursors your program can utilize to satisfy its processing requirements. This means that you can use more than one OPEN cursor at a time if you need to. Many specialized types of business reporting and updating requirements can be satisfied by using multiple cursors in a technique which can be described as a "multiple rolodex" method.

Picture two rolodexes on your desk, one for, say, Parts and one for Suppliers who supply parts. Both are in alphabetical order. Let's say you needed to update the Parts rolodex with supplier information from the Suppliers rolodex. You might thumb through the Parts rolodex starting from A and going to Z — maintaining position in the file with your left hand. For each part, you would then use your right hand to search the Suppliers rolodex looking at each supplier to see if they supplied the part you were positioned on with the other rolodex. At the end of the Suppliers rolodex, you would flip to the next card on the parts rolodex and continue this process until the last Z part in the file. An example of this technique using multiple cursors is shown in Figure 60:

6.11. REVIEW QUESTIONS

Because you will be coding SQL cursor statements for both retrieval and update processing, we will dispense with any additional coding exercises in this chapter.

1. What is a symbolic CURSOR?

2. What other file handling techniques are symbolic cursors similar to?

3. List the four steps used in processing rows for retrieval with symbolic cursors:

    _____

    _____

    _____

    _____

4. List some of the coding differences between specifying cursors for retrieval and specifying them for update processing.

5. What kinds of SELECT statements can be defined as FOR UPDATE OF?

6. (for IMS programmers) What IMS Database processing technique is equivalent to using multiple cursors?

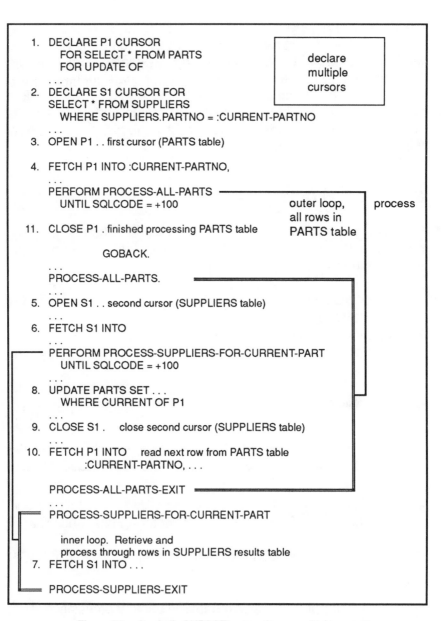

Figure 60. Symbolic CURSOR processing — multiple cursors.

6.12.   SOLUTIONS

1.   A symbolic CURSOR is a DB2 temporary structure that allows you to process multiple rows of a results table one at a time.

2.   Standard OS file processing, VSAM Browse processing, IMS Get-Next processing.

3.   The four steps used in processing rows for retrieval with symbolic cursors are:

   DECLARE CURSOR (define Cursor name and SELECT statement)

   OPEN CURSOR (activate Cursor — execute SELECT/build results table)

   FETCH CURSOR (retrieve current row into host variable fields)

   CLOSE CURSOR (deactivate Cursor — release resources)

4.   You must declare your CURSOR FOR UPDATE OF a column or columns you intend to update (you must do this even if you only intend to delete rows with a cursor). You also code the statement UPDATE or DELETE WHERE CURRENT OF <cursor_name> in the FETCH routine.

5.   Only SELECT statements that process a row/column subset of a single table are available FOR UPDATE OF.

6.   Processing through a database or databases using multiple PCBs.

6.13.   WORKSHOP — V,   USING A CURSOR FOR RETRIEVAL

Below you will find a skeleton program called CURSRAVG. This program uses a symbolic cursor to process a table join and produce a summary report. You will need to use the GROUP BY clause to create the report. You will also need to code several WORKING-STORAGE variables. Don't forget Null indicator variables.

My sample solution can be found in Appendix 1.

```
      IDENTIFICATION DIVISION.
      PROGRAM-ID. CURSRAVG.
     *REMARKS.  THIS PROGRAM JOINS TABLES, GROUPS DATA BY DEPT,
     *    AND DISPLAYS THE AVERAGE, MAXIMUM AND MINIMUM
     *    HOURS, AND PERFORMANCE EVALUATION BY DEPT.
     *
      ENVIRONMENT DIVISION.
      CONFIGURATION SECTION.
      SOURCE-COMPUTER. IBM-370.
      OBJECT-COMPUTER. IBM-370.


      DATA DIVISION.


      WORKING-STORAGE SECTION.


     *CODE THE NECESSARY DB2 INCLUDE STATEMENTS HERE


      01  WS-KTRS-SWITCHES.
          05 ROW-KTR          PIC S9(03) COMP-3 VALUE +0.


     *MODIFY THE TABLE-ROW PICTURE CLAUSES FOR THE HOST
     *PROGRAM VARIABLES — LOOK AT THE TABLE/COLUMN DEFINITIONS
     *    IN YOUR MANUAL (APPENDIX A FROM THE SQL PORTION)
     *    AND THE SQL TO COBOL DATATYPES IN CHAPTER 3
```

```
     01  TABLE-ROW.
         05  DEPT-TBL           PIC ?
         05  PERF-TBL-AVG       PIC ?
         05  PERF-TBL-MIN       PIC ?
         05  PERF-TBL-MAX       PIC ?
         05  HOURS-TBL-AVG      PIC ?
         05  HOURS-TBL-MAX      PIC ?
         05  HOURS-TBL-MIN      PIC ?
```

```
 01  OUTPUT-ROW.
     05     FILLER         PIC X(01   VALUE SPACES.
     05     DEPT-RPT       PIC X(03)  .
     05     FILLER         PIC X(03)  VALUE SPACES.
     05     PERF-RPT-AVG   PIC Z(03)  .99.
     05     FILLER         PIC X(01)  VALUE SPACES.
     05     PERF-RPT-MIN   PIC Z(03)  .99.
     05     FILLER         PIC X(01)  VALUE SPACES.
     05     PERF-RPT-MAX   PIC Z(03)  .99.
     05     FILLER         PIC X(03)  VALUE SPACES.
     05     HOURS-RPT-AVG  PIC Z(03)  .99.
     05     FILLER         PIC X(03)  VALUE SPACES.
     05     HOURS-RPT-MAX  PIC Z(03)  .99.
     05     FILLER         PIC X(03)  VALUE SPACES.
     05     HOURS-RPT-MIN  PIC Z(03)  .99.

*ERROR MSG AREA FOR CALLS TO DSNTIAR — WHICH DECODES YOUR
*SQL RETURN CODES (SQLCODE) FOR YOU.

 01  ERROR-MSG.
     05     ERROR-LEN      PIC S9(04) COMP VALUE +960.
     05     ERROR-TEXT     PIC X(120) OCCURS 8 TIMES
                INDEXED BY ERR-IDX.
 01  ERROR-TEXT-LEN        PIC S9(09) COMP VALUE +120.

PROCEDURE DIVISION.


000-SETUP-ERROR-TRAP-RTN.

*IF A SQLERROR CONDITION IS DETECTED (NEGATIVE RETURN CODE),
```

```
* SEND PROGRAM EXECUTION WILL BRANCH TO THE
* 999-ERROR-TRAP-RTN TO DISPLAY AN APPROPRIATE ERROR MSG.
┌─────────────────────────────────────────────────────────┐
│                                                         │
│                                                         │
│                                                         │
└─────────────────────────────────────────────────────────┘


  000-MAINLINE-RTN.

* THE MAINLINE CONTAINS THE DRIVER CODE TO PERFORM OUR DATA
* BASE ACCESS AND DISPLAY ROUTINES.

      PERFORM 100-DECLARE-CURSOR-RTN THRU 100-EXIT.

      PERFORM 150-OPEN-CURSOR-RTN THRU 150-EXIT.

*=>   PERFORM 200-FETCH-RTN THRU 200-EXIT        ┌──────────────────┐
*=>        UNTIL WHEN ?????                      │ loop through table│
                                                 │ until . . . . . . │
      PERFORM 300-CLOSE-CURSOR-RTN THRU 300-EXIT.└──────────────────┘

      MOVE ZERO TO RETURN-CODE.
      GOBACK.

  000-EXIT.
      EXIT.

  100-DECLARE-CURSOR-RTN.

* = = = > CODE THE SQL STATEMENT TO JOIN THE EMPL AND PAY TABLES
* = = = > GROUP THEM BY EMPL.DEPT AND DISPLAY THE DEPT AND:
* = = = > AVERAGE, MINIMUM AND MAXIMUM — HOURS AND PERF
┌─────────────────────────────────────────────────────────┐
│                                                         │
│                                                         │
│                                                         │
│                                                         │
│                                                         │
│                                                         │
└─────────────────────────────────────────────────────────┘
```

```
    100-EXIT.
        EXIT.

    150-OPEN-CURSOR-RTN.

*THIS STATEMENT OPENS THE "ACTIVE SET" IN PREPARATION OF
*ROW FETCH PROCESSING.
```

```
+--------------------------------------------------------------------+
|                                                                    |
|                                                                    |
|                                                                    |
+--------------------------------------------------------------------+
```

```
    150-EXIT.
        EXIT.

    200-FETCH-RTN.

*THIS PARAGRAPH SETS UP THE SQL PARAMETERS, PERFORMS THE
*PARAGRAPH TO FETCH THE ROW, AND DISPLAYS THE RESULTS.
*===> HINT <=== USE ISPF EXCLUDE (XX) OR BLOCK COPY
*FROM YOUR CURSOR DECLARE STATEMENT TO VERIFY PROPER
*SELECTED TABLE/COLUMN TO FETCHED HOST-VARIABLE MATCHING

        PERFORM 250-FETCH-A-ROW THRU 250-EXIT.

        IF SQLCODE = ZERO
        THEN
            MOVE DEPT-TBL        TO DEPT-RPT
            MOVE PERF-TBL-AVG         TO PERF-RPT-AVG
            MOVE PERF-TBL-MIN         TO PERF-RPT-MIN
            MOVE PERF-TBL-MAX         TO PERF-RPT-MAX
            MOVE HOURS-TBL-AVG   TO HOURS-RPT-AVG
            MOVE HOURS-TBL-MAX   TO HOURS-RPT-MAX
            MOVE HOURS-TBL-MIN   TO HOURS-RPT-MIN
            DISPLAY OUTPUT-ROW
        ELSE
            DISPLAY '*** END - OF - DATA ***'.

    200-EXIT.
        EXIT.
```

```
250-FETCH-A-ROW.
```

```
*THIS PARAGRAPH FETCHES A ROW FROM THE EMPL AND PAY TABLES
*AND MOVES SPECIFIC DATA INTO THE PROGRAM HOST VARIABLES
```

```
250-EXIT.
EXIT.
300-CLOSE-CURSOR-RTN.
* THIS STATEMENT CLOSES THE "ACTIVE SET"
```

```
300-EXIT.
    EXIT.

350-TERMINATE-RTN.

    MOVE ROW-KTR TO ROW-STAT.

    DISPLAY ROW-MSG.

350-EXIT.
    EXIT.

999-ERROR-TRAP-RTN.
****************************************************************
* ERROR TRAPPING ROUTINE FOR NEGATIVE SQLCODES                 *
****************************************************************

    DISPLAY '**** WE HAVE A SERIOUS PROBLEM HERE *****'.
    DISPLAY '999-ERROR-TRAP-RTN '.
```

```
   MULTIPLY SQLCODE BY -1 GIVING SQLCODE.
   DISPLAY 'SQLCODE ===> ' SQLCODE.
   DISPLAY SQLCA.
   DISPLAY SQLERRM.
   EXEC SQL ROLLBACK WORK END-EXEC.
   GOBACK.
999-EXIT.
   EXIT.
```

> rollback statement
> used to manually "undo"
> any updates processed

6.14.   WORKSHOP VI — USING A CURSOR FOR UPDATE

Below you will find a skeleton program called CURSRUPD. This program uses a symbolic cursor to UPDATE and DELETE from a table. The program is driven by a WORKING-STORAGE table you would populate with values read from a file at the beginning of your program. I have hard-coded the table values in WORK-ING-STORAGE for you. Notice that the table contains a code for the processing to be accomplished as well as the employee number. If the employee data on the DB2 table is to be updated as specified by a "U" in the field UPDATE-DEL-CODE, a new PERF is given in the program. If the employee is to be deleted off the table (as specified by a D in the same field), the employee is deleted from both tables.

You will need null-indicator(s) in this program.

```
 IDENTIFICATION DIVISION.
 PROGRAM-ID. CURSRUPD.
*REMARKS.      THIS PROGRAM UPDATES EMPLOYEE PERFORMANCE
 AND RATE
*     COLUMNS BASED ON VALUES STORED IN A TABLE IN
*     WORKING-STORAGE. THE PROGRAM USES A CURSOR TO
*     READ SEQUENTIALLY THROUGH THE EMPLOYEE TABLE. AS
*     EACH ROW IS RETURNED, THE WORKING-STORAGE TABLE IS
*     SEARCHED TO SEE IF THE EMPLOYEE IS GETTING:
*     *  DELETED --> UPDATE-DEL-CODE = 'D'
*     *  UPDATED --> UPDATE-DEL-CODE = 'U'
* YOU WILL UPDATE THE EMPL.PERF COLUMN AND PAY.RATE COLUMN.
```

```
*
*      IF A MATCH IS FOUND, UPDATE THE APPROPRIATE TABLE(S)
*      AND WRITE OUT A REPORT INDICATING THE ACTIONS TAKEN.
*      YOU WILL USE A CURSOR TO PROCESS THROUGH THE EMPL TABLE
*      (FOR UPDATE OF PERF). YOU WILL USE A STANDARD UPDATE
*      STATEMENT TO UPDATE THE RATE COLUMN ON THE PAY TABLE — USING
*      THE EMPL.NBR FETCHED INTO THE CURRENT ROW AS YOUR SEARCH
*      ARGUMENT.
*
 ENVIRONMENT DIVISION.
 CONFIGURATION SECTION.
 SOURCE-COMPUTER. IBM-370.
 OBJECT-COMPUTER. IBM-370.

 DATA DIVISION.

 WORKING-STORAGE SECTION.

*CODE THE INCLUDES FOR YOUR PROGRAM VARIABLES AND SQLCA HERE
```

```
┌─────────────────────────────────────────────────────────────┐
│                                                             │
│                                                             │
│                                                             │
└─────────────────────────────────────────────────────────────┘
```

```
*MISCELLANEOUS WORKING-STORAGE DATA ITEMS

 01  WS-SWITCHES.
     05    ROW-KTR          PIC S9(03) COMP-3 VALUE +0.
     05    NUL-IND          PIC S9(04) COMP.

 01  UPDATE-OUTPUT-ROW.
     05    FILLER           PIC X(25)   VALUE
           '*** EMPLOYEE NBR ==>'.
     05    NBR-RPT          PIC X(03).
     05    FILLER           PIC X(25) VALUE
           '*** EMPLOYEE PERF ==>'.
     05    PERF-RPT         PIC Z9.
     05    FILLER           PIC X(25) VALUE
```

```
                '*** PAY TABLE RATE ==>'.
        05      RATE-RPT        PIC Z99.99.


    01  DELETE-OUTPUT-ROW.
        05      FILLER          PIC X(25) VALUE
                '*** EMPLOYEE NBR ==>'.
        05      DEL-NBR-RPT     PIC X(03).
        05      FILLER          PIC X(25) VALUE
                '*** EMPLOYEE PERF ==>'.
        05      DEL-PERF-RPT    PIC Z9.


    01  ROW-MSG.
        05      FILLER          PIC X(24)
                VALUE '* * * ROWS READ ->'.
        05      ROW-STAT        PIC Z99.


    01  EMPL-TABLE-VALUES.
        05      EMPL-VALUES.
        10  EMPL-VALUE1     PIC X(06) VALUE 'U01210'.
        10  EMPL-VALUE2     PIC X(06) VALUE 'D02000'.
        10  EMPL-VALUE3     PIC X(06) VALUE 'U03208'.
        10  EMPL-VALUE4     PIC X(06) VALUE 'D10000'.
        05      EMPL-ROW-WS REDEFINES EMPL-VALUES OCCURS 4 TIMES
                    INDEXED BY EMPL-IDX.
        10  UPDATE-DEL-CODE PIC X(01).
          88 UPDATE-ROW VALUE 'U'.
          88 DELETE-ROW VALUE 'D'.
        10  EMPL-NBR-WS     PIC X(02).
        10  EMPL-PERF-WS    PIC 9(01).
        10  EMPL-RATE-WS    PIC 9(02).


    01  HIT-FLAG-WS             PIC X(01).
            88 TABLE-HIT        VALUE 'Y'.

 *ERROR MSG AREA FOR CALLS TO DSNTIAR — WHICH DECODES YOUR
 *SQL RETURN CODES (SQLCODE) FOR YOU.

    01  ERROR-MSG.
        05      ERROR-LEN       PIC S99(04) COMP VALUE +960.
        05      ERROR-TEXT      PIC X(120)  OCCURS 8 TIMES
                INDEXED BY ERR-IDX.
    01  ERROR-TEXT-LEN          PIC S9(09)  COMP VALUE +120.
```

```
PROCEDURE DIVISION.

 000-SETUP-ERROR-TRAP-RTN.

* IF A SQLERROR CONDITION IS DETECTED (NEGATIVE RETURN CODE),
* SEND PROGRAM EXECUTION WILL BRANCH TO THE
* 999-ERROR-TRAP-RTN TO DISPLAY AN APPROPRIATE ERROR MSG.
```

```
 000-MAINLINE-RTN.

* THE MAINLINE CONTAINS THE DRIVER CODE TO PERFORM OUR DATA
* BASE ACCESS AND DISPLAY ROUTINES.

     PERFORM 100-DECLARE-CURSOR-RTN THRU 100-EXIT.
     PERFORM 150-OPEN-CURSOR-RTN THRU 150-EXIT.

*=>  PERFORM 200-DISPLAY-RPT THRU 200-EXIT
*=>     UNTIL ???

     PERFORM 300-CLOSE-CURSOR-RTN THRU 300-EXIT.

     PERFORM 350-TERMINATE-RTN THRU 350-EXIT.

     MOVE ZERO TO RETURN-CODE.
     GOBACK.

 000-EXIT.
     EXIT.

 100-DECLARE-CURSOR-RTN.

* CODE YOUR CURSOR DEFINITION HERE. DECLARE IT FOR UPDATE OF PERF
```

```
100-EXIT.
    EXIT.

150-OPEN-CURSOR-RTN.
```

*OPEN THE CURSOR HERE

```



```

```
150-EXIT.
    EXIT.

200-DISPLAY-RPT.
```

*THIS PARAGRAPH SETS UP THE SQL PARAMETERS, PERFORMS THE
*PARAGRAPH TO MAKE THE CALL AND DISPLAYS THE RESULTS.

```
            PERFORM 275-FETCH-ROW-RTN THRU 275-EXIT.

    IF SQLCODE = ZERO
    THEN
            PERFORM 280-TABLE-SEARCH-RTN THRU 280-EXIT
            IF TABLE-HIT
            THEN
              IF UPDATE-ROW(EMPL-IDX)
              THEN
                PERFORM 290-UPDATE-ROW-RTN THRU 290-EXIT
              ELSE
                PERFORM 295-DELETE-ROW-RTN THRU 295-EXIT
            ELSE
              NEXT SENTENCE
    ELSE
            NEXT SENTENCE.

200-EXIT.
    EXIT.

275-FETCH-ROW-RTN.
```

Note: indexed 88-level
        field conditional

*THIS PARAGRAPH FETCHES A ROW FROM THE EMPL TABLE AND
*MOVES SPECIFIC DATA FIELDS INTO THE NBR AND PERF FIELDS.

```
```

   275-EXIT.
      EXIT.

   280-TABLE-SEARCH-RTN.

*THIS PARAGRAPH SEARCHES A WORKING-STORAGE TABLE TO FIND THE
*EMPLOYEE NBR. IF FOUND, IT MOVES THE NEW PERF AND RATE VALUES
*TO THE HOST PROGRAM VARIABLE FIELDS.

```
        MOVE 'N' TO HIT-FLAG-WS.
        SET EMPL-IDX TO 1.

        SEARCH EMPL-ROW-WS
           AT END GO TO 280-EXIT
           WHEN NBR OF DCLEMPL = EMPL-NBR-WS(EMPL-IDX)
               MOVE EMPL-PERF-WS(EMPL-IDX) TO PERF
               MOVE EMPL-RATE-WS(EMPL-IDX) TO RATE
               MOVE 'Y' TO HIT-FLAG-WS.
```

   280-EXIT.
      EXIT.

   290-UPDATE-ROW-RTN.

*THIS PARAGRAPH UPDATES THE DATABASE BY CHANGING THE PERF FIELD
*ON THE EMPL TABLE, AND THE RATE FIELD ON THE PAY TABLE. YOU
*SHOULD USE AN "UPDATE WHERE CURRENT OF" STATEMENT FOR THE EMPL
*TABLE, AND AN UPDATE STATEMENT (NON-CURSOR) FOR THE PAY TABLE.
*UPDATE THE PAY RATE BY SETTING DB2 PAY TABLE RATE EQUAL TO THE

*WORKING-STORAGE TABLE RATE

* =======> UPDATE EMPL TABLE

```



```

* =======> UPDATE PAY TABLE

```



```

```
 IF SQLCODE = ZERO
       MOVE NBR OF DCLEMPL
          TO NBR-RPT
          MOVE PERF        TO PERF-RPT
          MOVE RATE        TO RATE-RPT
          DISPLAY UPDATE-OUTPUT-ROW
          ADD +1 TO ROW-KTR.

 290-EXIT.
     EXIT.


 295-DELETE-ROW-RTN.
```

```
* THIS PARAGRAPH UPDATES THE DATABASE BY DELETING THE EMPLOYEE
*FROM THE EMPL AND PAY TABLES.
*YOU SHOULD USE A "DELETE WHERE CURRENT OF" STATEMENT FOR THE
*EMPL TABLE, AND A STANDARD DELETE STATEMENT FOR THE PAY TABLE.
*HINT — WHERE DO YOU GET THE SEARCH VALUES TO SPECIFY WHICH
*EMPLOYEE TO DELETE?
```

```
* =======> DELETE ROW FROM THE EMPL TABLE
```

```
┌─────────────────────────────────────────────────────────────────┐
│                                                                   │
│                                                                   │
│                                                                   │
└─────────────────────────────────────────────────────────────────┘
```

```
* =======> DELETE ROW FROM THE PAY TABLE
```

```
┌─────────────────────────────────────────────────────────────────┐
│                                                                   │
│                                                                   │
│                                                                   │
└─────────────────────────────────────────────────────────────────┘
```

```
   IF SQLCODE = ZERO
      MOVE NBR OF DCLEMPL
         TO DEL-NBR-RPT
               MOVE PERF TO DEL-PERF-RPT
               DISPLAY DELETE-OUTPUT-ROW
               ADD +1 TO ROW-KTR.

   295-EXIT.
      EXIT.

   300-CLOSE-CURSOR-RTN.

 *THIS STATEMENT CLOSES THE "ACTIVE SET"
```

```
┌─────────────────────────────────────────────────────────────────┐
│                                                                   │
│                                                                   │
│                                                                   │
└─────────────────────────────────────────────────────────────────┘
```

```
   300-EXIT.
      EXIT.

   999-ERROR-TRAP-RTN.
   ****************************************************************
   * ERROR TRAPPING ROUTINE FOR NEGATIVE SQLCODES               *
   ****************************************************************

       DISPLAY '**** WE HAVE A SERIOUS PROBLEM HERE *****'.
       DISPLAY '999-ERROR-TRAP-RTN '.
       MULTIPLY SQLCODE BY -1 GIVING SQLCODE.
       DISPLAY 'SQLCODE ==> ' SQLCODE.
```

```
EXEC SQL ROLLBACK WORK END-EXEC.
GOBACK.

999-EXIT.
    EXIT.
```

6.15. WORKSHOP VII — MAINTAINING REFERENTIAL INTEGRITY.

This is the final programming workshop in this book. It is an application that uses a symbolic cursor (retrieval) to sweep through table pairs and test for inter-table garbage on the database. By inter-table garbage I mean values that would not exist if referential integrity controls were in place. Referential integrity is a common problem in the relational database world. It refers to the synchronized control of updates across multiple tables, specifically control at the DBMS level — allowing or disallowing updates based on the relationships among the data.

For instance, in the EMPL table on the employee database, I am carrying each employee's project in the PROJ column. On the PROJ table is a master list of all projects and their unique numbers (NBR). The NBR column on the PROJ table, and the PROJ column on the EMPL table are used to link the EMPL and PROJ tables. Should DB2 allow me to insert or update a value in the PROJ column to some value that does not exist as a valid Project NBR on the PROJ table? No. But until DB2 version 2.1 (circa 1987) it did nothing at all to prevent such carryings on. In version 2.1 IBM implemented partial support of DBMS controlled referential integrity. Support is available for controlling INSERT and DELETE activity. However, little support was made available for "cascading updates."

What are "cascading updates"? In our example, if Project NBR 3 changed to Project NBR 9 on the PROJ table, we would be grateful if DB2 changed all values of 3 to 9 in the PROJ column of the EMPL table. Unfortunately, this would not occur. In fact, if we have defined referential integrity constraints on the EMPL and PROJ tables in DB2 Version 2.1 (PROJ.NBR would be a Primary Key, and EMPL.PROJ would be a Foreign Key), we would not even be allowed to UPDATE the Project NBR column to anything as long as there are rows on the EMPL table with the same values as the rows we intend to update on the Project table. (IMS programmer note: beginning to sound like the old "updating the primary key on the root segment" problem?) What we would need to do would depend on the way we implemented the referential integrity constraints between the two tables. It can get rather messy.

I have gone into this long diatribe to convince you of the necessity for application programs that monitor referential integrity. As of this writing, many production DB2 systems are not using the referential integrity constraints built in to the version 2.1 software. You will need a program like REFINTEG to scrub your tables and discover any values that - one way or another — are not "in synch" with the business rules behind the database design. Shown in Figure 61 are the business rules for the Employee database:

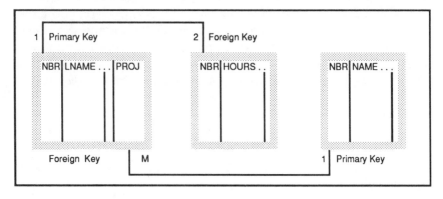

Figure 68. Business rules describing the relationships among the data in the video store database.

Please excuse the database design and column naming standards. This is a teaching database, and many lessons (both what to do and what not to do) can be learned from it.

6.15.1.   REFINTEG

The REFINTEG program uses the NOT EXISTS statement to join:

> EMPL and PAY tables — reporting on any employees receiving paychecks who are not on the employee master table;

> EMPL and PROJ tables — reporting on any employees doing work on fictitious projects.

You must code a correlated subquery with NOT EXISTS in the DECLARE CURSOR statements to satisfy this request. Most of the rest of the code is trivial. I would walk through the skeleton program listed below several times before attempting to solve the problem. And I would definitely try my SQL statements out in SPUFI or QMF before embedding it in the PROCEDURE DIVISION (just execute the interactive SELECT that is contained in the DECLARE CURSOR statement). You must be careful to understand which table is the parent and which is the child in coding your DECLARE CURSOR, and you may need to INSERT several bad rows on the PAY and EMPL tables to thoroughly test your solution. See appendix A for my solution if you get stuck.

```
 IDENTIFICATION DIVISION.
 PROGRAM-ID. REFINTEG.
*REMARKS.  THIS PROGRAM EXECUTES A SERIES OF CORRELATED
*    SUBQUERYS WITH THE EXISTS FUNCTION TO DETERMINE IF
*    THERE ARE ANY ROWS OUT OF SYNCH BETWEEN TWO TABLES
*    RELATED BY LINKING COLUMNS. A REPORT IS PRODUCED
*    DOCUMENTING ANY REFERENTIAL INTEGRITY PROBLEMS FOUND.
*
*
```

```
ENVIRONMENT DIVISION.
CONFIGURATION SECTION.
SOURCE-COMPUTER. IBM-370.
OBJECT-COMPUTER. IBM-370.

DATA DIVISION.

WORKING-STORAGE SECTION.

*
* HOST PROGRAM VARIABLES AND DB2 COMMUNICATIONS AREA COPYBOOKS
*
```

```
            EXEC SQL INCLUDE _ _ _ _ END-EXEC.
```

```
            EXEC SQL INCLUDE _ _ _ END-EXEC.
```

```
            EXEC SQL INCLUDE _ _ _ _ END-EXEC.
```

```
            EXEC SQL INCLUDE _ _ _ _ _ END-EXEC.
```

```
01   SQLCODE-OUT          PIC 9(03).

01   NULL-IND             PIC S9(04) COMP.

01   REPORT-LINE.
     05    FILLER         PIC X(16)  VALUE 'A FOREIGN KEY '.
     05    FILLER         PIC X(18)  VALUE 'COLUMN IN TABLE —'.
     05    TABLE-NAME-1   PIC X(19).
     05    FILLER         PIC X(19)  VALUE 'CONTAINS THE VALUE'.
     05    IDENT          PIC X(02).
     05    FILLER         PIC X(16)  VALUE 'WHICH DOES NOT '.
```

```
    05      FILLER          PIC X(17)  VALUE 'EXIST IN TABLE —'.
    05      TABLE-NAME-2    PIC X(19).


01  SQLCODE-OUT             PIC 9(03).
```

```
01  NULL-IND               PIC S9(04) COMP.
```
┌─────────────────────────────┐
│ Note: Null indicator . . . │
│   Why?   │
└─────────────────────────────┘

```
01  REPORT-LINE.
    05      FILLER          PIC X(16)  VALUE 'A FOREIGN KEY '.
    05      FILLER          PIC X(18)  VALUE 'COLUMN IN TABLE —'.
    05      TABLE-NAME-1    PIC X(19).
    05      FILLER          PIC X(19)  VALUE 'CONTAINS THE VALUE'.
    05      IDENT           PIC X(02).
    05      FILLER          PIC X(16)  VALUE 'WHICH DOES NOT '.
    05      FILLER          PIC X(17)  VALUE 'EXIST IN TABLE —'.
    05      TABLE-NAME-2    PIC X(19).
```

```
****************************************************************
*                                                              *
*    DECLARE YOUR SQL CURSORS HERE FOR THE SELECT              *
*    STATEMENTS WITH NOT EXISTS TO TEST FOR REFERENTIAL        *
*    INTEGRITY. NOTE THAT IT IS IMPORTANT TO UNDERSTAND        *
*    WHICH IS THE PRIMARY AN SECONDARY TABLE IN THIS           *
*    STATEMENT — APPLICATION RULES.                            *
*                                                              *
****************************************************************
```

```
┌────────────────────────────────────────────────────────────┐
│  EXEC SQL                                                    │
│     DECLARE EMPLPAY CURSOR FOR                               │
│        SELECT _ _ _ _ _ _ _ _ _ _ _ _ _ _ _                 │
│        FROM _ _ _ _ _ _ _ _ _                               │
│          WHERE _ _ _ _ _ _ _ _                              │
│          (SELECT _ _ _ _ _ _ _ _ _ _  FROM _ _ _ _ _        │
│          WHERE _ _ _ _ _ _ _ _ _ _ _ _ _ )                  │
│     END-EXEC.                                                │
└────────────────────────────────────────────────────────────┘
```

```
EXEC SQL
   DECLARE EMPLPROJ CURSOR FOR
      SELECT _ _ _ _ _ _ _ _ _ _ _ _ _ _ _ _ _ _ _ _
      FROM _ _ _ _ _ _ _ _ _ _ _ _
         WHERE _ _ _ _ _ _ _ _ _ _ _
         (SELECT _ _ _ _ _ _ _ _ _ _ _    FROM _ _ _ _ _ _ _ _
         WHERE _ _ _ _ _ _ _ _ _ _ _ _ _ _ _ _ _ _ )
END-EXEC.
```

Note: It is perfectly legal to DECLARE your CURSOR in the
        WORKING-STORAGE SECTION of a program. DECLARE CURSOR
        is not an executable statement like OPEN/FETCH/CLOSE.

```
PROCEDURE DIVISION.

    DISPLAY 'BEGINNING OF PROGRAM — REFINTEG'.
    DISPLAY SPACES.

000-SETUP-ERROR-TRAP-RTN.
*********************************************************************
*                                                                  *
*     CODE THE CORRECT ERROR-TRAPPING ROUTINES TO:                 *
*                                                                  *
*     BRANCH TO 999-ERROR-TRAP-RTN ON A NEGATIVE SQLCODE           *
*     CONTINUE PROCESSING UPON FINDING A POSITIVE SQLCODE          *
*     CONTINUE PROCESSING UPON END OF DATA                         *
*                                                                  *
*********************************************************************
```

```
EXEC SQL WHENEVER _ _ _ _ _ _    GOTO 999-ERROR-TRAP-RTN
END-EXEC.
EXEC SQL WHENEVER _ _ _ _ _ _ _ _ _    CONTINUE END-EXEC.
EXEC SQL WHENEVER _ _ _ _ _ _ _ _    CONTINUE END-EXEC.
```

```
000-MAINLINE-RTN.

    DISPLAY 'BEGINNING OF 000-MAINLINE'.
    DISPLAY SPACES.

    PERFORM 100-TEST-EMPL-PAY THRU 100-EXIT.

    PERFORM 200-TEST-EMPL-PROJ THRU 200-EXIT.

     MOVE ZERO TO RETURN-CODE.
     GOBACK.

 000-EXIT.
     EXIT.

 010-OPEN-EMPL-PAY-CURSOR.
 **************************************************************
 *                                                          *
 * CODE THE CURSOR OPEN STATEMENT HERE FOR THE PREVIOUSLY    *
 * DECLARED EMPLPAY CURSOR — SELECT.                         *
 *                                                          *
 **************************************************************
```

```
    EXEC SQL _ _ _ _ _ _ _ _ _ _ _ _ _ _  END-EXEC.
```

```
 010-EXIT.
     EXIT.


 020-OPEN-EMPL-PROJ-CURSOR.
 **************************************************************
 *                                                          *
 * CODE THE CURSOR OPEN STATEMENT HERE FOR THE PREVIOUSLY    *
 * DECLARED EMPLPROJ CURSOR — SELECT.                        *
 *                                                          *
 ***********************************************************************************
```

```
    EXEC SQL _ _ _ _ _ _ _ _ _ _ _ _ _ _ _  END-EXEC.
```

```
 020-EXIT.
    EXIT.

 030-FETCH-EMPL-PAY.
****************************************************************
*                                                              *
* CODE YOUR SQL FETCH RTN TO FETCH THE SELECTED ROW INTO       *
* YOUR WORKING STORAGE ROW DEFINITION.                         *
*                                                              *
****************************************************************

        MOVE 'PAYROLL' TO TABLE-NAME-1.
        MOVE SPACES TO IDENT.
        MOVE 'EMPLOYEE' TO TABLE-NAME-2.
```

```
 EXEC SQL _ _ _ _ _ _ _ _  _ _ _ _ _ _ _ _ _ _ _  END-EXEC.
```

```
        IF SQLCODE = ZERO
        THEN
             MOVE NBR OF DCLPAY TO IDENT
             DISPLAY REPORT-LINE.

 030-EXIT.
    EXIT.

 040-FETCH-EMPL-PROJ.
****************************************************************
*                                                              *
* CODE YOUR SQL FETCH RTN TO FETCH THE SELECTED ROW INTO       *
* YOUR WORKING STORAGE ROW DEFINITION.                         *
*                                                              *
****************************************************************

        MOVE 'EMPLOYEE' TO TABLE-NAME-1.
        MOVE SPACES TO IDENT.
        MOVE 'PROJECT' TO TABLE-NAME-2.
```

```
        EXEC SQL _ _ _ _  _ _ _ _ _ _ _ _  _ _ _ _
 _ _ _ _ _ _ _ _ _ _ _ _ _ _ _ _ _ _ _ _ _ _  END-EXEC.
```

```
        IF SQLCODE = ZERO
        THEN
              IF NULL-IND < ZERO
              THEN
                    MOVE '**' TO IDENT
                    DISPLAY REPORT-LINE
        ELSE
                    MOVE PROJ OF DCLEMPL TO IDENT
                    DISPLAY REPORT-LINE.

    040-EXIT.
        EXIT.


    050-CLOSE-EMPL-PAY.
    ****************************************************************
    *                                                              *
    * CODE THE CURSOR CLOSE STATEMENT HERE FOR THE PREVIOUSLY       *
    * DECLARED SELECT STATEMENT FOR CURSOR — EMPLPAY.               *
    *                                                              *
    ****************************************************************
```

```
              EXEC SQL CLOSE _ _ _ _ _ _ _ _   END-EXEC.
```

```
    050-EXIT.
        EXIT.


    060-CLOSE-EMPL-PROJ.
    ****************************************************************
    *                                                              *
    * CODE THE CURSOR CLOSE STATEMENT HERE FOR THE PREVIOUSLY       *
    * DECLARED SELECT STATEMENT FOR CURSOR EMPLPROJ.                *
    *                                                              *
    ****************************************************************
```

```
              EXEC SQL _ _ _ _ _ _ _ _ _ _ _ _ _ _ _ _ _   END-EXEC.
```

```
    060-EXIT.
        EXIT.
```

```
100-TEST-EMPL-PAY.
******************************************************************
*                                                                *
*CODE THE COBOL LOGIC TO PERFORM THE OPEN - FETCH -              *
*CLOSE                                                           *
*ROUTINES TO CHECK FOR REFERENTIAL INTEGRITY FOR EMPL/PAY        *
*                                                                *
******************************************************************

        PERFORM 010-OPEN-EMPL-PAY-CURSOR THRU 010-EXIT.
        PERFORM 030-FETCH-EMPL-PAY THRU 030-EXIT
```

```
    UNTIL _ _ _ _ _ _ _ _ _ _ _ _ _ _ _ _ _ _ _ _ _ _ _ _ .
```

```
        PERFORM 050-CLOSE-EMPL-PAY THRU 050-EXIT.

100-EXIT.
    EXIT.

200-TEST-EMPL-PROJ.
******************************************************************
*                                                                *
*CODE THE COBOL LOGIC TO PERFORM THE OPEN - FETCH - CLOSE        *
*ROUTINES TO CHECK FOR REFERENTIAL INTEGRITY FOR EMPL/PROJ       *
*                                                                *
******************************************************************

        PERFORM 020-OPEN-EMPL-PROJ-CURSOR THRU 020-EXIT.
        PERFORM 040-FETCH-EMPL-PROJ THRU 040-EXIT
```

```
    UNTIL _ _ _ _ _ _ _ _ _ _ _ _ _ _ _ _ _ _ _ _ _ _ _ _ .
```

```
        PERFORM 060-CLOSE-EMPL-PROJ THRU 060-EXIT.

200-EXIT.
    EXIT.
```

```
999-ERROR-TRAP-RTN.
***********************************************************
***   ERROR TRAPPING ROUTINE FOR NEGATIVE SQLCODES        *
***********************************************************

        DISPLAY '**** WE HAVE A SERIOUS PROBLEM HERE *****'.
        DISPLAY '999-ERROR-TRAP-RTN
        MULTIPLY SQLCODE BY -1 GIVING SQLCODE.
        DISPLAY 'SQLCODE ==> ' SQLCODE.
        DISPLAY SQLCA.
        DISPLAY SQLERRM.
        EXEC SQL ROLLBACK WORK END-EXEC.
        GOBACK.

999-EXIT.
    EXIT.
```

6.16. WORKSHOP TABLES

EMPLOYEE DATABASE

BASE TABLE — EMPL:

NBR	LNAME	FNAME	DOB	HIREDTE	PERF	JOB	DEPT	PROJ
01	LOWE	ROB	53012	85012	4	PROG	FIN	01
02	SHIELDS	BROOKE	59131	87001	3	MAN	MKT	01
03	MOORE	ROGER	48111	86002	1	DIR	MKT	04
04	EASTWOOD	CLINT	41091	60120	3	PROG	FIN	03
05	MOSTEL	ZERO	21365	84211		PRES		
06	BURNS	GEORGE	11178	49001	2	SYS	FIN	01
07	O'NEAL	RYAN	42189	60121	3	DIR	ACC	05
08	MARVIN	LEE	32187	51876	2	VP	ACC	02
09	LANCASTER	BURT	41091	79092	1	AN	R&D	02
10	BLAIR	LINDA	54013	85012	1	PROG	MKT	

BASE TABLE — PAY:

NBR	HOURS	RATE	DED	YTD
01	8.89	43	128.78	11890.66
02	13.23	40	204.45	15840.78
03	6.11	49	94.76	11890.66
04	26.75	45	132.58	17605.66
05	67.82	37	394.69	79990.99
06	32.45	32	121.99	53421.23
07	26.75	49	101.56	32758.11
08	15.99	52	327.98	67870.01
09	43.59	24	0	28090.91
10	32.41	52	112.78	27000.01

BASE TABLE — PROJ:

NBR	NAME	DEPT	MAJPROJ
01	PHASERS	MKT	
02	SYSTEM X	MKT	03
03	SYSTEM R	FIN	
04	LASERS	ACC	01
05	R*	FIN	03
06	NEW PROJ	F&D	02

Chapter 7

Performance-Oriented Application Design

After completing this chapter you will be able to describe specific considerations and guidelines for fine-tuning the SQL statements in a DB2 application program. You will also be able to describe several BIND parameter options which affect certain aspects of DB2 application performance. Topics include:

7.1. Performance Considerations: When and Why
7.2. How DB2 Accesses Your Data
7.3. Using SQL Statements Effectively
7.4. SQL Statement/Index Usage
7.5. Recoding SQL Statements to Take Advantage of Available Indexes
7.6. The EXPLAIN Statement
7.7. Using EXPLAIN
7.8. Overview of BIND
7.9. BIND Options for Locking
7.10. BIND Options for DB2 Object Authorization
7.11. Review Exercises —Workshop VIII

7.1. PERFORMANCE CONSIDERATIONS: WHEN AND WHY

SQL is a high-level data access language with much power and flexibility. In fact, SQL is so flexible that you can often code the same query several different ways to retrieve the same data. This would be wonderful if all the different combinations of SQL clauses and operators performed equally well. Unfortunately, this is far from the case. There are usually one or two most efficient ways to code an SQL query to solve a problem. This situation gives rise to a modern dilemma of all relational systems developers which is articulated as: "Do you want it to work, or do you want it to work well?" The answer of course is "Yes!"

What you will be learning in this chapter are guidelines to help you design and code your application programs, specifically, your application programs' SQL statements. You will learn how to code SQL that minimizes the use of DB2 and system resources without compromising your program's specification requirements.

The amount of time you devote to optimizing your SQL statements should grow in direct proportion to the Size of the DB2 tables your statements access. There are two basic high-water marks:

*   If you are accessing a table of over 10,000 rows (or 1,000 pages) you should spend some amount of time optimizing your SQL statements.
*   If you are accessing a table of over 100,000 rows (or 10,000 pages), or you are accessing multiple tables (joins, correlated subqueries, etc.), or you are writing an online program with response time service levels measured in seconds, you should plan on spending enough time on SQL statement optimization to ensure that you are accessing DB2 data as efficiently as possible.

Of course, you should *always try* to code your programs so that they run efficiently without compromising your coding specifications, but if your target production table sizes are as large or larger than the above two categories, you *must* optimize your SQL code. Until the hardware catches up to the software "Desperate times call for desperate measures!"

7.2.   HOW DB2 ACCESSES YOUR DATA

So what are the guidelines for using SQL statements effectively? Patience, we'll get to them presently. First, you must learn a little about how DB2 processes your SQL statements before we can discuss specifics on what, and what not, to do.

In accessing data in tables, DB2 chooses between two methods:

* Using an index to access the data.
* Reading all pages of a tablespace[1]

Notice that I said reading all pages of a *TABLESPACE* — not table. This is not a typo and is illustrated for you in Figure 69:

As illustrated in Figure 69, when DB2 uses an index to access your data, it is able to read a sorted file of keys (indexed columns) and use a row identifier (pointer) stored with the key to go directly to the row requested. When DB2 is forced to perform a full tablespace scan, it must retrieve each and every page in the tablespace in order to examine the rows in the page.

7.2.1.   TABLESPACE SCAN versus INDEX SCAN

If, by the nature of the business request, your query will be accessing over ⅓ of the rows in a table, then a tablespace scan

---

[1]With DB2 Version 2.1 you are able to define segmented tablespaces. This allows DB2 to access only the pages corresponding with the tables referenced in your query.

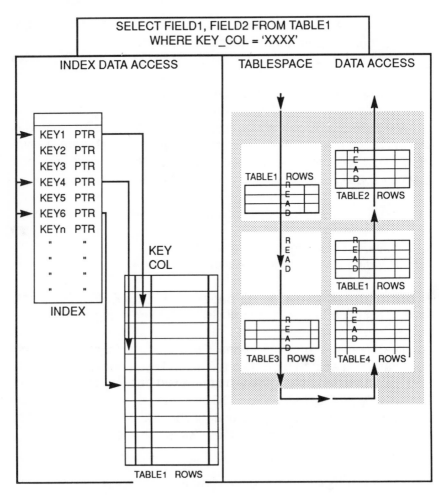

Figure 69. Two ways of accessing DB2 data.

will be more efficient than an index scan. The reason for this has to do with certain efficient internal sequential pre-fetching mechanisms, and that in accessing data through an index, DB2 may need to perform two physical I/O operations for each row:

- The first I/O operation to read the index and get the row pointer.
- The second I/O operation to access the row on the base table.

What kinds of queries access over $1/3$ the rows in a table? Detail and summary reports, year- or period-end processing, and any SQL statement without a WHERE clause or with a "non-selective" WHERE clause.

Example:

- List all customer information, sorted by city within state.
- List all movies costing over $10.
- List all customers whose last names begin after the letter G of the alphabet.
- List all employees hired after January 1, 1940, etc.
- Summarize the statistics on the first quarter's hiring.
- List all employee information for employees outside of the marketing department.

Now for a bit more on indexes and indexed data access.

7.2.2.   The Different Types of Index Access

There are basically three types of index access to DB2 data.[2] In order of decreasing performance they are:

- Index only access
- Clustered index access
- Unclustered index access

---

[2]IBM defines several other types of index accesses to your data. For more information about them consult the *DB2 Systems Programming and Administration Guide.*

Index Only Access

If DB2 can satisfy your SQL statement by accessing only the data stored in an index, you will get the best possible performance out of the system. Situations where DB2 can do this include:

- SELECT a single indexed column or columns that are all part of a multi-column index.
- SELECT the MIN or MAX function on an indexed column.
- SELECT COUNT(*) on a table with an indexed column.

Index only access to DB2 data is illustrated in Figure 70:

In the situation in Figure 70, DB2 only needs to read the index pages, because all the data needed to satisfy the SELECT statement is contained in the index.

Clustered Index Access

A clustered index is a type of DB2 index that maintains the data rows in your table in the same physical order as the key values in the indexed column. In other words, your physical data is in the same order as its logical order — by key value. This can be very beneficial for sequential access to your data (BETWEEN operator, <, >, <=, >= operators, etc.). You can only define one clustered index on a table.

If a clustered index exists on a column in your search condition, DB2 may be able to search for your rows using the clustered index. This will give efficient performance (two physical I/Os or less per data page containing rows to satisfy your query), and the process is illustrated in Figure 71:

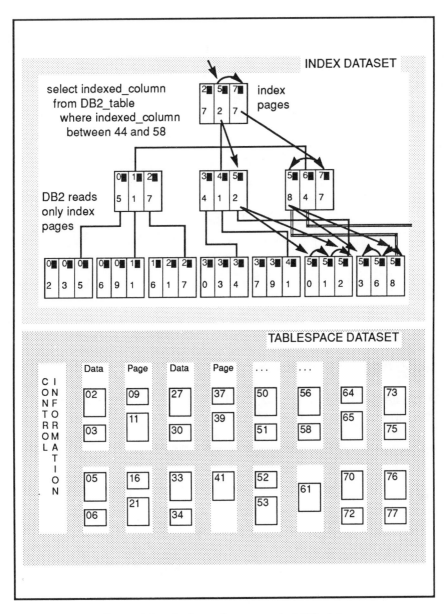

Figure 70.   Index only access to DB2 data.

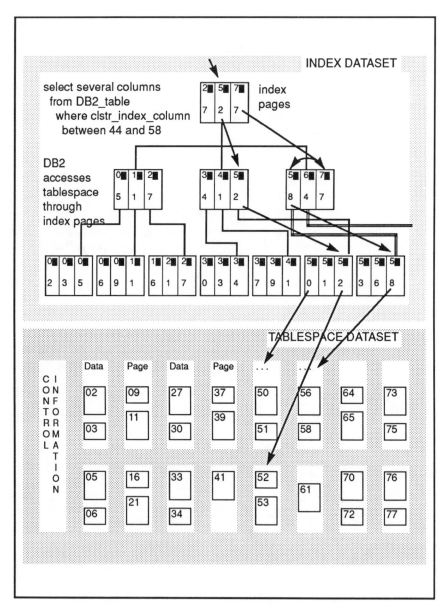

Figure 71.   Clustered index access to DB2 data.

In the situation in Figure 71, we are retrieving columns that are not contained in the index. DB2 uses the index to retrieve the correct tablespace pages that contain the rows to satisfy the search condition.

Unclustered Index Access

An unclustered index is simply a unique or non-unique index that is not defined as clustered. No attempt is made by DB2 to maintain the physical data rows in order by logical key. This is not an issue if DB2 uses the index to randomly access the table using the equal operator. It can become an issue if DB2 uses the index to access the data sequentially, as DB2 may have to read a single page more than once.

Unclustered index access is illustrated in Figure 72. As you study the diagram notice two things:

1.   In the clustered index scan, fewer total pages were needed because many rows were grouped sequentially on the same page.

2.   DB2 must read several pages more than once because data is stored randomly on each page.

In the situation in Figure 72, we are retrieving columns that are not contained in the index. DB2 uses the index to retrieve the correct tablespace pages that contain the rows to satisfy the search condition. Certain pages may be read more than once.

Note that if we are doing random data access

        where colm = value
        where colm IN(val,val . . .)

whether or not the data pages are clustered makes no difference.

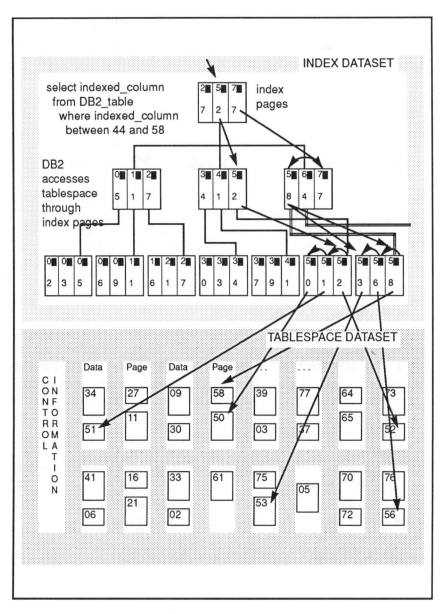

Figure 72. Unclustered index access to DB2 data.

7.3.   USING SQL STATEMENTS EFFECTIVELY

In general, it is important to try and minimize the input/output processing DB2 has to do in order to satisfy your query. This boils
down to reading fewer tablespace data pages, and there are four
aspects to this:

1.   Number of columns selected: Unless your program actually
     uses all the columns in a row, avoid coding SELECT *. This
     is particularly important if your SELECT statement generates
     a sort operation (ORDER BY, GROUP BY, JOINS, UNION,
     DISTINCT all generate sorts).

2.   Number of columns FOR UPDATE: Along the same lines,
     DB2 places internal locks on columns DECLAREd FOR
     UPDATE OF. Don't list columns in your UPDATE OF clause
     unless you intend to update them in your program.

3.   Number of rows selected: What this requirement boils down
     to is learning how to avoid DB2 tablespace scans by coding
     your SQL statements to allow DB2 to take advantage of
     existing indexes. In the next section you will learn various
     dos and don'ts regarding this.

4.   Obtain index access: The fastest access will always be
     index-only access. If your specification doesn't allow you to
     obtain index-only access (and not many will):

     • For sequential types of processing requests, the most effi-
        cient access will be via a clustered index scan.
     • For random access, efficient processing can be obtained
        using a unique or clustered unique index.

However, if you anticipate that your request will be accessing a
large percentage of the tablespace pages, employ a tablespace
scan.

7.4.   SQL STATEMENT/INDEX USAGE

7.4.1.   Performance Guideline #1 — Employ the Best Tool for the Job

If, due to processing requirements, your program will be accessing (either reading or updating) most of the pages in a tablespace,
you will get the best performance from a tablespace scan. If you
know ahead of time that this will be the situation for your program,
you can force DB2 out of choosing an index scan by coding your
SQL statement a certain way. For instance, DB2 will not choose
index access to your data if a search column uses the operator
¬= (not equal). You can force DB2 to use a tablespace scan for a
query by changing the WHERE clause as follows:

```
SELECT COLUMNS FROM DB2_TABLE WHERE INDEX_COLUMN
       BETWEEN 44 AND 58 AND INDEX_COLUMN ¬ = 0
```

For most other types of statements you will want DB2 to use an
index to access your data.

Recall from the beginning of the chapter that DB2 (specifically the
DB2 optimizer) decides on the access path to your data. You can
only influence the optimizer's decision in this respect. However,
many types of SQL keyword/operator combinations make the
choice of index access unlikely. Figure 73 is an important chart
that should be used during code reviews to analyze potential
application efficiency problems. The chart in Figure 73 outlines
the types of SQL statements and their influence on the optimizer's
decision on access path selection. It contains three columns:

 The first is simply a column showing different types of
 WHERE clause operators (COL = value, T1.COL = T2.COL,
 etc.). "Op" is any of the allowable simple operators (=, <, >,
 <= etc.). "Expression" is an arithmetic expression or DB2 row
 function (see *SQL as a Second Language,* chapter 12, for
 information on the DB2 row functions).

WHERE Clause Operators	Use Index?	Sargable?
COL = *value* COL IS NULL COL *op value* COL BETWEEN *value1* AND *value2* COL LIKE *'char%'* COL IN (*list*)	Yes	Yes
COL ¬ = *value* COL IS NOT NULL COL NOT BETWEEN (*value1, value2*) COL NOT IN (*list*) COL NOT LIKE *'char'* COL LIKE *'%char'* COL LIKE *'_char'* COL LIKE *host variable*	No	Yes
COL = (correlated subquery) COL *op* (correlated subquery) COL ¬ = (correlated subquery)	No	No
T1.COL = T2.COL (different tables) T1.COL *op* T2.COL T1.COL ¬ = T2.COL	Yes No	Yes
T1.COL1 = T1.COL2 (same table) T1.COL1 *op* T1.COL2 T1.COL1 ¬ = T1.COL2	No	No
COL (...) IN (subquery) COL (...) ANY (subquery) COL (...) ALL (subquery) (NOT) EXISTS (subquery)	No	No
COL = *expression* *expression = value* *expression* ¬ = *value* *expression op value*	No	No
predicate 1 AND predicate 2	Maybe	Yes
prediate1 OR predicate 2	No	Yes

Figure 73.   Combinations of SQL statements/index usage.

The second column shows whether or not a specific predicate (WHERE clause) can access data using an available index.

The third column shows the internal processing efficiency of the various WHERE clauses. A sargable[3] predicate is a predicate that can be evaluated by lower level internal DB2 processing, saving CPU cycles. Non-sargable predicates must be evaluated at a higher level and by a different module in the DB2 workspace. Many MVCL (Move Character Long) machine instructions are needed to move rows around within DB2. This can be avoided by using sargable predicates as your WHERE clauses.

In Figure 73 you can see that many combinations of keywords and operators are not "indexable" (i.e., will force DB2 to use a tablespace scan).

Now let's begin looking at guidelines to recode SQL queries so that they can take better advantage of available DB2 indexes.

7.5.   RECODING SQL STATEMENTS TO TAKE ADVANTAGE OF AVAILABLE INDEXES

7.5.1.   Using UNION in Place of OR

DB2 will not use an index to access your data if you connect multiple conditions with OR — unless you refer to single column and the operator is the equal sign:

---

[3]Sargable means Search Argument Able. Starting with DB2 Version 2.1, IBM started calling sargable "Stage 1," a better description of the lower level predicate evaluation taking place.

```
             WHERE COLUMN_1 = 'X' OR COLUMN_1 = 'Y'
```

Only OR condition where DB2 can choose index access

You can recode most OR conditions as a union:

```
change:
     SELECT COL_1 FROM DB2_TABLE WHERE COL_2 = 'X' OR
     COL_3 < 'Y'
to:
     SELECT COL_1 FROM DB2_TABLE WHERE COL_2 = 'X'
     UNION
     SELECT COL_1 FROM DB2_TABLE WHERE COL_3 < 'Y'
```

OR condition recoded as union to take advantage of existing index

The above example is significant in light of another DB2 restriction. DB2 can only use one index per table/per SELECT. This means that if indexes existed on COL_2 and COL_3, DB2 could only use one index for the original form of the query with OR. When we recoded the query using UNION, we in effect coded two independent SELECTs, and DB2 could potentially utilize both indexes in searching for our data rows.

You should realize that UNION will force a DB2 internal sort of your final results table. If your query will return many rows, this must be weighed against gains made by obtaining indexed access to your data.

7.5.2. Useing Table Joins in Place of Subqueries

DB2 is optimized to process table joins fairly efficiently, probably much more efficiently than subqueries — particularly if the subquery is correlated or if the subselect is linked with IN (see example). As a general rule of thumb, choose joins in place of sub-queries whenever possible:

To retrieve Employee last names of employees who worked over 40 hours:

```
change:
     SELECT LNAME FROM EMPL WHERE NBR IN
        (SELECT NBR FROM PAY WHERE HOURS > 40)
to:
     SELECT LNAME FROM EMPL.PAY WHERE EMPL.NBR = PAY.NBR
        AND HOURS > 40
```

Recode subquery as table join

You should realize that joins may return more data rows than cor-responding subqueries if there are duplicate values in the JOIN condition columns. If you have installed my test tables try these queries out to see for yourself:

1.   SELECT * from EMPL
        WHERE PROJ IN(SELECT NBR from PROJ)

2.   SELECT EMPL.* from EMPL.PROJ
        WHERE EMPL.PROJ = PROJ.NBR

     Before you do this, insert a few extra rows in the PROJECT table.

     Duplicate PROJECT numbers 03, 04.

7.5.3. Avoid Datatype Conversion Problems

DB2 will not use available indexes if the host variable or literal value you are comparing to a column has a greater precision or length than the column.

If you are comparing a value to the PERF column of the employee table which is defined as SMALLINT (halfword integer value):

```
change:
    WHERE PERF > 1.0

to:
    WHERE PERF > 1
```

Avoid numeric conversions

If you are comparing a value to the DEPT column of the employee table which is defined as CHAR(3) (fixed length character, 3 bytes long):

```
change:
    WHERE DEPT = 'XYZ

to:
    WHERE DEPT = 'XYZ'
```

Avoid character string padding

7.5.4.   Avoid Arithmetic Expressions in a WHERE Clause

DB2 will not use available indexes if the WHERE clause contains an arithmetic expression. In embedded SQL this should not present a problem (see example). In interactive SQL there may not be a way to avoid this.

If you have obtained a salary base figure and percent increase from a file, and want to see how many employees earn as much as

the salary figure multiplied by the percent increase

```
change:
     WHERE YTD > :SALARY-BASE * PERCENT-INCREASE

to:
     COMPUTE SALARY-BASE = SALARY-BASE *
     PERCENT-INCREASE
        .
        .
     WHERE YTD > :SALARY-BASE
```

Avoid arithmetic expressions

7.5.5.   Avoid Using LIKE in Embedded SQL Statements

The percent (%) wildcard specifier can cause DB2 to search a majority of rows in a table. This may prevent DB2 from using an index that is defined on the search column. Why? When you use LIKE in an embedded SQL statement, the optimizer has no way of knowing what kind of search string you may be assigning to the LIKE operator. For all the optimizer knows, the percent sign (%) might be in position 1 of your search string, forcing a full table scan to determine row eligibility.

If you are using COBOL II, you may be able to recode the SQL statements using LIKE as dynamic SQL statements. Dynamic

SQL statements are statements that are built by your program, prepared (BINDed), and executed at run-time. The optimizer sees the entire LIKE predicate when it does a BIND of a dynamic SQL statement and will make more effective use of available indexes.

You also may be able to recode some LIKE statements using BETWEEN. Find all DEPTs that begin with the letters E and F:

```
change:
     WHERE DEPT LIKE 'E%' or DEPT LIKE 'F%'

to:
     WHERE DEPT BETWEEN 'EAA' AND 'FZZ'
```

Recode LIKE using BETWEEN

7.5.6. Indexes on Columns DECLAREd FOR UPDATE OF

DB2 will not use available indexes if you are updating a column declared with the FOR UPDATE OF — except if your WHERE clause specifies the equal condition.

If indexes exist on DEPT and JOB:

```
change:
    DECLARE UPDT CURSOR FOR SELECT NBR, DEPT, JOB FROM EMPL
       WHERE DEPT IS NOT NULL AND JOB IN ('PROG','DBA')
          FOR UPDATE OF DEPT, JOB
              .
              .
    UPDATE EMPL SET DEPT = :NEW-DEPT,JOB = ;NEW-JOB WHERE CURRENT OF UPDT
to:
    DECLARE UPDT CURSOR FOR SELECT NBR, DEPT, JOB FROM EMPL
       WHERE DEPT IS NOT NULL AND JOB IN ('PROG','DBA')
              .
              o
              . read each row, use NBR as search argument in
             standard update statement
    UPDATE EMPL SET DEPT = :NEW-DEPT, JOB = :NEW-JOB WHERE NBR = :NBR
```

Use standard UPDATE statement in place of FOR UPDATE OF

7.6.   THE EXPLAIN STATEMENT

Considering the importance of obtaining index access to DB2 data for large tables or online processing, it was universally applauded when, in DB2 Version 1.2 (circa 1986), IBM announced support for an SQL statement that allows you to determine:

*   Whether or not your SQL statement will be processed using an index;
*   The level of index support (which index, how many columns of a multi-column index are used, etc.);
*   Whether or not your SQL statement requires DB2 to sort any data rows;
*   The locking level imposed by DB2 on your statement;
*   The method DB2 chooses for processing your table joins;

and other information about the access path chosen for your SQL statement's execution. Armed with this information, you can analyze the access path chosen and determine whether or not your SQL statement needs further optimization. To the best of my knowledge, IBM relational products[4] (DB2 and SQL/DS) are the only commercial products that have this feature. And considering the fact that you must rely on the optimizer for choosing the access path to your data (you cannot directly influence its decision), the ability to find out "just what was the verdict" is truly an important feature.

EXPLAIN does not execute your statement. It merely describes (explains) the internal access path choices made by DB2. The format of the EXPLAIN looks like this:

```
EXPLAIN PLAN
   SET QUERYNO = <integer> FOR
   <sql statement>
```

EXPLAIN statement format

[4]Ingres by RTI has a similar function, with a very different format

Where:

- EXPLAIN PLAN inserts one or more rows into a DB2 table called a PLAN_TABLE for your statement.
- SET QUERYNO allows you to associate a specific PLAN_TABLE row with the SQL statement it describes.
- FOR specifies the SQL statement to be analyzed:

  SELECT, INSERT, UPDATE, DELETE.

To use EXPLAIN, you must first create a PLAN_TABLE on your ID (i.e., you must be the "owner" of the PLAN_TABLE). The statements to create a PLAN_TABLE are shown in Figure 74.

```
CREATE TABLE PLAN_TABLE
   (QUERYNO              INTEGER    NOT NULL      ,
    QBLOCKNO             SMALLINT   NOT NULL      ,
    APPLNAME             CHAR(8)    NOT NULL      ,
    PROGNAME             CHAR(8)    NOT NULL      ,
    PLANNO               SMALLINT   NOT NULL      ,
    METHOD               SMALLINT   NOT NULL      ,
    CREATOR              CHAR(8)    NOT NULL      ,
    TNAME                CHAR(18)   NOT NULL      ,
    TABNO                SMALLINT   NOT NULL      ,
    ACCESSTYPE           CHAR(2)    NOT NULL      ,
    MATCHCOLS            SMALLINT   NOT NULL      ,
    ACCESSCREATOR        CHAR(8)    NOT NULL      ,
    ACCESSNAME           CHAR(18)   NOT NULL      ,
    INDEXONLY            CHAR(1)    NOT NULL      ,
    SORTNUNIQ            CHAR(1)    NOT NULL      ,
    SORTNJOIN            CHAR(1)    NOT NULL      ,
    SORTNORDERBY         CHAR(1)    NOT NULL      ,
    SORTNGROUPBY         CHAR(1)    NOT NULL      ,
    SORTCUNIQ            CHAR(1)    NOT NULL      ,
    SORTCJOIN            CHAR(1)    NOT NULL      ,
    SORTCORDERBY         CHAR(1)    NOT NULL      ,
    SORTCGROUPBY         CHAR(1)    NOT NULL      ,
    TSLOCKMODE           CHAR(3)    NOT NULL      ,
    TIMESTAMP            CHAR(16)   NOT NULL      ,
    REMARKS              VARCHAR(254)  NOT NULL  );
```

Figure 74.   Statements needed to create plan_table.

Each of the columns in the PLAN_TABLE contain information about your SQL statement. They include:

QUERYNO: Allows you to distinguish among EXPLAIN statements in your PLAN_TABLE by assigning each query a unique number.

QBLOCKNO: An integer value used to identify subselects within an SQL statement.

APPLNAME: The name of the application plan. It is set to blanks for an interactive EXPLAIN statement.

PROGNAME: The name of the SQL/COBOL program in which the EXPLAIN statement is embedded.

PLANNO: An integer indicating the order in which DB2 undertakes the action of a plan.

METHOD: An integer indicating an internal DB2 process at work in this step:

0 First table accessed (PLANNO = 1).

1 Nested/loop join — usually the most efficient table join technique you can get from DB2. Indexes must be available on both joining columns.

2 Merge/Scan join — usually a less efficient table join technique consisting of multiple sort steps and "match/merge" style logic.

3 Additional sorts (needed by ORDER BY, GROUP BY, or SELECT DISTINCT).

CREATOR: CREATOR of any new (temporary work) tables built during this step.

TNAME: Name of any new (temporary work) tables.

TABNO: An integer used to distinguish among multiple references to the same table (joining a table to itself, correlated subquery, etc.).

ACCESSTYPE: Either R for full-table scan of all data pages or I for Index access. This is the critical information.

MATCHCOLS: The number of index keys (columns that make up an index) DB2 was able to use in accessing your data. If a three part, multi-column index exists on LNAME, FNAME, and NBR from the EMPL, DB2 may be able to use all three columns, two of the three columns, or one of the three columns, depending on your SQL statement coding, the order of the columns in the index, and other factors.

ACCESSNAME: The name of the index DB2 is using to access your data (if ACCESSTYPE = I above).

ACCESSNAME: The name of the creator of the index (if ACCESSTYPE = I above).

INDEXONLY: Whether or not DB2 will be able to satisfy your query using data obtained only from the index (Y), or whether it will need to access data pages (N).

Sort indicators: A series of four Y/N indicators that describe whether or not DB2 will need to perform a sort during execution. The four types of statements that may force DB2 to sort are indicated by the columns:

U   UNIQUE
J   Table join
O   ORDER BY clause
G   GROUP BY clause

Composite Sort
indicators: Another set of sort indicators used to denote sorts forced during intermediate phases of SQL statement execution on composite (internal work) tables.

TSLOCKMODE: The locking level imposed by DB2 on the tablespace while executing your SQL statement.

The critical columns in dealing with performance analysis are (in order of importance):

---

* ACCESSTYPE (did you get the type of access you wanted?)
  If ACCESSTYPE = 'I'

  * ACCESSNAME (did DB2 use the index you wanted it to use?)
  * MATCHCOLS (how many of the index keys are being used?)
  * INDEXONLY (potentially)

* METHOD (if joining tables — did you get a Nested/Loop join?)

* Sort indicators (Sorting is very easy to do in DB2, many SQL statements force sorts of either internal tables or results tables. Nevertheless, sorts are no less expensive in DB2 than in OS processing)

Critical performance columns in PLAN TABLE

Before we analyze a few EXPLAIN results, let's go over the steps in using EXPLAIN one more time, in Figure 75:

---

1. Create your PLAN_TABLE using the statements shown in Figure 73.

2. Code your SQL statements using the EXPLAIN format:

```
EXPLAIN PLAN
   SET QUERYNO = <integer> FOR
      <sql statement>
```

3. SELECT your results from the PLAN_TABLE using SPUFI or QMF. Use a statement like:

```
SELECT * FROM PLAN_TABLE
   WHERE QUERYNO = <n>
END-EXEC.
```

Where n is the value you set your EXPLAIN statement to.

Figure 75. Summary of steps to use EXPLAIN

There are three methods of obtaining EXPLAIN data:

1. Code and execute EXPLAIN statements to analyze your queries interactively using SPUFI or QMF.

2. BIND your program with the EXPLAIN option set to YES. When you do this, multiple rows will be inserted into your PLAN_TABLE. You will be able to distinguish your program's rows by looking at the APPLNAME column, which will be valued with your program's APPLICATION PLAN name, and the QUERYNO will be set to the statement number (line number) of your program's SQL statements.

3. Use a third party DB2 performance tool such as DB/Optimizer.[5] Several vendors have created SQL execution analysis tools to help you tune the performance of your program. DB/Optimizer is a product that allows you to capture EXPLAIN and other DB2 performance and tuning information easily and quickly — for both interactive and embedded SQL statements.

7.7. USING EXPLAIN

Let's look at a few examples of EXPLAIN and analyze the values in the critical performance columns, shown in Figure 76.

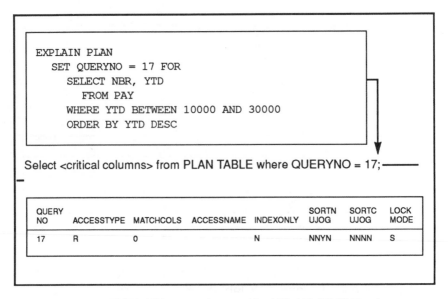

```
EXPLAIN PLAN
    SET QUERYNO = 17 FOR
        SELECT NBR, YTD
            FROM PAY
            WHERE YTD BETWEEN 10000 AND 30000
            ORDER BY YTD DESC
```

Select <critical columns> from PLAN TABLE where QUERYNO = 17;

QUERY NO	ACCESSTYPE	MATCHCOLS	ACCESSNAME	INDEXONLY	SORTN UJOG	SORTC UJOG	LOCK MODE
17	R	0		N	NNYN	NNNN	S

Figure 76. EXPLAIN example — critical PLAN_TABLE columns.

---

[5] Information on DB/Optimizer is available from Systems Center, 125 Technology Drive, Waltham, Ma 02154 (617-891-7676).

Assuming that our PAY table is production size (35,000 rows) and has an index built on the NBR column, Figure 76 shows the results of running EXPLAIN. Note that we are getting a full tablespace scan and that a sort is performed for the ORDER BY clause.

If this query is part of a critical online inquiry process, the DBA might decide to index the YTD field Descending. After REBINDing the application a new access path is chosen, as shown in Figure 77 (Why no more Sort for the ORDER BY clause?).

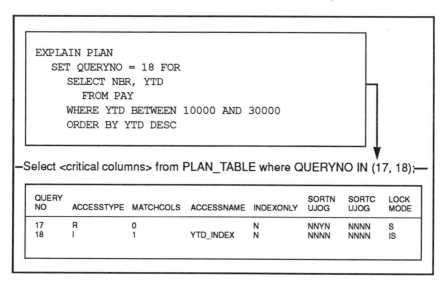

Figure 77.   EXPLAIN of query after adding index.

Now an example of a table join. Figure 78 shows an EXPLAIN of a join of the EMPL and PAY tables. Assume indexes on employee number, payroll number, and employee department columns.

The ORDER BY PLANNO in our SELECT to look at the EXPLAIN information is necessary so that we can see the order in which the tables are joined.

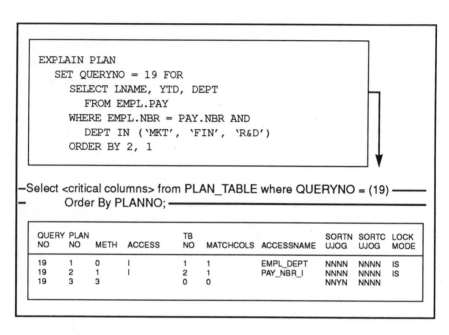

Figure 78.   EXPLAIN example — critical PLAN_TABLE columns.

1.   The first row (PLANNO 1) represents access to the "outer table" a table chosen by DB2 to drive the join process. This table is accessed through the index on the department column, using a matching index scan of referenced tablespace data pages.

2.   The second row (PLANNO 2) describes the access to the "inner table" and the join operation itself (a nested/loop join). Again, a matching index scan with referenced data pages is used.

3.   The third row (PLANNO 3) shows that a sort will be performed on the join results (Method 3). The sort indicator for ORDER BY is set to "Y."

EXPLAIN is a very powerful tool in designing and tuning your DB2 applications for optimum performance. It is my opinion that all critical application programs should undergo a design review which includes an EXPLAIN analysis of the SQL statements included in the programs.

7.8.   OVERVIEW OF BIND

There are several BIND options that can affect the performance of not only your individual program, but the overall DB2 system performance. Before we discuss the various options of BIND, let's review the BIND process.

As illustrated in Figure 79, BIND:

- Accepts as input the various DBRMs that compose your application's SQL statements.
- Checks the statements for syntax.
- Checks the DB2 objects referenced in the statements:
  — For spelling, etc.,
  — For user/object authorization.
- Compiles the DBRMs into an application plan and chooses the:
  — Most efficient access path
  — Locking protocol

Many of the decisions made during BIND are beyond your direct control (although we've just finished learning how to "influence" the optimizer for or against index access path selection). However, recall that on the BIND panel there were several choices you could make regarding:

- Resource Acquisition/Release
- Program Isolation Level
- Authority Validation

We continue our discussion with these BIND parameters.

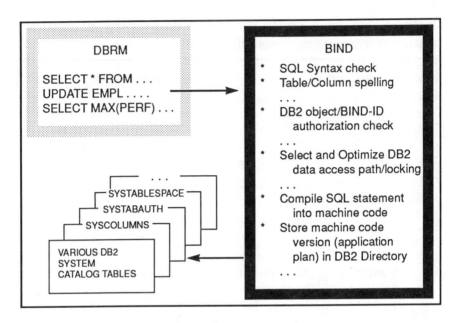

Figure 79.   BIND.

7.9.   BIND OPTIONS FOR LOCKING

There are two DB2 locking aspects affected by your choice of lock options on the BIND panel: ISOLATION LEVEL and resource acquisition/release.

7.9.1.   ISOLATION LEVEL: CS/RR

This option refers to the manner in which data pages are held (locked) after you are finished accessing them. Simply, when you choose the isolation level of CS (Cursor Stability), your program relinquishes its locks on individual pages of data when your symbolic cursor moves to a row on a new page. When you choose the isolation level of RR (Repeatable Read), your program retains locks on individual pages of data when your symbolic cursor moves to a new page. This is illustrated in Figure 80:

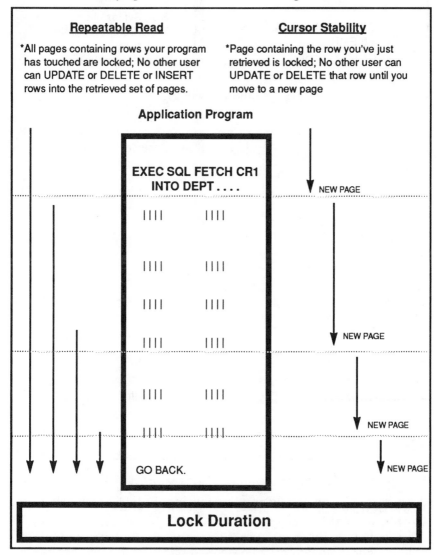

Figure 80. Cursor Stability vs Repeatable Read.

Considerations for choosing CS versus RR are fairly straightforward:

• If, due to processing requirements, you must guarantee that data referenced and REREFERENCED by your program will not change during your program's execution, choose ISOLATION LEVEL ==> RR.
• Otherwise, choose isolation level CS.

CS allows for greater concurrency (more users accessing a table at the same time). RR guarantees that another program may not update values you have previously accessed in your program.

7.9.2. Resource Acquisition/Release

There are several options you can choose that dictate when DB2 acquires locks on the tablespaces you process against, and when DB2 releases those locks. You specify the options on the BIND panel:

RESOURCE ACQUISITION ===> (Allocate/Use)

RESOURCE RELEASE   ===> (DeAllocate/Commit)

The allowable combinations include:

```
Acquire ALLOCATE    —    Release DEALLOCATE
Acquire USE         —    Release COMMIT
Acquire ALLOCATE    —    Release COMMIT
```

A short description of the various options follows:

Acquire allocate

This option acquires locks on all — that is, *all* — DB2 objects referenced in your application plan when the plan is allocated — at the highest locking level possible for your plan's execution — *whether or not the SQL statements that use the DB2 objects ever actually execute!*

Acquire use

This option acquires locks on the DB2 object referenced in your application plan *only* when your program decides to use the object.

Release deallocate

This option releases all locks held on DB2 objects when the application plan is deallocated (in TSO, usually after returning to the TSO Terminal Monitor Program).

Release commit

This option releases all locks held on DB2 objects when your program reaches a commit point (via explicit or implicit COMMIT).

The tradeoffs among these options are discussed below.

Assuming your program executes most of its SQL code, the tradeoffs shown in Figure 81 apply.

If your program contains many SQL statements, most of which are not executed in a single program run, consider using Acquire(USE) Release(COMMIT).

Acquire(USE) Release(COMMIT) will give you:

* Better multi-program concurrency

* More locking activity — hence increased CPU usage

* Better system-wide access to DB2 objects — Tablespaces not being used are not locked

Acquire(ALLOCATE) Release(DEALLOCATE) will give you:

* Less multi-program concurrency

* Less locking activity — decreased CPU usage

* Less system-wide access to DB2 objects — Tablespaces not being used <u>are</u> locked

* Less potential for dead-locks and timeouts

Figure 81.   Trade-offs in the duration of tablespace locks.

If your online program is designed to reuse the control blocks (THREADS) established by the online supervisor (IMS, CICS), consider using Acquire(ALLOCATE) Release(DEALLOCATE). This will reduce the allocation cost for each program invocation.

7.10.   BIND OPTIONS FOR DB2 OBJECT AUTHORIZATION

The options for object authorization include:

* VALIDATE(BIND)   Check all authorizations against the BINDing ID during the BIND operation.
* VALIDATE(RUN)   Defer authorization checks until the plan (program) is executed.

This one is easy. Unless your program is issuing Dynamic SQL statements or you're in development/test mode and don't have your tables defined yet, *always* BIND with the VALIDATE(BIND) option. This will save substantial overhead and DB2 System Catalog contention at execute time.

7.11. REVIEW EXERCISES

One final workshop for this book. Below you will find the SQL/COBOL program FRIDGE, so named for its vast consumption of both I/O overhead and CPU processing cycles. Your job is to recode the SQL statements in the program, based on the guidelines established in this chapter, and to streamline the FRIDGE, making it lean and mean. My solution can be found in Appendix A.

I hope you've enjoyed this book as much as I enjoyed writing it.

Best Wishes,

Jonathan Sayles

```
IDENTIFICATION DIVISION.
PROGRAM-ID. FRIDGE.
REMARKS.    THIS PROGRAM CONTAINS SEVERAL PERFORMANCE
PROBLEMS.
        RE-CODE THE SQL STATEMENTS IN THE PROCEDURE DIVISION
        TO OPTIMIZE THE PROGRAM ACCORDING TO THE SUGGESTIONS
        MADE IN THE APPLICATION DESIGN SECTION OF YOUR MANUAL.
        INDEXES EXIST ON THE FOLLOWING COLUMNS:
        *    EMPL.NBR
        *    PROJ.NBR
        *    PAY.NBR
```

```
*      EMPL.LNAME
*      EMPL.DEPT
*      PAY.YTD

ENVIRONMENT DIVISION.
CONFIGURATION SECTION.
SOURCE-COMPUTER. IBM-370.
OBJECT-COMPUTER. IBM-370.

DATA DIVISION.

WORKING-STORAGE SECTION.

****************************************************************
* DCLGEN TABLE(EMPL)                                           *
****************************************************************

      EXEC SQL DECLARE EMPL TABLE
        ( NBR              CHAR(2),
          LNAME            CHAR(10),
          FNAME            CHAR(6),
          DOB              INTEGER,
          HIREDTE          INTEGER,
          PERF             SMALLINT,
          JOB              CHAR(4),
          DEPT             CHAR(3),
          PROJ             CHAR(2)
        )  END-EXEC.


****************************************************************
* COBOL DECLARATION FOR TABLE EMPL                            *
****************************************************************

01   DCLEMPL.
     10   NBR          PIC X(2).
     10   LNAME        PIC X(10).
     10   FNAME        PIC X(6).
```

```
10   DOB            PIC S9(9)      USAGE COMP.
10   HIREDTE        PIC S9(9)      USAGE COMP.
10   PERF           PIC S9(4)      USAGE COMP.
10   JOB            PIC X(4).
10   DEPT           PIC X(3).
10   PROJ           PIC X(2).
*****************************************************************
* DCLGEN TABLE(PAY)                                             *
*****************************************************************

     EXEC SQL DECLARE PAY TABLE
     ( NBR                CHAR(2),
       HOURS              DECIMAL(5, 2),
       RATE               DECIMAL(5, 2),
       DED                DECIMAL(5, 2),
       YTD                DECIMAL(8, 2)
     ) END-EXEC.


*****************************************************************
* COBOL DECLARATION FOR TABLE PAY                              *
*****************************************************************

     01   DCLPAY.
     10   NBR            PIC X(2).
     10   HOURS          PIC S999V99      USAGE COMP-3.
     10   RATE           PIC S999V99      USAGE COMP-3.
     10   DED            PIC S999V99      USAGE COMP-3.
     10   YTD            PIC S999999V99   USAGE COMP-3.


*****************************************************************
* THE NUMBER OF COLUMNS DESCRIBED BY THIS DECLARATION IS 5     *
*****************************************************************

* SQL COMMUNICATIONS AREA - DATA ITEMS PULLED IN VIA INCLUDE

     EXEC SQL INCLUDE SQLCA END-EXEC.
```

```
01  MISC-DATA-ITEMS.
    05   CHAR-FIELD       PIC X(04).
    05   NUMERIC-FIELD  PIC S9(05)V99     COMP-3.
    05   SQLCODE-OUT      PIC 9(03).
    05   NUL-FIELD        PIC S9(04)       COMP.
    05   NUL-FIELD-1      PIC S9(04)       COMP.
    05   DRIVER-SRCH      PIC X(20).
    05   NUL-STRUCT.
         10 NUL          PIC S9(04)       COMP OCCURS 8 TIMES.
    05   SMALL-SRCH.
    49   SMALL-SRCH-LEN  PIC S9(04)       COMP.
         49   SMALL-SRCH-TEXT    PIC X(04).
```

```
PROCEDURE DIVISION.

000-SETUP-ERROR-TRAP-RTN.

000-MAINLINE-RTN.

    DISPLAY 'BEGINNING OF PROGRAM — FRIDGE'.
    DISPLAY SPACES.

    PERFORM 200-TEST-RTN THRU 200-EXIT.

    MOVE ZERO TO RETURN-CODE.
    GOBACK.

000-EXIT.
    EXIT.

200-TEST-RTN.

****************************************************************
* 1) RETRIEVE AND DISPLAY EMPLOYEE LAST-NAMES THAT CONTAIN AN  *
* A, B, OR C IN THE FIRST CHAR — Disregard Cursor Usage        *
****************************************************************
```

```
EXEC SQL SELECT * INTO :DCLEMPL
    FROM EMPL
    WHERE       LNAME LIKE 'A%'
    OR          LNAME LIKE 'B%'
    OR          LNAME LIKE 'C%' END-EXEC.
```

Recode here:

```
    EXEC SQL



    END-EXEC.
```

```
****************************************************************
* 2) RETRIEVE AND DISPLAY ALL EMPLOYEE NUMBERS FOR EMPLOYEES   *
* MAKING OVER $20,000                                         *
****************************************************************
```

```
EXEC SQL DECLARE FRIDGE1 CURSOR FOR
    SELECT * FROM EMPL
        WHERE NBR IN
         (SELECT NBR FROM PAY
         WHERE YTD > 20000)
END-EXEC.
```

```
        EXEC SQL




        END-EXEC.
```

```
****************************************************************
* 3) RETRIEVE AND DISPLAY EMPLOYEE NBRs, FOR EMPLOYEES         *
*    WHOSE LAST NAMES ARE BETWEEN 'G' AND 'M' or WHO           *
*    MAKE OVER $20,000;                                        *
****************************************************************
```

```
  EXEC SQL DECLARE FRIDGE2 CURSOR FOR
      SELECT * FROM EMPL, PROJ
          WHERE EMPL.PROJ = PROJ.NBR
          AND (LNAME BETWEEN 'G' AND 'M' OR
            YTD > 20000)
  END-EXEC.
```

```
        EXEC SQL




        END-EXEC.
```

```
****************************************************************
* 4) UPDATE THE PAY TABLE — GIVE ALL MANAGERS A 10% RAISE      *
****************************************************************
```

```
  EXEC SQL UPDATE PAY
      SET YTD = YTD * 1.10
          WHERE NBR IN (SELECT NBR
            FROM EMPL WHERE JOB = 'MAN') END-EXEC.
```

```
    EXEC SQL



    END-EXEC.
```

```
*****************************************************************
* 5) SELECT ALL EMPLOYEES WHO ARE ON PROJECT NBRS 01, 02, 03    *
*     AND ALL EMPLOYEES IN THE MARKETING DEPT.                  *
*****************************************************************
```

```
EXEC SQL SELECT * FROM EMPL
    WHERE PROJ IN ('01','02','03') OR
        DEPT = 'MKT' END-EXEC.
```

```
    EXEC SQL



    END-EXEC.
```

```
*****************************************************************
* 6) SELECT ALL EMPLOYEE INFORMATION FOR EMPLOYEES WHOSE LAST   *
* NAMES DO NOT BEGIN WITH G OR H                                *
*****************************************************************
```

```
EXEC SQL SELECT * FROM EMPL
    WHERE LNAME NOT LIKE 'G%' OR LNAME NOT LIKE 'H%'
END-EXEC.
```

```
      EXEC SQL



      END-EXEC.
```

```
**************************************************************
* 7) SELECT ALL EMPLOYEE NBRS FOR EMPLOYEES WITH PERFORMANCE  *
* EVALUATIONS OVER 5                                          *
**************************************************************
```

```
MOVE 5 TO NUMERIC-FIELD.

EXEC SQL SELECT * FROM EMPL
    WHERE PERF > NUMERIC-FIELD
        END-EXEC.
```

```
      EXEC SQL



      END-EXEC.
```

```
**************************************************************
* 8) SELECT ALL EMPLOYEE NBRS FOR EMPLOYEES IN THE MARKETING  *
* AND FINANCE DEPARTMENTS.                                    *
**************************************************************
```

```
MOVE 'MKT' TO DEPT.
MOVE 'FIN' TO CHAR-FIELD.

EXEC SQL SELECT NBR FROM EMPL
      WHERE DEPT = :DEPT
    UNION
    SELECT NBR FROM EMPL
      WHERE DEPT = :CHAR-FIELD      END-EXEC.
```

```
    EXEC SQL




    END-EXEC.
```

```
**************************************************************
* 9) SELECT ALL EMPLOYEE NUMBERS FOR EMPLOYEES WHERE THE     *
*    SALARY IS NOT EQUAL TO THE HOST VARIABLE SAL * 1.07     *
**************************************************************
```

```
EXEC SQL SELECT * FROM EMPL, PAY
      WHERE EMPL.NBR = PAY.NBR
    AND YTD = :SAL * 1.07 END-EXEC.
```

```
    EXEC SQL



    END-EXEC.
```

```
**************************************************************
*10) UPDATE THE SALARY COLUMN. GIVE ALL SALARIES UNDER $20,000   *
*    A PAY RAISE OF 10 PERCENT.                                  *
**************************************************************
```

```
EXEC SQL UPDATE PAY
      SET YTD = YTD * 1.1
      WHERE YTD < 20000 END-EXEC.
```

```
EXEC SQL




END-EXEC.
```

Appendix 1

Workshop Program Solutions

WORKSHOP I: EZPROG PROGRAM

```
 IDENTIFICATION DIVISION.
 PROGRAM-ID. EZPROG.
*REMARKS.  THIS PROGRAM REINFORCES THE CONCEPTS COVERED IN
*    CHAPTER TWO OF THIS BOOK.
*    YOU MUST SATISFY THE THREE REQUESTS LISTED IN THE
*    PROCEDURE DIVISION USING EMBEDDED SQL STATEMENTS. THE PROGRAM
*    LOGIC BASICALLY FALLS THROUGH THESE REQUESTS AND EXECUTES
*    THEM SEQUENTIALLY. YOU MAY USE LITERALS OR HOST VARIABLES.
*    IF YOU CHOOSE TO USE HOST VARIABLES FOR REQUESTS 2 AND 3 YOU
*    WILL HAVE TO CREATE YOUR OWN IN THE WORKING-STORAGE SECTION.
*
*    EZPROG USES THE VIDEO STORE DATABASE WHICH IS ILLUSTRATED
*    IN APPENDIX B OF THIS BOOK
*
 ENVIRONMENT DIVISION.
 CONFIGURATION SECTION.
 SOURCE-COMPUTER. IBM-370.
 OBJECT-COMPUTER. IBM-370.
 INPUT-OUTPUT SECTION.
 DATA DIVISION.
```

```
FILE SECTION.

WORKING-STORAGE SECTION.

*HOST PROGRAM VARIABLES — DATA ITEMS EXPLICITLY DEFINED
*THESE COPYBOOKS WERE CREATED BY DCLGEN, AND COPIED INTO THE
*MANUALLY. IF I WANTED TO COPY THEM IN USING THE INCLUDE VERB
*I WOULD HAVE CODED:
*EXEC SQL INCLUDE MOV END-EXEC.
*EXEC SQL INCLUDE CUST END-EXEC.
*

****************************************************************
*COBOL DECLARATION FOR TABLE MOV                              *
****************************************************************
01   DCLMOV.
       10  NBR            PIC S9(4) USAGE      COMP.
       10  TITLE-X        PIC X(20).
       10  TYPE-X         PIC X(6).
       10  RATING         PIC X(4).
       10  STAR           PIC X(10).
       10  QTY            PIC S9(4) USAGE      COMP.
       10  PRICE          PIC S999V99 USAGE    COMP-3.
****************************************************************
*THE NUMBER OF COLUMNS DESCRIBED BY THIS DECLARATION IS 7     *
****************************************************************

****************************************************************
*COBOL DECLARATION FOR TABLE CUST                            *
****************************************************************
01   DCLCUST.
       10  ID-X           PIC X(2).
       10  LNAME          PIC X(12).
       10  FNAME          PIC X(6).
       10  CITY           PIC X(15).
       10  ST             PIC X(2).
****************************************************************
*THE NUMBER OF COLUMNS DESCRIBED BY THIS DECLARATION IS 5     *
****************************************************************
```

*CODE THE INCLUDE STATEMENT HERE FOR THE SQL COMMUNICATIONS AREA

```
EXEC SQL INCLUDE SQLCA END-EXEC.
```

*MISCELLANEOUS WORKING-STORAGE DATA ITEMS
```
     01   WS-KTRS-SWITCHES.
      05  SQLCODE-OUT    PIC 9(03) VALUE 0.
```

```
      05  LO-VAL         PIC S9(03)V99 VALUE 0 COMP-3.
      05  HI-VAL         PIC S9(03)V99 VALUE 0 COMP-3.
```

New host variable fields for request #2.   Why comp-3? You
will learn about valid host variable definitions in chapter 4.

```
PROCEDURE DIVISION.
000-SETUP-ERROR-TRAP-RTN.
```

*THIS PORTION OF THE PROGRAM ACTIVATES THE SQL ERROR TRAPPING
*FACILITIES. AT PRECOMPILE TIME, THE DB2 PRE-COMPILER
*GENERATES COBOL INSTRUCTIONS TO INTERROGATE THE SQLCODE
* (RETURN CODE) FROM EACH CALL. IF A SQLERROR CONDITION IS
*DETECTED (NEGATIVE RETURN CODE), EXECUTION WILL BRANCH TO THE
* 999-ERROR-TRAP-RTN TO DISPLAY AN APPROPRIATE ERROR MSG.

```
EXEC SQL
        WHENEVER SQLERROR GOTO 999-ERROR-TRAP-RTN
END-EXEC.
```

```
    000-MAINLINE-RTN.
```

```
****************************************************************
*                      REQUEST 1                              *
* CODE AN EMBEDDED SELECT STATEMENT TO RETURN THE             *
* MOVIE NUMBER, TITLE, AND PRICE FOR TOOTSIE                  *
****************************************************************
```

```
    MOVE SPACES TO DCLMOV.
    MOVE 'TOOTSIE' TO TITLE-X OF DCLMOV.
```

```
EXEC SQL
    SELECT NBR, TITLE, PRICE
    INTO :NBR, :TITLE-X, :PRICE
    FROM MOV
    WHERE TITLE = :TITLE-X
END-EXEC.
```

```
 DISPLAY '****** REQUEST 1 ******'.
 IF SQLCODE = ZERO
     DISPLAY DCLMOV.
 DISPLAY SPACES.
 *****************************************************************
 *                        REQUEST 2                             *
 *CODE AN EMBEDDED SELECT STATEMENT TO RETURN THE               *
 *MOVIE QTY, PRICE AND TITLE FOR ALL COMEDIES COSTING           *
 *OVER $200 BUT LESS THAN $400(USE BETWEEN). *
 *HARD CODE THE BETWEEN PORTION OF YOUR WHERE CLAUSE            *
 *USING LITERALS VALUES - NOT HOST VARIABLES *
 *****************************************************************
```

```
    MOVE SPACES TO DCLMOV.
    MOVE 200 TO LO-VAL.
    MOVE 400 TO HI-VAL.
```

```
EXEC SQL
    SELECT QTY, PRICE, TITLE
    INTO            :QTY, :PRICE, :TITLE-X
    FROM    MOV
    WHERE   PRICE       BETWEEN :LO-VAL AND :HI-VAL
END-EXEC.
```

```
    DISPLAY '****** REQUEST 2 ******'.
    IF SQLCODE = ZERO
        DISPLAY DCLMOV.
    DISPLAY SPACES.
```

```
****************************************************************
*                        REQUEST 3                           *
* CODE AN EMBEDDED SELECT STATEMENT TO RETURN                 *
* ALL CUSTOMER INFORMATION FOR CUSTOMERS FROM HAWAII          *
* WYOMING AND VERMONT *** (USE IN) ***                        *
* HARD CODE THE IN PORTION OF YOUR WHERE CLAUSE               *
* USING LITERALS VALUES — NOT HOST VARIABLES                  *
****************************************************************

       MOVE SPACES TO DCLCUST.
```

```
EXEC SQL
    SELECT ID, LNAME, FNAME, CITY, ST
    INTO       :ID-X, :LNAME, :FNAME, :CITY, :ST
    FROM       CUST
    WHERE      ST IN ('HA','WY','VT')
    END-EXEC.
```

```
        DISPLAY '****** REQUEST 3 ******'.
       IF SQLCODE = ZERO
           DISPLAY DCLCUST.
       DISPLAY SPACES.

       DISPLAY '**** NORMAL END-OF-JOB ****'.
       MOVE ZERO TO RETURN-CODE.
    GOBACK.

    999-ERROR-TRAP-RTN.
****************************************************************
* ERROR TRAPPING ROUTINE FOR NEGATIVE SQLCODES               *
****************************************************************

       DISPLAY '**** WE HAVE A SERIOUS PROBLEM HERE ****'.
       DISPLAY '999-ERROR-TRAP-RTN '.
       MOVE SQLCODE TO SQLCODE-OUT.
       DISPLAY 'SQLCODE ==> ' SQLCODE-OUT.
       DISPLAY SQLCA.
       DISPLAY SQLERRM.
       EXEC SQL ROLLBACK WORK END-EXEC.
       GOBACK.
```

```
999-EXIT.
   EXIT.
```

WORKSHOP II: SINGLTON SELECT PROGRAM

```
IDENTIFICATION DIVISION.
PROGRAM-ID. SINGLTON.
*REMARKS. THIS PROGRAM READS IN AN EMPLOYEE NUMBER FROM A
*    FILE, SEARCHES A DB2 TABLE FOR THE EMPLOYEE ON THE
*    FILE, JOINS THE EMPL AND PAY TABLES, AND PRODUCES
*    A REPORT LINE FOR EMPLOYEES ON THE FILE, WHO:
*        * MAKE OVER $30,000, AND WHOSE PERF IS 1, 3 OR 5
*    OR . . . . . . . . . . .
*        * ARE IN THE MARKETING DEPARTMENT
*
ENVIRONMENT DIVISION.
CONFIGURATION SECTION.
SOURCE-COMPUTER. IBM-370.
OBJECT-COMPUTER. IBM-370.

INPUT-OUTPUT SECTION.
FILE-CONTROL.
    SELECT EMPL-FILE-IN ASSIGN TO UT-S-EMPFILE.

DATA DIVISION.

FILE SECTION.

FD EMPL-FILE-IN
RECORDING MODE IS F
BLOCK CONTAINS 0 RECORDS
RECORD CONTAINS 80 CHARACTERS
LABEL RECORDS ARE OMITTED
DATA RECORD IS EMPL-REC-IN.

01   EMPL-REC-IN.
        05  EMPL-NBR-IN    PIC X(02).
        05  FILLER         PIC X(78).
```

WORKING-STORAGE SECTION.

*HOST PROGRAM VARIABLES — DATA ITEMS EXPLICITLY DEFINED

*** CODE INCLUDE STATEMENTS HERE TO COPY IN THE TABLE DECLARATIONS
*** FOR THE EMPL AND PAY TABLES — DESCRIPTIONS CAN BE FOUND IN
*** APPENDIX B.
*** THE INCLUDED COPYBOOKS WILL HAVE TO BE CREATED BY RUNNING
*** DCLGEN


```
EXEC SQL INCLUDE EMPL END-EXEC.
```


```
EXEC SQL INCLUDE PAY END-EXEC.
```


*** CODE THE STATEMENT(S) HERE TO INCLUDE THE SQLCA

```
EXEC SQL INCLUDE SQLCA END-EXEC.
```


*MISCELLANEOUS WORKING-STORAGE DATA ITEMS

```
01   WS-KTRS-SWITCHES.
        05  SW-EOF            PIC X(01) VALUE 'N'.
            88 END-OF-FILE      VALUE 'Y'.
        05  EMPL-FILE-IN-KTR PIC S9(03) COMP-3 VALUE +0.
        05  EMPL-ROW-KTR     PIC S9(03) COMP-3 VALUE +0.

01   OUTPUT-ROW.
        05  FILLER           PIC X(01)     VALUE SPACES.
        05  NBR-RPT          PIC X(02).
        05  FILLER           PIC X(04)     VALUE SPACES.
        05  LNAME-RPT        PIC X(14).
        05  FILLER           PIC X(04)     VALUE SPACES.
```

```
        05  FNAME-RPT      PIC X(08).
        05  FILLER         PIC X(04)     VALUE SPACES.
        05  HOURS-RPT      PIC Z(02).99.
        05  FILLER         PIC X(04)     VALUE SPACES.
        05  RATE-RPT       PIC Z(02).99.

01  EMPL-FILE-MSG.
        05  FILLER         PIC X(26)
            VALUE '* * * EMPL FILE RECS IN —>'.
        05  EMPL-FILE-IN-STAT  PIC Z99.


01  EMPL-REC-WS.
        05  EMPL-NBR-WS    PIC X(02).


01  EMPL-ROW-MSG.
        05  FILLER            PIC X(24)
            VALUE '* * * EMPL ROWS READ —>'.
        05  EMPL-ROW-STAT  PIC Z99.

* ERROR MSG AREA FOR CALLS TO DSNTIAR — WHICH DECODES YOUR SQL
* RETURN CODES (SQLCODE) FOR YOU.

01  ERROR-MSG.
        05  ERROR-LEN      PIC S9(04)    COMP VALUE +960.
        05  ERROR-TEXT     PIC X(120)    OCCURS 8 TIMES
            INDEXED BY ERR-IDX.
01  ERROR-TEXT-LEN PIC S9(09) COMP VALUE +120.


    PROCEDURE DIVISION.

    000-SETUP-ERROR-TRAP-RTN.

* THIS PORTION OF THE PROGRAM ACTIVATES THE SQL ERROR TRAPPING
* FACILITIES. AT PRECOMPILE TIME, THE D82 PRECOMPILER
* GENERATES COBOL INSTRUCTIONS TO INTERROGATE THE SQLCODE
* (RETURN CODE) FROM EACH CALL. IF A SQLERROR CONDITION IS
* DETECTED (NEGATIVE RETURN CODE), EXECUTION WILL BRANCH TO
* 999-ERROR-TRAP-RTN WHICH WILL DISPLAY AN APPROPRIATE ERROR MSG.
```

```
*= = = = > CODE YOUR ERROR TRAPPING STATEMENT(S) HERE
```

```
EXEC SQL WHENEVER SQLERROR GOTO 999-ERROR-TRAP-RTN
END-EXEC.
```

```
 000-MAINLINE-RTN.

*THE MAINLINE CONTAINS THE DRIVER CODE TO PERFORM OUR DATABASE
*ACCESS AND DISPLAY ROUTINES.

     OPEN INPUT EMPL-FILE-IN.

     PERFORM 100-READ-INFILE THRU 100-EXIT.

     PERFORM 200-DISPLAY-RPT THRU 200-EXIT
       UNTIL END-OF-FILE.

     PERFORM 300-TERMINATE-RTN THRU 300-EXIT.
     MOVE ZERO TO RETURN-CODE.
     GOBACK.

 000-EXIT.
     EXIT.

 100-READ-INFILE.

     READ EMPL-FILE-IN
         AT END
       MOVE 'Y' TO SW-EOF
       GO TO 100-EXIT.

     ADD 1 TO EMPL-FILE-IN-KTR.

 100-EXIT.
     EXIT.
```

```
200-DISPLAY-RPT.

*THIS PARAGRAPH SETS UP THE SQL PARAMETERS, PERFORMS THE
*PARAGRAPH TO MAKE THE CALL AND DISPLAYS THE RESULTS.

    PERFORM 250-CALL-DB2-RTN THRU 250-EXIT.

    IF SQLCODE = ZERO
    THEN
        MOVE NBR OF DCLEMPL TO NBR-RPT
        MOVE LNAME TO LNAME-RPT
        MOVE FNAME TO FNAME-RPT
        MOVE HOURS TO HOURS-RPT
        MOVE RATE TO RATE-RPT
        DISPLAY OUTPUT-ROW
        ADD +1 TO EMPL-ROW-KTR
      ELSE
        NEXT SENTENCE.

PERFORM 100-READ-INFILE THRU 100-EXIT.

200-EXIT.
    EXIT.


250-CALL-DB2-RTN.

*THIS PARAGRAPH SELECTS A ROW FROM THE EMPL AND PAY TABLES
*JOINED ON EMPLOYEE NUMBER — WHICH IS OBTAINED FROM THE CURRENT
*RECORD IN EMPL-FILE-IN. SELECT CRITERIA INCLUDE:
*—   EMPLOYEE NUMBER FROM INPUT FILE USED AS SEARCH CONDITION
*—   (EARNINGS (YTD ON THE PAY TABLE) OVER $30,000 AND
*    PERFORMANCE EVALUATION = 1, 3, 5) OR
*—   (EMPLOYEE IS IN THE MARKETING DEPT)
```

```
        MOVE EMPL-NBR-IN TO EMPL-NBR-WS.
```

```
    EXEC SQL
        SELECT    EMPL.NBR, LNAME, FNAME, HOURS, RATE
        INTO`     :DCLEMPL.NBR, :LNAME, :FNAME, :HOURS, :RATE
        FROM      EMPL, PAY
        WHERE     EMPL.NBR = PAY.NBR AND EMPL.NBR = :EMPL-NBR-WS
        AND ((PERF IN (1,3,5) OR YTD > 30000.00) OR
              DEPT = 'MKT')
    END-EXEC.
```

```
     250-EXIT.
         EXIT.

     300-TERMINATE-RTN.

         CLOSE EMPL-FILE-IN.

         MOVE EMPL-FILE-IN-KTR TO EMPL-FILE-IN-STAT.
         MOVE EMPL-ROW-KTR TO EMPL-ROW-STAT.

         DISPLAY EMPL-FILE-MSG.
         DISPLAY EMPL-ROW-MSG.

     300-EXIT.
         EXIT.

     999-ERROR-TRAP-RTN.
    ****************************************************************
    *ERROR TRAPPING ROUTINE FOR NEGATIVE SQLCODES                 *
    ****************************************************************

         DISPLAY '****WE HAVE A SERIOUS PROBLEM HERE *****'.
         DISPLAY '999-ERROR-TRAP-RTN '.
         MULTIPLY SQLCODE BY -1 GIVING SQLCODE.
         DISPLAY 'SQLCODE ==> ' SQLCODE.
         DISPLAY SQLCA.
         DISPLAY SQLERRM.
         EXEC SQL ROLLBACK WORK END-EXEC.
         GOBACK.
```

```
999-EXIT.
   EXIT.
```

WORKSHOP IV: VARIOUS TECHNIQUES PROGRAM[1]

```
 IDENTIFICATION DIVISION.
 PROGRAM-ID. VARIOUS.
*REMARKS.   THIS PROGRAM USES SEVERAL DIFFERENT DATATYPES AND
*    PROGRAMMING TECHNIQUES TO REINFORCE THE LESSONS ON
*    HOST PROGRAM VARIABLES AND ERROR HANDLING ROUTINES
*    COVERED DURING CHAPTERS FOUR AND FIVE.
*
 ENVIRONMENT DIVISION.
 CONFIGURATION SECTION.
 SOURCE-COMPUTER. IBM-370.
 OBJECT-COMPUTER. IBM-370.

 DATA DIVISION.

 WORKING-STORAGE SECTION.

*HOST PROGRAM VARIABLES — DATA ITEMS EXPLICITLY DEFINED

     EXEC SQL INCLUDE CELEBRIT END-EXEC.

     EXEC SQL INCLUDE SQLCA END-EXEC.
```

Note: "CELEBRIT" is what I called my PDS copybook member

```
01 MISC-DATA-ITEMS.
    05    SMALL-FIELD    PIC X(02).
    05    LONG-FIELD     PIC X(22).
    05    AVG-MILEAGE    PIC S9(5)V99  COMP-3.
    05    SQLCODE-OUT    PIC 9(03).
    05    NUL-FIELD      PIC S9(04)    COMP.
    05    NUL-FIELD-1    PIC S9(04)    COMP.
    05    NUL-STRUCT.
       10    NUL    PIC S9(04)   COMP OCCURS 8 TIMES.
```

Note: I want to get decimal precision for my AVG-MILEAGE

---

[1]Recall that no solution is given for Workshop III in Chapter 3.

```
*
  PROCEDURE DIVISION.
*
  000-SETUP-ERROR-TRAP-RTN.
  ***************************************************************
  *     CODE THE CORRECT ERROR-TRAPPING ROUTINES TO:           *
  *                                                            *
  *BRANCH TO 999-ERROR-TRAP-RTN ON A NEGATIVE SQLCODE          *
  *CONTINUE PROCESSING UPON FINDING A POSITIVE SQLCODE         *
  *CONTINUE PROCESSING UPON END OF DATA                        *
  ***************************************************************
       EXEC SQL
            WHENEVER SQLERROR GOTO 999-ERROR-TRAP-RTN
       END-EXEC.
*
       EXEC SQL WHENEVER SQLWARNING CONTINUE END EXEC.
*
       EXEC SQL WHENEVER NOT FOUND CONTINUE END EXEC.
*
  000-MAINLINE-RTN.
*
       DISPLAY 'BEGINNING OF PROGRAM - VARIOUS'.
       DISPLAY SPACES.
*
       PERFORM 200-TEST-RTN THRU 200-EXIT.
*
       MOVE ZERO TO RETURN-CODE.
       GOBACK.
*
  000-EXIT.
       EXIT.


  200-TEST-RTN.
*
  ***************************************************************
  ***    CODE AND EXECUTE THE FOLLOWING DATABASE REQUESTS    ***
  ***                                                        ***
  ***    (AFTER EACH CALL, DISPLAY THE REQUEST NUMBER,       ***
  ***    THE ROW RETURNED (IF APPROPRIATE) AND THE SQLCODE)  ***
  ***************************************************************
```

```
*
****************************************************************
*1)  UPDATE THE CELEBRITY_RACE TABLE:                         *
*    SET THE PURCHASE EQUAL TO THE CURRENT DATE — AND         *
*    THE QUALIFYING TIME EQUAL TO 71 SECONDS *** be careful ****
*    DB2 is very picky about valid times, *** FOR ALL ROWS IN *
*    THE TABLE. AFTER THE CALL DISPLAY SQLERRD(3) TO VERIFY   *
*    THE NBR OF ROWS UPDATED BY THE CALL.                     *
****************************************************************
```

```
EXEC SQL UPDATE CELEBRITY_RACE
        SET PURCHASE = CURRENT DATE,
            QUAL_TIM = '00.01.11'
END-EXEC.
```

```
     DISPLAY '*** REQUEST 1 ***, SQLCODE'.
     MOVE SQLCODE TO SQLCODE-OUT.
     DISPLAY SQLCODE-OUT.
     DISPLAY '*** WARNING #4 = > ' SQLWARN4.
     DISPLAY '*** NBR ROWS UPDATED = > ' SQLERRD(3).
*
****************************************************************
*2)  CALCULATE THE AVG(MILEAGE) FOR THE MERCEDES BENZ         *
***  YOU WILL NEED A NULL-INDICATOR FOR YOUR HOST VARIABLE-WHY?*
****************************************************************
```

```
EXEC SQL                             ***** NOTE *****
    SELECT AVG(MILEAGE) INTO         A null value is the result
    :AVG-MILEAGE:NUL-FIELD           of a DB2 function on an
     FROM CELEBRITY_RACE             empty set (there is no
        WHERE  CAR = 'MERCEDES BENZ' Mercedes Benz)
END-EXEC.
```

```
     DISPLAY '*** REQUEST 2 ***'.
     DISPLAY '*** NULL-VALUE ===> ' NUL-FIELD.
     DISPLAY '*** SQLCODE AND AVG-MILEAGE'.
     MOVE SQLCODE TO SQLCODE-OUT.
     DISPLAY SQLCODE-OUT.
     DISPLAY AVG-MILEAGE.
```

```
*
*****************************************************************
* 3)   CALCULATE THE AVERAGE ENTRANT CAR MILEAGE FOR ALL CARS.  *
*      AFTER THE CALL DISPLAY THE SQLWARNINGS TO CHECK FOR      *
*      NULL VALUE IN THE ROWS.                                  *
*****************************************************************
```

```
EXEC SQL
        SELECT   AVG(MILEAGE)
                 INTO :AVG-MILEAGE
        FROM     CELEBRITY_RACE
END-EXEC.
```

```
    DISPLAY `*** REQUEST 3 ***'.
    DISPLAY `*** AVERAGE ===> ` AVG-MILEAGE.
    DISPLAY `*** SQLCODE ***'.
    MOVE SQLCODE TO SQLCODE-OUT.
    DISPLAY SQLCODE-OUT.
*
    DISPLAY `*** WARNINGS ***, SQLWARN0, SQLWARN2 `.
    DISPLAY SQLWARN0.
    DISPLAY SQLWARN2.
*
```

> Note: Null value elimination warning
>   "W". SQLCODE will be Zero.

```
*****************************************************************
* 4)   SELECT DRIVER INTO SMALL-FIELD FOR DRIVER `MARIO SPAGHETTI'*
*          CHECK AND DISPLAY SQLWARN(S) AFTER THE CALL          *
*****************************************************************
*
    MOVE `MARIO SPAGHETTI' TO LONG-FIELD.
```

```
EXEC SQL SELECT DRIVER
        INTO :SMALL-FIELD
            FROM CELEBRITY_RACE

    WHERE DRIVER = :LONG-FIELD
END-EXEC.
```

```
*
 DISPLAY '*** REQUEST 4 ***'.
 DISPLAY '*** SMALL-FIELD ===> ' SMALL-FIELD.
 DISPLAY '*** SQLCODE ***'.
 MOVE SQLCODE TO SQLCODE-OUT.
 DISPLAY SQLCODE-OUT.
 DISPLAY '*** WARNINGS ***, SQLWARN0, SQLWARN2 '.
 DISPLAY SQLWARN0.
 DISPLAY SQLWARN1.
```

Note: Field Truncation warning
"W". SQLCODE will be Zero.

```
*********************************************************************
* 5A) INSERT A ROW INTO CELEBRITY_RACE.        IF SQLCODE = ZERO *
*     ISSUE A COMMIT WORK STATEMENT.                            *
* 5B) RETRIEVE AND DISPLAY THE ROW YOU JUST INSERTED            *
*********************************************************************
*
      MOVE 11  TO ENTRANT, DRIVER-LEN.
      MOVE 'LEE IACOCCA'      TO DRIVER-TEXT.
      MOVE 'ARIES K'          TO CAR.
      MOVE 1   TO MILEAGE.
      MOVE 7900              TO PRICE.
      MOVE '1988-10-01'       TO PURCHASE.
      MOVE '00.01.00'         TO QUAL-TIM.
```

```
EXEC SQL
      INSERT INTO CELEBRITY_RACE VALUES
      (:ENTRANT,
       :CAR,
       :DRIVER,
       :MILEAGE,
       :PRICE,
       :PURCHASE,
       :QUAL_TIM )
END-EXEC.
```

```
*
 DISPLAY '*** REQUEST 5A ***'.
 DISPLAY '*** SQLCODE ***'.
```

```
MOVE SQLCODE TO SQLCODE-OUT.
DISPLAY SQLCODE-OUT.
```

```
IF SQLCODE = 0
    EXEC SQL COMMIT WORK END-EXEC.
```

```
EXEC SQL                                    Note use of SELECT
    SELECT * INTO :DCLCELEBRITY_RACE        into Host Structure.
        FROM CELEBRITY_RACE                 DCLCELEBRITY_RACE
                                            is the name of 01 level
    WHERE ENTRANT = 11                      Working-Storage struc-
END-EXEC.                                   ture that describes the
                                            Celebrity_Race table
```

```
*
 DISPLAY '*** REQUEST 5B ***'.
 DISPLAY '*** TABLE-ROW ===> ' DCLCELEBRITY_RACE.
 DISPLAY '*** SQLCODE ***'.
 MOVE SQLCODE TO SQLCODE-OUT.
 DISPLAY SQLCODE-OUT.
*
```

```
***************************************************************
* 6)  DELETE ALL ROWS FROM CELEBRITY_RACE — WHERE            *
*     PURCHASE = THE CURRENT DATE.                           *
*      **** DISPLAY SQLWARNINGS AND SQLERRD(3) ****          *
*     IF SQLERRD(3) INDICATES THAT YOU HAVE ERASED OVER FOUR *
*     ROWS IN THE TABLE, ISSUE THE ROLLBACK WORK COMMAND.    *
***************************************************************
```

```
EXEC SQL
    DELETE FROM CELEBRITY_RACE WHERE PURCHASE =
    CURRENT DATE
END-EXEC.
```

```
*
 DISPLAY SPACES.
 DISPLAY '*** REQUEST 6 ***'.
```

```
  DISPLAY '*** SQLCODE ***'.
  MOVE SQLCODE TO SQLCODE-OUT.
  DISPLAY SQLCODE-OUT.
*
  DISPLAY '*** NBR ROWS DELETED = ' SQLERRD(3).
```

```
  IF SQLERRD(3) > 4
      EXEC SQL ROLLBACK WORK          END-EXEC.
```

```
*
  DISPLAY '*** SQLCODE AFTER ROLLBACK ***'.
  MOVE SQLCODE TO SQLCODE-OUT.
  DISPLAY SQLCODE-OUT.

  200-EXIT.
      EXIT.


  999-ERROR-TRAP-RTN.
 ****************************************************************
 *ERROR TRAPPING ROUTINE FOR NEGATIVE SQLCODES                 *
 ****************************************************************

  DISPLAY '**** WE HAVE A SERIOUS PROBLEM HERE *****'.
  DISPLAY '999-ERROR-TRAP-RTN '.
  MULTIPLY SQLCODE BY -1 GIVING SQLCODE.
  DISPLAY 'SQLCODE ==> ' SQLCODE.
  DISPLAY SQLCA.
  DISPLAY SQLERRM.
  EXEC SQL ROLLBACK WORK END-EXEC.
  GOBACK.

  999-EXIT.
      EXIT.
```

WORKSHOP V: CURSRAVG — SYMBOLIC RETRIEVAL CURSOR

```
IDENTIFICATION DIVISION.
PROGRAM-ID. CURSRAVG.
*REMARKS.   THIS PROGRAM JOINS TABLES, GROUPS DATA BY DEPT,
*    AND DISPLAYS THE AVERAGE, MAXIMUM AND MINIMUM
*    HOURS, AND PERFORMANCE EVALUATION BY DEPT.
*
ENVIRONMENT DIVISION.
CONFIGURATION SECTION.
SOURCE-COMPUTER. IBM-370.
OBJECT-COMPUTER. IBM-370.


DATA DIVISION.

WORKING-STORAGE SECTION.

*CODE THE NECESSARY DB2 INCLUDE STATEMENTS HERE


01   WS-KTRS-SWITCHES.
     05   ROW-KTR         PIC S9(03)    COMP-3 VALUE +0.

*MODIFY THE TABLE-ROW PICTURE CLAUSES FOR THE HOST
*PROGRAM VARIABLES — LOOK AT THE TABLE/COLUMN DEFINITIONS
*IN YOUR MANUAL (APPENDIX A FROM THE SQL PORTION)
*AND THE SQL TO COBOL DATATYPES IN CHAPTER 3


01   TABLE-ROW.
     05   DEPT-TBL        PIC X(3).
     05   PERF-TBL-AVG    PIC S9(5)V99    COMP-3.
     05   PERF-TBL-MIN    PIC S9(4)       COMP.
     05   PERF-TBL-MAX    PIC S9(4)       COMP.
     05   HOURS-TBL-AVG PIC S9(5)V99    COMP-3.
     05   HOURS-TBL-MAX PIC S9(4)       COMP.
     05   HOURS-TBL-MIN PIC S9(4)       COMP.


01   OUTPUT-ROW.
     05   FILLER          PIC X(01)  VALUE SPACES.
     05   DEPT-RPT        PIC X(03).
     05   FILLER          PIC X(03)  VALUE SPACES.
     05   PERF-RPT-AVG    PIC Z(03).99.
```

```
05   FILLER          PIC X(01)  VALUE SPACES.
05   PERF-RPT-MIN    PIC Z(03).99.
05   FILLER          PIC X(01)  VALUE SPACES.
05   PERF-RPT-MAX    PIC Z(03).99.
05   FILLER          PIC X(03)  VALUE SPACES.
05   HOURS-RPT-AVG   PIC Z(03).99.
05   FILLER          PIC X(03)  VALUE SPACES.
05   HOURS-RPT-MAX   PIC Z(03).99.
05   FILLER          PIC X(03) VALUE SPACES.
05   HOURS-RPT-MIN   PIC Z(03).99.
```

```
*ERROR MSG AREA FOR CALLS TO DSNTIAR — WHICH DECODES YOUR
*SQL RETURN CODES (SQLCODE) FOR YOU.

01   ERROR-MSG.
     05   ERROR-LEN    PIC S9(04)   COMP VALUE +960.
     05   ERROR-TEXT   PIC X(120)   OCCURS 8 TIMES
              INDEXED BY ERR-IDX.
01   ERROR-TEXT-LEN PIC S9(09) COMP VALUE +120.

01   NULL-FIELD-WS.
     05   NULL-IND-DEPT PIC S9(04)   COMP VALUE +0.
     05   NULL-IND-PERF PIC S9(04)   COMP VALUE +0.

 PROCEDURE DIVISION.

  000-SETUP-ERROR-TRAP-RTN.

*THIS PORTION OF THE PROGRAM ACTIVATES THE SQL ERROR TRAPPING
*FACILITIES. AT PRE-COMPILE TIME, THE DB2 PRE-COMPILER
*GENERATES COBOL INSTRUCTIONS TO INTERROGATE THE SQLCODE
* (RETURN CODE) FROM EACH CALL. IF A SQLERROR CONDITION IS
*DETECTED (NEGATIVE RETURN CODE), EXECUTION WILL BRANCH TO THE
*999-ERROR-TRAP-RTN TO DISPLAY AN APPROPRIATE ERROR MSG.
```

```
EXEC SQL
    WHENEVER SQLERROR GOTO 999-ERROR-TRAP-RTN
END-EXEC.
```

```
 000-MAINLINE-RTN.
```

```
*THE MAINLINE CONTAINS THE DRIVER CODE TO PERFORM OUR DATA
*BASE ACCESS AND DISPLAY ROUTINES.

     PERFORM 100-DECLARE-CURSOR-RTN THRU 100-EXIT.

     PERFORM 150-OPEN-CURSOR-RTN THRU 150-EXIT.

     PERFORM 200-FETCH-RTN THRU 200-EXIT
         UNTIL WHEN SQLCODE = +100.

     PERFORM 300-CLOSE-CURSOR-RTN THRU 300-EXIT.

     MOVE ZERO TO RETURN-CODE.
     GOBACK.

 000-EXIT.
     EXIT.


 100-DECLARE-CURSOR-RTN.
```

loop through table
until . . . . . .

```
*= = = > CODE THE SQL STATEMENT TO JOIN THE EMPL AND PAY TABLES
*= = = > GROUP THEM BY EMPL.DEPT AND DISPLAY THE DEPT AND:
*= = = > AVERAGE, MINIMUM AND MAXIMUM — HOURS AND PERF
```

```
EXEC SQL
    DECLARE DEPT _AVG CURSOR FOR
    SELECT  DEPT,   AVG(PERF), MIN(PERF), MAX(PERF)
                    AVG(HOURS), MIN(HOURS), MAX(HOURS)
         FROM EMPL, PAY
    WHERE EMPL.NBR = PAY.NBR
    GROUP BY DEPT
END-EXEC.
```

```
 100-EXIT.
     EXIT.
```

```
150-OPEN-CURSOR-RTN.

*THIS STATEMENT OPENS THE "ACTIVE SET" IN PREPARATION OF
*ROW FETCH PROCESSING.
```

```
    EXEC SQL OPEN DEPT_AVG        END-EXEC.
```

```
150-EXIT.
    EXIT.


200-FETCH-RTN.

*THIS PARAGRAPH SETS UP THE SQL PARAMETERS, PERFORMS THE
*PARAGRAPH TO FETCH THE ROW, AND DISPLAYS THE RESULTS.
*===>HINT <=== USE ISPF EXCLUDE (XX) OR BLOCK COPY
*FROM YOUR CURSOR DECLARE STATEMENT TO VERIFY PROPER
*SELECTED TABLE/COLUMN TO FETCHED HOST-VARIABLE MATCHING

    PERFORM 250-FETCH-A-ROW THRU 250-EXIT.

    IF SQLCODE = ZERO
    THEN
        MOVE DEPT-TBL  TO DEPT-RPT
        MOVE PERF-TBL-AVG          TO PERF-RPT-AVG
        MOVE PERF-TBL-MIN          TO PERF-RPT-MIN
        MOVE PERF-TBL-MAX          TO PERF-RPT-MAX
        MOVE HOURS-TBL-AVG         TO HOURS-RPT-AVG
        MOVE HOURS-TBL-MAX         TO HOURS-RPT-MAX
        MOVE HOURS-TBL-MIN         TO HOURS-RPT-MIN
        DISPLAY OUTPUT-ROW
    ELSE
        DISPLAY '*** END - OF - DATA ***'.


200-EXIT.
    EXIT.
250-FETCH-A-ROW.
```

```
*THIS PARAGRAPH FETCHES A ROW FROM THE EMPL AND PAY TABLES
*AND MOVES SPECIFIC DATA FIELDS INTO THE AVG, MIN AND MAX FIELDS
```

```
EXEC SQL
        FETCH DEPT_AVG INTO
          :DEPT-TBL:NULL-FIELD-DEPT,
          :PERF-TBL-AVG:NULL-FIELD-PERF,
          :PERF-TBL-MIN:NULL-FIELD-PERF,
          :PERF-TBL-MAX:NULL-FIELD-PERF,
          :HOURS-TBL-AVG,
          :HOURS-TBL-MIN,
          :HOURS-TBL-MAX
END-EXEC
```

Note: Presence of Null indicators.

Why am I using the same one for all functions on PERF?

```
IF NULL-FIELD-DEPT < ZERO
THEN
        MOVE 'NUL' TO DEPT-TBLE.
IF NULL-FIELD-PERF < ZERO
THEN
        MOVE ZEROS TO
                      PERF-TBL-MIN,
                      PERF-TBL-MAX,
                      PERF-TBL-AVG.
```

Note: COBOL logic necessary to initialize COBOL host variables if nulls encountered (DB2 does not move any table values into your program's fields if null values are detected).

```
    250-EXIT.
       EXIT.

    300-CLOSE-CURSOR-RTN.

*THIS STATEMENT CLOSES THE "ACTIVE SET"
```

```
EXEC SQL CLOSE DEPT_AVG END-EXEC.
```

```
300-EXIT.
    EXIT.

350-TERMINATE-RTN.

    MOVE ROW-KTR TO ROW-STAT.
    DISPLAY ROW-MSG.

350-EXIT.
EXIT.

999-ERROR-TRAP-RTN.
****************************************************************
*ERROR TRAPPING ROUTINE FOR NEGATIVE SQLCODES                 *
****************************************************************

    DISPLAY '**** WE HAVE A SERIOUS PROBLEM HERE *****'.
    DISPLAY '999-ERROR-TRAP-RTN '.
    MULTIPLY SQLCODE BY —1 GIVING SQLCODE.
    DISPLAY 'SQLCODE ==> ' SQLCODE.
    DISPLAY SQLCA.
    DISPLAY SQLERRM
    EXEC SQL ROLLBACK WORK END-EXEC.
    GOBACK.
999-EXIT.
    EXIT.
```

> rollback statement
> used to manually "undo"
> any updates processed

WORKSHOP VI: CURSRUPD — SYMBOLIC UPDATE CURSOR PROCESSING

```
IDENTIFICATION DIVISION.
PROGRAM-ID. CURSRUPD.
*REMARKS.   THIS PROGRAM UPDATES EMPLOYEE PERFORMANCE AND RATE
*     COLUMNS BASED ON VALUES STORED IN A TABLE IN
*     WORKING-STORAGE. THE PROGRAM USES A CURSOR TO
*     READ SEQUENTIALLY THROUGH THE EMPLOYEE TABLE. AS
*     EACH ROW IS RETURNED, THE WORKING-STORAGE TABLE IS
*     *     SEARCHED TO SEE IF THE EMPLOYEE IS GETTING:
*     *     DELETED —> UPDATE-DEL-CODE = 'D'
```

```
*    *    UPDATED --> UPDATE-DEL-CODE = 'U'
*YOU WILL UPDATE THE EMPL.PERF COLUMN AND PAY.RATE COLUMN.
*
*IF A MATCH IS FOUND, UPDATE THE APPROPRIATE TABLE(S)
*AND WRITE OUT A REPORT INDICATING THE ACTIONS TAKEN.
*YOU WILL USE A CURSOR TO PROCESS THROUGH THE EMPL TABLE
*(FOR UPDATE OF PERF). YOU WILL USE A STANDARD UPDATE
*STATEMENT TO UPDATE THE RATE COLUMN ON THE PAY TABLE — USING
*THE EMPL.NBR FETCHED INTO THE CURRENT ROW AS YOUR SEARCH
*ARGUMENT.
*
 ENVIRONMENT DIVISION.
 CONFIGURATION SECTION.
 SOURCE-COMPUTER. IBM-370.
 OBJECT-COMPUTER. IBM-370.

 DATA DIVISION.

 WORKING-STORAGE SECTION.
```

```
┌────────────────────────────────────────────────────────────────┐
│                                                                │
│   EXEC SQL INCLUDE EMPL END-EXEC.                              │
│                                                                │
│                                                                │
│   EXEC SQL INCLUDE EMPL END-EXEC.                              │
│                                                                │
└────────────────────────────────────────────────────────────────┘
```

```
*MISCELLANEOUS WORKING-STORAGE DATA ITEMS

01  WS-SWITCHES.
    05   ROW-KTR        PIC S9(03)    COMP-3 VALUE +0.
    05   NUL-IND        PIC S9(04)    COMP.

01  UPDATE-OUTPUT-ROW.
    05   FILLER         PIC X(25)     VALUE
         '***   EMPLOYEE NBR ==>'.
    05   NBR-RPT        PIC X(03).
    05   FILLER         PIC X(25)     VALUE
         '***   EMPLOYEE PERF ==>'.
    05   PERF-RPT       PIC Z9.
    05   FILLER         PIC X(25) VALUE
```

```
         '***  PAY TABLE RATE ==>'.
      05   RATE-RPT          PIC Z99.99.


01  DELETE-OUTPUT-ROW.
      05   FILLER            PIC X(25)      VALUE
           '***  EMPLOYEE NBR ==>'.
      05   DEL-NBR-RPT       PIC X(03).
      05   FILLER            PIC X(25)      VALUE
           '***  EMPLOYEE PERF ==>'.
      05   DEL-PERF-RPT      PIC Z9.


01  ROW-MSG.
      05   FILLER            PIC X(24)
           VALUE '* * * ROWS READ ->'.
      05   ROW-STAT          PIC Z99.


01  EMPL-TABLE-VALUES.
      05   EMPL-VALUES.
      10   EMPL-VALUE1  PIC X(06)      VALUE 'U01210'.
      10   EMPL-VALUE2  PIC X(06)      VALUE 'D02000'.
      10   EMPL-VALUE3  PIC X(06)      VALUE 'U03208'.
      10   EMPL-VALUE4  PIC X(06)      VALUE 'D10000'.
      05   EMPL-ROW-WS REDEFINES EMPL-VALUES OCCURS 4 TIMES
                INDEXED BY EMPL-IDX.
      10   UPDATE-DEL-CODE    PIC X(01).
           88 UPDATE-ROW VALUE 'U'.
           88 DELETE-ROW VALUE 'D'.
      10   EMPL-NBR-WS   PIC X(02).
      10   EMPL-PERF-WS  PIC 9(01).
      10   EMPL-RATE-WS  PIC 9(02).


01  HIT-FLAG-WS          PIC X(01).
      88 TABLE-HIT       VALUE 'Y'.

*ERROR MSG AREA FOR CALLS TO DSNTIAR - WHICH DECODES YOUR
*SQL RETURN CODES (SQLCODE) FOR YOU.

01  ERROR-MSG.
      05 ERROR-LEN        PIC S99(04)   COMP VALUE +960.
      05 ERROR-TEXT       PIC X(120)    OCCURS 8 TIMES
         INDEXED BY ERR-IDX.
```

```
01  ERROR-TEXT-LEN      PIC S9(09)    COMP VALUE +120.
```

```
PROCEDURE DIVISION.
```

```
000-SETUP-ERROR-TRAP-RTN.
```

```
EXEC SQL
    WHENEVER SQLERROR GOTO 999-ERROR-TRAP-RTN
END-EXEC.
```

```
000-MAINLINE-RTN.
```

```
* THE MAINLINE CONTAINS THE DRIVER CODE TO PERFORM OUR DATA
* BASE ACCESS AND DISPLAY ROUTINES.
```

```
PERFORM 100-DECLARE-CURSOR-RTN THRU 100-EXIT.
```

```
PERFORM 150-OPEN-CURSOR-RTN THRU 150-EXIT.
```

```
PERFORM 200-DISPLAY-RPT THRU 200-EXIT
    UNTIL SQLCODE = +100.
```

```
PERFORM 300-CLOSE-CURSOR-RTN THRU 300-EXIT.
```

```
PERFORM 350-TERMINATE-RTN THRU 350-EXIT.
```

```
MOVE ZERO TO RETURN-CODE.
GOBACK.
```

```
000-EXIT.
    EXIT.
```

```
100-DECLARE-CURSOR-RTN.
```

```
* CODE YOUR CURSOR DEFINITION HERE. DECLARE IT FOR UPDATE OF
* PERF.
```

```
EXEC SQL
      DECLARE UPDT_CURSOR FOR
      SELECT NBR, PERF
                     FROM EMPL
      FOR UPDATE OF PERF
END-EXEC.
```

```
  100-EXIT.
      EXIT.

  150-OPEN-CURSOR-RTN.

* OPEN THE CURSOR HERE
```

```
EXEC SQL OPEN UPDT_CURSOR END-EXEC.
```

```
  150-EXIT.
      EXIT.


  200-DISPLAY-RPT.

* THIS PARAGRAPH SETS UP THE SQL PARAMETERS, PERFORMS THE
* PARAGRAPH TO MAKE THE CALL AND DISPLAYS THE RESULTS.

        PERFORM 275-FETCH-ROW-RTN THRU 275-EXIT.

      IF SQLCODE = ZERO
      THEN
          PERFORM 280-TABLE-SEARCH-RTN THRU 280-EXIT
          IF TABLE-HIT
          THEN
              IF UPDATE-ROW(EMPL-IDX)
              THEN
                  PERFORM 290-UPDATE-ROW-RTN THRU 290-EXIT
              ELSE
                  PERFORM 295-DELETE-ROW-RTN THRU 295-EXIT
```

Note: indexed 88-level
field conditional

```
        ELSE
              NEXT SENTENCE
     ELSE
         NEXT SENTENCE.

  200-EXIT.
     EXIT.

  275-FETCH-ROW-RTN.

*THIS PARAGRAPH FETCHES A ROW FROM THE EMPL TABLE AND
*MOVES SPECIFIC DATA FIELDS INTO THE NBR AND PERF FIELDS.
```

```
EXEC SQL
       FETCH UPDT_CURSOR INTO :NBR, :PERF:NUL-IND
END-EXEC.
```

```
  275-EXIT.
     EXIT.

  280-TABLE-SEARCH-RTN.

*THIS PARAGRAPH SEARCHES A WORKING-STORAGE TABLE TO FIND THE
*EMPLOYEE NBR. IF FOUND, IT MOVES THE NEW PERF AND RATE VALUES
*TO THE HOST PROGRAM VARIABLE FIELDS.

     MOVE 'N' TO HIT-FLAG-WS.
     SET EMPL-IDX TO 1.

     SEARCH EMPL-ROW-WS
         AT END GO TO 280-EXIT
         WHEN NBR OF DCLEMPL = EMPL-NBR-WS(EMPL-IDX)
             MOVE EMPL-PERF-WS(EMPL-IDX) TO PERF
             MOVE EMPL-RATE-WS(EMPL-IDX) TO RATE
             MOVE 'Y' TO HIT-FLAG-WS.

  280-EXIT.
     EXIT.
```

```
290-UPDATE-ROW-RTN.
```

```
*THIS PARAGRAPH UPDATES THE DATABASE BY CHANGING THE PERF FIELD
*ON THE EMPL TABLE, AND THE RATE FIELD ON THE PAY TABLE. YOU
*WILL NEED AN "UPDATE WHERE CURRENT OF" STATEMENT FOR THE EMPL
*TABLE, AND AN UPDATE STATEMENT (NON-CURSOR) FOR THE PAY TABLE.
*UPDATE THE PAY RATE BY SETTING DB2 PAY TABLE RATE EQUAL TO THE
*WORKING-STORAGE TABLE RATE
```

```
*=======>   UPDATE EMPL TABLE
```

```
EXEC SQL
      UPDATE EMPL
        SET PERF = :PERF
        WHERE CURRENT OF UPDT_CURSOR
END-EXEC.
```

```
*=======>   UPDATE PAY TABLE
```

```
EXEC SQL
      UPDATE PAY
        SET RATE = :RATE
        WHERE PAY.NBR = :DCLEMPL.NBR
END-EXEC.
```

```
IF SQLCODE = ZERO
   MOVE NBR OF DCLEMPL
      TO NBR-RPT
   MOVE PERF          TO PERF-RPT
   MOVE RATE          TO RATE-RPT
   DISPLAY UPDATE-OUTPUT-ROW
   ADD +1 TO ROW-KTR.
```

```
290-EXIT.
   EXIT.

295-DELETE-ROW-RTN.
```

```
* THIS PARAGRAPH UPDATES THE DATABASE BY DELETING THE EMPLOYEE
* FROM THE EMPL AND PAY TABLES.
* YOU WILL NEED A "DELETE WHERE CURRENT OF" STATEMENT FOR THE
* EMPL TABLE, AND A DELETE STATEMENT FOR THE PAY TABLE.
* HINT — WHERE DO YOU GET THE SEARCH VALUES TO SPECIFY WHICH
* EMPLOYEE TO DELETE?

* =======> DELETE ROW FROM THE EMPL TABLE
```

```
EXEC SQL DELETE FROM EMPL
        WHERE CURRENT OF UPDT_CURSOR END-EXEC.
```

```
* =======> DELETE ROW FROM THE PAY TABLE
```

```
EXEC SQL DELETE FROM PAY
WHERE PAY.NBR = :DCLEMPL.NBR
```

```
IF SQLCODE = ZERO
   MOVE NBR OF DCLEMPL
      TO DEL-NBR-RPT
           MOVE PERF TO DEL-PERF-RPT
           DISPLAY DELETE-OUTPUT-ROW
           ADD +1 TO ROW-KTR.

295-EXIT.
   EXIT.
```

```
300-CLOSE-CURSOR-RTN.

*THIS STATEMENT CLOSES THE "ACTIVE SET"
```

```
EXEC SQL CLOSE UPDT_CURSOR END-EXEC.
```

```
 300-EXIT.
     EXIT.

 999-ERROR-TRAP-RTN.
 *************************************************************
 *ERROR TRAPPING ROUTINE FOR NEGATIVE SQLCODES              *
 *************************************************************

     DISPLAY '**** WE HAVE A SERIOUS PROBLEM HERE *****'.
     DISPLAY '999-ERROR-TRAP-RTN '.
     MULTIPLY SQLCODE BY -1 GIVING SQLCODE.
     DISPLAY 'SQLCODE ==> ' SQLCODE.
     EXEC SQL ROLLBACK WORK END-EXEC.
     GOBACK.
 999-EXIT.
     EXIT.
```

WORKSHOP VI: REFINTEG — REFERENTIAL INTEGRITY MAINTENANCE

```
 IDENTIFICATION DIVISION.
 PROGRAM-ID. REFINTEG.
*REMARKS.    THIS PROGRAM EXECUTES A SERIES OF CORRELATED
*    SUBQUERYS WITH THE EXISTS FUNCTION TO DETERMINE IF
*    THERE ARE ANY ROWS OUT OF SYNCH BETWEEN TWO TABLES
*    RELATED BY LINKING COLUMNS. A REPORT IS PRODUCED
*    DOCUMENTING ANY REFERENTIAL INTEGRITY PROBLEMS FOUND.
*
*
 ENVIRONMENT DIVISION.
 CONFIGURATION SECTION.
 SOURCE-COMPUTER. IBM-370.
```

```
OBJECT-COMPUTER. IBM-370.

DATA DIVISION.

WORKING-STORAGE SECTION.

*
* HOST PROGRAM VARIABLES AND DB2 COMMUNICATIONS AREA COPYBOOKS
*
```

```
EXEC SQL INCLUDE EMPL END-EXEC.
```

```
EXEC SQL INCLUDE PAY END-EXEC.
```

```
EXEC SQL INCLUDE PROJ END-EXEC.
```

```
EXEC SQL INCLUDE SQLCA END-EXEC.
```

```
01  SQLCODE-OUT        PIC 9(03).

01  NULL-IND           PIC S9(04) COMP.

01  REPORT-LINE.
    05   FILLER        PIC X(16)    VALUE 'A FOREIGN KEY '.
    05   FILLER        PIC X(18)    VALUE 'COLUMN IN TABLE —'.
    05   TABLE-NAME-1  PIC X(19).
    05   FILLER        PIC X(19)    VALUE 'CONTAINS THE VALUE'.
    05   IDENT         PIC X(02).
    05   FILLER        PIC X(16)    VALUE 'WHICH DOES NOT '.
    05   FILLER        PIC X(17)    VALUE 'EXIST IN TABLE —'.
    05   TABLE-NAME-2  PIC X(19).
```

.

```
01  SQLCODE-OUT PIC 9(03).


01  NULL-IND PIC S9(04) COMP.
```

Note: Null indicator. . . Why?

```
01  REPORT-LINE.
    05   FILLER        PIC X(16)    VALUE 'A FOREIGN KEY '.
    05   FILLER        PIC X(18)    VALUE 'COLUMN IN TABLE —'.
    05   TABLE-NAME-1  PIC X(19).
    05   FILLER        PIC X(19)    VALUE 'CONTAINS THE VALUE'.
    05   IDENT         PIC X(02).
    05   FILLER        PIC X(16)    VALUE 'WHICH DOES NOT '.
    05   FILLER        PIC X(17)    VALUE 'EXIST IN TABLE —'.
    05   TABLE-NAME-2  PIC X(19).
```

```
****************************************************************
*                                                              *
* DECLARE YOUR SQL CURSORS HERE FOR THE SELECT STATEMENTS WITH *
* NOT EXISTS TO TEST FOR REFERENTIAL INTEGRITY. NOTE THAT IT   *
* IS IMPORTANT TO UNDERSTAND WHICH IS THE PRIMARY AND SECONDARY*
* TABLE IN THIS STATEMENT — APPLICATION RULES.                 *
*                                                              *
****************************************************************
```

```
EXEC SQL
    DECLARE EMPLPAY CURSOR FOR
        SELECT NBR
            FROM PAY_CORR_VAR
                WHERE NOT EXISTS
            (SELECT * FROM EMPL WHERE
                EMPL.NBR = PAY_CORR_VAR.NBR)
END-EXEC.
```

```
EXEC SQL
     DECLARE EMPLPROJ CURSOR FOR
          SELECT PROJ
               FROM EMPL_CORR_VAR
                    WHERE NOT EXISTS
                    (SELECT * FROM PROJ WHERE
                         PROJ.NBR = EMPL_CORR_VAR.PROJ
END-EXEC.
```

Note: It is perfectly legal to DECLARE your CURSOR in the
      WORKING-STORAGE SECTION of a program. DECLARE CURSOR
      is not an executable statement like OPEN/FETCH/CLOSE.

```
PROCEDURE DIVISION.

     DISPLAY 'BEGINNING OF PROGRAM - REFINTEG'.
     DISPLAY SPACES.

000-SETUP-ERROR-TRAP-RTN.
****************************************************************
*                                                             *
* CODE THE CORRECT ERROR-TRAPPING ROUTINES TO:                *
*                                                             *
* BRANCH TO 999-ERROR-TRAP-RTN ON A NEGATIVE SQLCODE          *
* CONTINUE PROCESSING UPON FINDING A POSITIVE SQLCODE          *
* CONTINUE PROCESSING UPON END OF DATA                         *
*                                                             *
****************************************************************
```

```
EXEC SQL WHENEVER SQLERROR GOTO 999-ERROR-TRAP-RTN
END-EXEC.

EXEC SQL WHENEVER SQLWARNING CONTINUE END-EXEC.

EXEC SQL WHENEVER NOT FOUND CONTINUE END-EXEC.
```

```
000-MAINLINE-RTN.

    DISPLAY 'BEGINNING OF 000-MAINLINE'.
    DISPLAY SPACES.

    PERFORM 100-TEST-EMPL-PAY THRU 100-EXIT.

    PERFORM 200-TEST-EMPL-PROJ THRU 200-EXIT.

    MOVE ZERO TO RETURN-CODE.
    GOBACK.

000-EXIT.
    EXIT.

010-OPEN-EMPL-PAY-CURSOR.
*****************************************************************
*                                                               *
* CODE THE CURSOR OPEN STATEMENT HERE FOR THE PREVIOUSLY         *
* DECLARED EMPLPAY CURSOR — SELECT.                             *
*                                                               *
*****************************************************************
```

```
    EXEC SQL OPEN EMPLPAY END-EXEC.
```

```
010-EXIT.
    EXIT.

020-OPEN-EMPL-PROJ-CURSOR.
*****************************************************************
*                                                               *
* CODE THE CURSOR OPEN STATEMENT HERE FOR THE PREVIOUSLY         *
* DECLARED EMPLPROJ CURSOR — SELECT.                            *
*                                                               *
*****************************************************************
```

```
    EXEC SQL OPEN EMPLPROJ END-EXEC.
```

```
   020-EXIT.
      EXIT.

   030-FETCH-EMPL-PAY.
 ************************************************************
 *                                                          *
 *CODE YOUR SQL FETCH RTN TO FETCH THE SELECTED ROW INTO    *
 *YOUR WORKING STORAGE ROW DEFINITION.                      *
 *                                                          *
 ************************************************************

         MOVE 'PAYROLL' TO TABLE-NAME-1.
         MOVE SPACES TO IDENT.
         MOVE 'EMPLOYEE' TO TABLE-NAME-2.
```

```
   EXEC SQL FETCH EMPLPAY INTO :DCLPAY.NBR END-EXEC.
```

```
         IF SQLCODE = ZERO
         THEN
             MOVE NBR OF DCLPAY TO IDENT
             DISPLAY REPORT-LINE.

   030-EXIT.
      EXIT.

   040-FETCH-EMPL-PROJ.
 ************************************************************
 *                                                          *
 *CODE YOUR SQL FETCH RTN TO FETCH THE SELECTED ROW INTO    *
 *YOUR WORKING-STORAGE ROW DEFINITION.                      *
 *                                                          *
 ************************************************************

         MOVE 'EMPLOYEE' TO TABLE-NAME-1.
         MOVE SPACES TO IDENT.
         MOVE 'PROJECT' TO TABLE-NAME-2.
```

```
   EXEC SQL FETCH EMPLPROJ INTO :PROJ:NULL-IND
   END-EXEC.
```

```
        IF SQLCODE = ZERO
        THEN
             IF NULL-IND < ZERO
             THEN
                       MOVE '**' TO IDENT
                       DISPLAY REPORT-LINE
             ELSE
                       MOVE PROJ OF DCLEMPL TO IDENT
                       DISPLAY REPORT-LINE.

    040-EXIT.
        EXIT.

    050-CLOSE-EMPL-PAY.
   ****************************************************************
   *                                                              *
   * CODE THE CURSOR CLOSE STATEMENT HERE FOR THE PREVIOUSLY      *
   * DECLARED SELECT STATEMENT FOR CURSOR - EMPLPAY.             *
   *                                                              *
   ****************************************************************
```

```
    EXEC SQL CLOSE EMPLPAY END-EXEC.
```

```
    050-EXIT.
        EXIT.


    060-CLOSE-EMPL-PROJ.
   ****************************************************************
   *                                                              *
   * CODE THE CURSOR CLOSE STATEMENT HERE FOR THE PREVIOUSLY      *
   * DECLARED SELECT STATEMENT FOR CURSOR EMPLPROJ.              *
   *                                                              *
   ****************************************************************
```

```
    EXEC SQL CLOSE EMPLPROJ END-EXEC.
```

```
    060-EXIT.
        EXIT.
```

```
 100-TEST-EMPL-PAY.
 ****************************************************************
 *                                                            *
 *CODE THE COBOL LOGIC TO PERFORM THE OPEN — FETCH — CLOSE     *
 *ROUTINES TO CHECK FOR REFERENTIAL INTEGRITY FOR EMPL/PAY     *
 *                                                            *
 ****************************************************************

        PERFORM 010-OPEN-EMPL-PAY-CURSOR THRU 010-EXIT.
        PERFORM 030-FETCH-EMPL-PAY THRU 030-EXIT
```

```
        UNTIL SQLCODE = +100.
```

```
        PERFORM 050-CLOSE-EMPL-PAY THRU 050-EXIT.

  100-EXIT.
      EXIT.


  200-TEST-EMPL-PROJ.
 ****************************************************************
 *                                                            *
 *CODE THE COBOL LOGIC TO PERFORM THE OPEN — FETCH — CLOSE     *
 *ROUTINES TO CHECK FOR REFERENTIAL INTEGRITY FOR EMPL/PROJ    *
 *                                                            *
 ****************************************************************

        PERFORM 020-OPEN-EMPL-PROJ-CURSOR THRU 020-EXIT.
        PERFORM 040-FETCH-EMPL-PROJ THRU 040-EXIT
```

```
        UNTIL SQLCODE = +100.
```

```
     PERFORM 060-CLOSE-EMPL-PROJ THRU 060-EXIT.
 200-EXIT.
      EXIT.
```

```
999-ERROR-TRAP-RTN.
****************************************************************
***   ERROR TRAPPING ROUTINE FOR NEGATIVE SQLCODES            *
****************************************************************

         DISPLAY '**** WE HAVE A SERIOUS PROBLEM HERE *****'.
         DISPLAY '999-ERROR-TRAP-RTN '.
         MULTIPLY SQLCODE BY -1 GIVING SQLCODE.
         DISPLAY 'SQLCODE ==> ' SQLCODE.
         DISPLAY SQLCA.
         DISPLAY SQLERRM.
         EXEC SQL ROLLBACK WORK END-EXEC.
         GOBACK.

 999-EXIT.
    EXIT.
```

WORKSHOP VI: FRIDGE — SQL RECODE FOR PERFORMANCE

```
IDENTIFICATION DIVISION.
PROGRAM-ID. FRIDGE.
REMARKS.      THIS PROGRAM CONTAINS SEVERAL PERFORMANCE
PROBLEMS.
    RE-CODE THE SQL STATEMENTS IN THE PROCEDURE DIVISION
    TO OPTIMIZE THE PROGRAM ACCORDING TO THE SUGGESTIONS MADE
    IN THE APPLICATION DESIGN SECTION OF YOUR MANUAL. INDEXES
    EXIST ON THE FOLLOWING COLUMNS:
         *  EMPL.NBR
         *  PROJ.NBR
         *  PAY.NBR
         *  EMPL.LNAME
         *  EMPL.DEPT
         *  PAY.YDT

ENVIRONMENT DIVISION.
CONFIGURATION SECTION.
```

```
      SOURCE-COMPUTER. IBM-370.
      OBJECT-COMPUTER. IBM-370.

      DATA DIVISION.

      WORKING-STORAGE SECTION.

      ****************************************************************
      * DCLGEN TABLE (EMPL)                                         *
      ****************************************************************

            EXEC SQL DECLARE EMPL TABLE
            ( NBR              CHAR(2),
              LNAME            CHAR(10),
              FNAME            CHAR(6),
              DOB              INTEGER,
              HIREDTE          INTEGER,
              PERF             SMALLINT,
              JOB              CHAR(4),
              DEPT             CHAR(3),
              PROJ             CHAR(2)
            ) END-EXEC.


      ****************************************************************
      * COBOL DECLARATION FOR TABLE EMPL                            *
      ****************************************************************

      01  DCLEMPL.
            10   NBR        PIC X(2).
            10   LNAME      PIC X(10).
            10   FNAME      PIC X(6).
            10   DOB        PIC S9(9)     USAGE COMP.
            10   HIREDTE    PIC S9(9)     USAGE COMP.
            10   PERF       PIC S9(4)     USAGE COMP.
            10   JOB        PIC X(4).
            10   DEPT       PIC X(3).
            10   PROJ       PIC X(2).
```

```
******************************************************************
* DCLGEN TABLE (PAY)                                              *
******************************************************************

      EXEC SQL DECLARE PAY TABLE
      ( NBR                CHAR (2),
        HOURS              DECIMAL (5, 2),
        RATE               DECIMAL (5, 2),
        DED                DECIMAL (5, 2),
        YTD                DECIMAL (8, 2)
      ) END-EXEC.

******************************************************************
* COBOL DECLARATION FOR TABLE PAY                                 *
******************************************************************

 01  DCLPAY.
     10   NBR          PIC X(2).
     10   HOURS        PIC S999V99      USAGE COMP-3.
     10   RATE         PIC S999V99      USAGE COMP-3.
     10   DED          PIC S999V99      USAGE COMP-3.
     10   YTD          PIC S999999V99   USAGE COMP-3.

******************************************************************
* THE NUMBER OF COLUMNS DESCRIBED BY THIS DECLARATION IS 5        *
******************************************************************

* SQL COMMUNICATIONS AREA — DATA ITEMS PULLED IN VIA INCLUDE

      EXEC SQL INCLUDE SQLCA END-EXEC.
```

```
 01  MISC-DATA-ITEMS.
     05   CHAR-FIELD        PIC X(03).
     05   NUMERIC-FIELD     PIC S9(04)     COMP.
     05   SQLCODE-OUT       PIC 9(03).
     05   NUL-FIELD         PIC S9(04)     COMP.
     05   NUL-FIELD-1       PIC S9(04)     COMP.
     05   DRIVER-SRCH       PIC X(20).
     05   NUL-STRUCT.
          10   NUL          PIC S9(04)     COMP OCCURS 8 TIMES.
     05   SMALL-SRCH.
          49   SMALL-SRCH-LEN    PIC S9(04)     COMP.
          49   SMALL-SRCH-TEXT   PIC X(04).
```

Note: I fixed up Numeric-field and Char-field which were the wrong datatypes for the columns

```
PROCEDURE DIVISION.

000-SETUP-ERROR-TRAP-RTN.

000-MAINLINE-RTN.

    DISPLAY 'BEGINNING OF PROGRAM — FRIDGE'.
    DISPLAY SPACES.

    PERFORM 200-TEST-RTN THRU 200-EXIT.

    MOVE ZERO TO RETURN-CODE.
    GOBACK.

000-EXIT.
    EXIT.

200-TEST-RTN.
*****************************************************************
*1) RETRIEVE AND DISPLAY EMPLOYEE LAST-NAMES THAT CONTAIN AN   *
*A, B, OR C IN THE FIRST CHAR — Disregard Cursor Usage         *
*****************************************************************
```

```
EXEC SQL SELECT * INTO :DCLEMPL
    FROM EMPL
    WHERE    LNAME LIKE 'A%'
    OR       LNAME LIKE 'B%'
    OR       LNAME LIKE 'C%' END-EXEC.
```

Recode here:

Recode using BETWEEN

```
EXEC SQL
    SELECT   LNAME INTO :LNAME FROM EMPL
             WHERE LNAME BETWEEN 'AAAA'
                   AND 'C999'
END-EXEC.
```

Note: 10 byte literals,
to avoid precision
problems — see
LNAME PIC in WS

```
*************************************************************
*2) RETRIEVE AND DISPLAY ALL EMPLOYEE NUMBERS FOR          *
* EMPLOYEES                                                 *
* MAKING OVER $20,000                                       *
*************************************************************
```

```
EXEC SQL DECLARE FRIDGE1 CURSOR FOR
    SELECT * FROM EMPL
        WHERE NBR IN
            (SELECT NBR FROM PAY
            WHERE YTD > 20000)
END-EXEC.
```

Note: Recode as
table join

```
EXEC SQL
    DECLARE FRIDGE1 CURSOR FOR
        SELECT LNAME FROM EMPL, PAY WHERE EMPL.NBR = PAY.NBR
            AND YTD > 20000.00
END-EXEC.
```

```
*************************************************************
*3) RETRIEVE AND DISPLAY EMPLOYEE NBRs, FOR EMPLOYEES      *
* WHOSE LAST NAMES ARE BETWEEN 'G' AND 'M' or WHO          *
* MAKE OVER $20,000                                         *
*************************************************************
```

```
EXEC SQL DECLARE FRIDGE2 CURSOR FOR
    SELECT * FROM EMPL, PAY
        WHERE EMPL.PAY = PAY.NBR
        AND (LNAME BETWEEN 'G' AND 'M' OR
            YTD > 20000)
END-EXEC.
```

Note: Recode
using union

```
EXEC SQL
    DECLARE    FRIDGE2 CURSOR FOR
               SELECT EMPL.NBR FROM EMPL
               WHERE LNAME BETWEEN 'G . . . . . . . . .' AND
               'M . . . . . . . . '
    UNION
               SELECT PAY.NBR FROM PAY
               WHERE YTD > 20000.00
END-EXEC.
```

```
*****************************************************************
* 4) UPDATE THE PAY TABLE — GIVE ALL MANAGERS A 10% RAISE      *
*****************************************************************
```

```
EXEC SQL UPDATE PAY
    SET YTD = YTD * 1.10
        WHERE NBR IN (SELECT NBR
            FROM EMPL WHERE JOB = 'MAN') END-EXEC.
```

```
EXEC SQL
     DECLARE UPDATEM CURSOR FOR
         SELECT PAY.NBR, YTD FROM EMPL, PAY
     WHERE EMPL.NBR = PAY.NBR
             AND JOB = 'MAN'
END-EXEC.
     . . .
EXEC SQL OPEN UPDATEM END-EXEC.
     . . .
     . . .                    Loop until no more rows

 ┌──────────────────────────────────────────────────────┐
 │ EXEC SQL FETCH UPDATEM INTO  :DCLPAY.NBR,   :YTD       │
 │ END-EXEC.                                              │
 └──────────────────────────────────────────────────────┘


COMPUTE YTD = YTD * 1.1
     . . .
EXEC SQL
     UPDATE PAY
         WHERE NBR = :DCLPAY.NBR
         SET YTD = :YTD
END-EXEC.
```

Note: Recode as multi-step procedure using Cursor Select and Standard Update

```
**************************************************************
*5) SELECT ALL EMPLOYEES WHO ARE ON PROJECT NBRS 01, 02, 03  *
*    AND ALL EMPLOYEES IN THE MARKETING DEPT.                *
**************************************************************
```

```
EXEC SQL SELECT * FROM EMPL
    WHERE PROJ IN ('01','02','03') OR
          DEPT = 'MKT' END-EXEC.
```

Recode using UNION

```
EXEC SQL
    SELECT * FROM EMPL
            WHERE PROJ IN ('01','02','03')
UNION
    SELECT * FROM EMPL
            WHERE DEPT = 'MKT'
END-EXEC.
```

```
****************************************************************
* 6) SELECT ALL EMPLOYEE INFORMATION FOR EMPLOYEES WHOSE LAST  *
*    NAMES DO NOT BEGIN WITH G OR H                            *
****************************************************************
```

```
EXEC SQL SELECT * FROM EMPL
    WHERE LNAME NOT LIKE 'G%' OR LNAME NOT LIKE 'H%'
END-EXEC.
```

Recode using UNION

```
EXEC SQL
    SELECT  LNAME FROM EMPL
            WHERE LNAME < 'F999999999'
UNION
    SELECT  LNAME FROM EMPL
            WHERE LNAME > 'H999999999'
END-EXEC.
```

```
****************************************************************
* 7)  SELECT ALL EMPLOYEE NBRS FOR EMPLOYEES WITH PERFORMANCE   *
*     EVALUATIONS OVER 5                                        *
****************************************************************
```

```
MOVE 5 TO NUMERIC-FIELD.

EXEC SQL SELECT * FROM EMPL
    WHERE PERF > NUMERIC-FIELD
END-EXEC.
```

Note: Numeric-field was fixed up in WS

```
MOVE 5 TO NUMERIC-FIELD

EXEC SQL
    SELECT NBR FROM EMPL WHERE PERF > :NUMERIC-FIELD
END-EXEC.
```

```
**************************************************************
* 8)  SELECT ALL EMPLOYEE NBRS FOR EMPLOYEES IN THE MARKETING  *
*     AND FINANCE DEPARTMENTS                                  *
**************************************************************
```

```
MOVE 'MKT' TO DEPT.
MOVE 'FIN' TO CHAR-FIELD.

EXEC SQL SELECT NBR FROM EMPL
    WHERE DEPT = :DEPT
    UNION
    SELECT NBR FROM EMPL
    WHERE DEPT = :CHAR-FIELD     END-EXEC.
```

Note: Char-field was fixed
up in Working-Storage
  . . .

```
MOVE 'MKT' TO DEPT.
MOVE 'FIN' TO CHAR-FIELD.

EXEC SQL SELECT NBR FROM EMPL
    WHERE DEPT = :DEPT
    UNION
    SELECT NBR FROM EMPL
    WHERE DEPT = :CHAR-FIELD END-EXEC.
```

```
*****************************************************************
*9)  SELECT ALL EMPLOYEE NUMBERS FOR EMPLOYEES WHERE THE        *
*     SALARY IS NOT EQUAL TO THE HOST VARIABLE SAL * 1.07       *
*****************************************************************
```

```
EXEC SQL SELECT * FROM EMPL, PAY
    WHERE EMPL.NBR = PAY.NBR
    AND YTD = :SAL * 1.07 END-EXEC.
```

Note: Keep arithmetic expressions out of SQL statements (do them in COBOL).

```
COMPUTE SAL = SAL * 1.07
    . . .
EXEC SQL
    SELECT NBR FROM EMPL, PAY
        WHERE EMPL.NBR = PAY.NBR
        AND YTD = :SAL
END-EXEC.
```

```
******************************************************************
*10) UPDATE THE SALARY COLUMN. GIVE ALL SALARIES UNDER $20,000 *
*     A PAY RAISE OF 10 PERCENT                                 *
******************************************************************
```

```
EXEC SQL UPDATE PAY
SET YTD = YTD * 1.1
WHERE YTD < 20000       END-EXEC.
```

Recode using
multi-step procedure

```
EXEC SQL
      DECLARE UPD CURSOR FOR SELECT NBR FROM PAY
                 WHERE YTD < 20000
END-EXEC.
   . . .

EXEC SQL OPEN UPD END-EXEC.
   . . .

EXEC SQL                      Loop until end-of-results
    FETCH UPD INTO :NBR
END-EXEC.

EXEC SQL UPDATE PAY SET YTD = YTD * 1.1 WHERE NBR = :NBR
     END-EXEC.
```

Appendix 2

Database Definition Statements

```
-THESE ARE THE DATA DEFINITION LANGUAGE STATEMENTS TO DEFINE AND
-LOAD THE TABLES USED IN THE QED DB2 COURSES.
-THE TABLE NAMES ARE:
-                        MOV
-                        CUST
-                        INV
-                        IM
-                        EMPL
-                        PAY
-                        PROJ
-                        CELEBRITY_RACE

-THE DDL STATEMENTS TO GENERATE THESE TABLES CONSIST OF CREATE
-TABLE STATEMENTS AND CORRESPONDING FORMAT ONE
-INSERT STATEMENTS. THE TABLE CREATE STATEMENTS NEED TO BE EDITED
-SO THAT THE CORRECT DATABASE (AND/OR) TABLESPACE CAN BE USED TO
-HOLD THEM.
-
-THE ISPF EDIT COMMAND TO CHANGE THE DATABASE SHOULD LOOK LIKE
  THIS:
-C '????????' 'DBSENAME' ALL
-
-THE CREATE TABLE STATEMENTS FOR THE MOVIE TABLE.
-
CREATE TABLE MOV (NBR SMALLINT,
TITLE CHAR(20),
```

```
TYPE CHAR(6),
RATING CHAR(4),
STAR CHAR(10),
QTY SMALLINT,
PRICE DECIMAL(5,2) )
IN DATABASE ????????;
—
—THE INSERT STATEMENTS FOR THE MOVIE TABLE.
—
INSERT INTO MOV
  VALUES (1,'GONE WITH THE WIND','DRAMA',NULL,'GABLE',4,39.95);
INSERT INTO MOV
  VALUES (2,'FRIDAY THE 13TH','HORROR','R','JASON',2,69.95);
INSERT INTO MOV
  VALUES (3,'TOP GUN','DRAMA','PG','CRUISE',7,49.95);
INSERT INTO MOV
  VALUES (4,'SPLASH','COMEDY','PG13','HANKS',3,29.95);
INSERT INTO MOV
  VALUES (5,'101 DALMATIONS','COMEDY','G',NULL,3,59.95);
INSERT INTO MOV
  VALUES (6,'BODY HEAT','DRAMA','R','TURNER',3,19.95);
INSERT INTO MOV
  VALUES (7,'RISKY BUSINESS','COMEDY','R','CRUISE',2,44.55);
INSERT INTO MOV
  VALUES (8,'COCOON','SCIFI','PG','AMECHE',2,NULL);
INSERT INTO MOV
  VALUES (9,'CROCODILE DUNDEE','COMEDY','PG13','HARRIS',2,69.95);
INSERT INTO MOV
  VALUES (10,'TOOTSIE','COMEDY','PG','HOFFMAN',1,29.95);
—
—THE CREATE TABLE STATEMENTS FOR THE INVOICE TABLE
—
CREATE TABLE INV (NBR SMALLINT,
CUSTID CHAR(2),
TOT DECIMAL(5,2),
RENT INTEGER,
RETURN INTEGER)
  IN DATABASE ????????;
```

```
—
—THE INSERT STATEMENTS FOR THE INVOICE TABLE
—
INSERT INTO INV
  VALUES (1,'01',9.55,87055,NULL);
INSERT INTO INV
  VALUES (2,'02',13.55,87030,NULL);
INSERT INTO INV
  VALUES (3,'02',21.01,87041,87042);
INSERT INTO INV
  VALUES (4,'01',11.25,87042,87072);
INSERT INTO INV
  VALUES (5,'03',12.55,87045,87051);
INSERT INTO INV
  VALUES (6,'02',9.75,87047,87051);
INSERT INTO INV
  VALUES (7,'04',10.35,86355,NULL);
INSERT INTO INV
  VALUES (8,'04',12.55,87051,87053);
INSERT INTO INV
  VALUES (9,'05',10.35,87052,NULL);
INSERT INTO INV
  VALUES (10,'02',7.55,87030,87060);
—
—THE CREATE TABLE STATEMENTS FOR THE CUSTOMER TABLE
—
CREATE TABLE CUST (ID CHAR(2),
LNAME CHAR(12),
FNAME CHAR(6),
CITY CHAR(15),
ST CHAR(2) )
  IN DATABASE ????????;
—
—THE INSERT STATEMENTS FOR THE CUSTOMER TABLE
—
INSERT INTO CUST
  VALUES ('01','DANGERFIELD','RODNEY','HARTFORD','CT');
INSERT INTO CUST
  VALUES ('02','FIELD','SALLY','FRANKLIN','NY');
```

```
INSERT INTO CUST
  VALUES ('03','NICHOLSON','JACK','HARTFORD','CA');
INSERT INTO CUST
  VALUES ('04','MURRAY','FRED','BOZRAH','CT');
INSERT INTO CUST
  VALUES ('05','MADDEN','JOHN','BRATTLEBORO','VT');
INSERT INTO CUST
  VALUES ('06','WEST','MAE','PARK PLACE','CA');
INSERT INTO CUST
  VALUES ('07','WOODWARD','JOANNE','GETTYSBURG','PA');
INSERT INTO CUST
  VALUES ('08','ROGERS','ROY','HAPPY TRAILS','TX');
INSERT INTO CUST
  VALUES ('09','RINGWALD','MOLLY','PINKSVILLE','CA');
INSERT INTO CUST
  VALUES ('10','ROGERS','FRED','PARK PLACE','CA');
--

--THE CREATE TABLE STATEMENTS FOR THE INVOICE MOVIE TABLE
--

CREATE TABLE I_M (INBR SMALLINT,
MNBR SMALLINT)
  IN DATABASE ????????;
--

--THE INSERT STATEMENTS FOR THE CUSTOMER TABLE
--

INSERT INTO I_M
  VALUES (1,4);
INSERT INTO I_M
  VALUES (1,5);
INSERT INTO I_M
  VALUES (2,3);
INSERT INTO I_M
  VALUES (3,1);
INSERT INTO I_M
  VALUES (3,10);
INSERT INTO I_M
  VALUES (4,6);
INSERT INTO I_M
  VALUES (4,3);
```

```
INSERT INTO I_M
  VALUES (4,5);
INSERT INTO I_M
  VALUES (4,1);
INSERT INTO I_M
  VALUES (5,1);
INSERT INTO I_M
  VALUES (5,7);
INSERT INTO I_M
  VALUES (7,1);
INSERT INTO I_M
  VALUES (7,3);
INSERT INTO I_M
  VALUES (7,5);
INSERT INTO I_M
  VALUES (8,4);
INSERT INTO I_M
  VALUES (8,7);
INSERT INTO I_M
  VALUES (9,9);
INSERT INTO I_M
  VALUES (9,2);
INSERT INTO I_M
  VALUES (10,4);
INSERT INTO I_M
  VALUES (10,4);
INSERT INTO I_M
  VALUES (10,1);
INSERT INTO I_M
  VALUES (10,5);
INSERT INTO I_M
  VALUES (10,4);
—
—THE CREATE TABLE STATEMENTS FOR THE EMPLOYEE TABLE
—
CREATE TABLE EMPL (NBR CHAR(2),
LNAME CHAR(10),
FNAME CHAR(8),
DOB INTEGER,
```

```
HIREDTE INTEGER,
PERF SMALLINT,
JOB CHAR(4),
DEPT CHAR(3),
PROJ CHAR(2) )
  IN DATABASE ????????;
-

-THE INSERT STATEMENTS FOR THE EMPLOYEE TABLE
-

INSERT INTO EMPL
  VALUES ('01','LOWE','ROB',53012,85012,4,'PROG','FIN','01');
INSERT INTO EMPL
  VALUES ('02','SHIELD','BROOKE',59131,87001,3,'MAN','MKT','01');
INSERT INTO EMPL
  VALUES ('03','MOORE','ROGER',48111,86002,1,'DIR','MKT','04');
INSERT INTO EMPL
  VALUES ('04','EASTWOOD','CLINT',41091,60120,3,'PROG','FIN','03');
INSERT INTO EMPL
  VALUES ('05','MOSTEL','ZERO',21365,84211,NULL,'PRES',NULL,NULL);
INSERT INTO EMPL
  VALUES ('06','BURNS','GEORGE',11178,49001,2,'SYS','FIN','01');
INSERT INTO EMPL
  VALUES ('07','O'NEAL','RYAN',42189,60121,3,'DIR','ACC','05');
INSERT INTO EMPL
  VALUES ('08','MARVIN','LEE',32187,51876,2,'VP','ACC','02');
INSERT INTO EMPL
  VALUES ('09','LANCASTER','BURT',41091,79092,1,'MAN','R&D','02');
INSERT INTO EMPL
  VALUES ('10','BLAIR','LINDA',54013,85012,1,'PROG','MKT',NULL);
-

-THE CREATE TABLE STATEMENTS FOR THE PROJECT TABLE
-

CREATE TABLE PROJ (NBR CHAR(2),
NAME CHAR(10),
DEPT CHAR(3),
MAJPROJ CHAR(2) )
  IN DATABASE ????????;
```

```
-
-THE INSERT STATEMENTS FOR THE PROJECT TABLE
-
INSERT INTO PROJ
 VALUES ('01','PHASERS','MKT',NULL);
INSERT INTO PROJ
 VALUES ('05','SYSTEM X','MKT','03');
INSERT INTO PROJ
 VALUES ('03','SYSTEM R','FIN',NULL);
INSERT INTO PROJ
 VALUES ('04','LASERS','ACC','01');
INSERT INTO PROJ
 VALUES ('02','R*','FIN','03');
INSERT INTO PROJ
 VALUES ('06','NEW PROJ','R&D','02');
-
-THE CREATE TABLE STATEMENTS FOR THE PAYROLL TABLE
-
CREATE TABLE PAY (NBR CHAR(2),
HOURS DECIMAL(5,2),
RATE DECIMAL(5,2),
DED DECIMAL(5,2),
YTD DECIMAL(7,2) )
 IN DATABASE ????????;
-
-THE INSERT TABLE STATEMENTS FOR THE PAYROLL TABLE
-
INSERT INTO PAY
 VALUES ('01',8.89,43,128.78,11890.66);
INSERT INTO PAY
 VALUES ('02',13.23,40,204.45,15840.78);
INSERT INTO PAY
 VALUES ('03',6.11,49,94.76,11890.66);
INSERT INTO PAY
 VALUES ('04',26.75,45,132.58,17605.66);
INSERT INTO PAY
 VALUES ('05',67.82,37,394.69,79990.99);
INSERT INTO PAY
 VALUES ('06',32.45,32,121.99,53421.23);
```

```
INSERT INTO PAY
 VALUES ('07',26.75,49,101.56,32758.11);
INSERT INTO PAY
 VALUES ('08',15.99,52,327.98,67870.01);
INSERT INTO PAY
 VALUES ('09',43.59,24,0,28090.91);
INSERT INTO PAY
 VALUES ('10',32.41,52,112.78,27000.01);
—
—CREATE TABLE STATEMENT FOR CELBRITY_RACE TABLE
—

CREATE TABLE CELBRITY_RACE
  ( ENTRANT            SMALLINT,
    CAR                CHAR(10),
    DRIVER             VARCHAR(15),
    PRICE              DEC(7,2),
    MILEAGE            INTEGER,
    PURCHASE           DATE,
    QUALTIM            TIME )
  IN DATABASE ????????;
—
—INSERT STATEMENTS FOR CELBRITY_RACE TABLE
—
INSERT INTO CELBRITY_RACE VALUES
  (1,'LINCOLN','MARIO SPAGHETTI',3400.88,5400,'1987-01-01',
     '01.14.39');
INSERT INTO CELBRITY_RACE VALUES
  (2,'SEAHAWK','MRS. PAUL',1940.25,2100,'1984-05-29',
     '07.23.51');
INSERT INTO CELBRITY_RACE VALUES
  (3,'300 ZX','PAUL NEWMAN',189.99,12788,'1988-05-22',
     '00.54.33');
INSERT INTO CELBRITY_RACE VALUES
  (4,'LAND ROVER','MAGGIE THATCHER',NULL,15400,'1985-12-25',
     '11.55.24');
INSERT INTO CELBRITY_RACE VALUES
  (5,NULL,'MILLARD FILLMORE',1999.99,NULL,'1983-10-31',
     '08.33.56');
```

Appendix 3

Common DB2 Return Codes

```
000 SUCCESSFUL EXECUTION
```

The SQL statement has probably executed successfully. Check SQLWARN0 to ensure that it is blank. If it is blank, the statement executed successfully. If it is not blank, a warning condition exists. Check the other warning indicators to determine the particular warning condition. For example, if SQLWARN1 is not blank, a string has been truncated.

```
+100 ROW NOT FOUND FOR FETCH, UPDATE, OR DELETE,
     OR THE RESULT OF A QUERY IS AN EMPTY TABLE
```

One of the following conditions has occurred:

No row was found that met the search conditions specified in an UPDATE or DELETE statement.

The result of an imbedded SELECT statement was an empty table.

A FETCH statement was executed when the cursor was positioned after the last row of the result table.

The result of the subselect of an INSERT statement is empty.

319

When a SELECT statement is executed using SPUFI, this SQL code indicates normal completion.

```
+304 A VALUE WITH DATA TYPE [data_type1] CANNOT
    BE ASSIGNED TO A HOST VARIABLE BECAUSE THE
    VALUE IS NOT WITHIN THE RANGE OF THE HOST
    VARIABLE IN POSITION [position number] WITH
              DATA TYPE [data_type2]
```

A FETCH or SELECT into a host variable list or structure, position number 'position_number' failed because the host variable having data type 'data_type2' was not large enough to hold the retrieved value having data type 'data_type1'.

```
+802 EXCEPTION ERROR [exception type] HAS OCCURRED
    DURING [operation type] OPERATION ON [data_type]
          DATA, POSITION [position_number]
```

The exception error indicated by 'exception type' has occurred while doing either an ADDITION, SUBTRACTION, MULTIPLICA-TION, DIVISION, or NEGATION operation on a field whose 'data_type' can be either DECIMAL, FLOAT, SMALLINT, or INTE-GER while processing an arithmetic expression in the SELECT list of an outer SELECT statement, position in the select list is denoted by 'position_number'. The possible exception types are FIXED POINT OVERFLOW< DECIMAL OVERFLOW< DIVIDE EXCEPTION, and EXPONENT OVERFLOW. The datatype displayed in the message may indicate the datatype of the temporary internal copy of the data, which may differ from the actual column or literal datatype due to conversions by DB2.

A fixed point overflow can occur during any arithmetic operation on either INTEGER or SMALLINT fields.

A decimal overflow exception can occur when one or more non-zero digits are lost because the destination field in any decimal operation is too short to contain the result.

A divide exception can occur on a division operation on any numeric field type (DECIMAL, FLOAT, SMALLINT, or INTEGER) by zero, or on a decimal division operation when the quotient exceeds the specified data-field size.

An exponent overflow can occur when the result characteristic of any floating point operation exceeds 127 and the result fraction is not zero, i.e., the magnitude of the result exceeds approximately 7.2E+75.

-084 UNACCEPTABLE SQL STATEMENT

The precompiler noted an error in this SQL statement in your application program.

The statement cannot be executed.

Correct all errors that were found by the precompiler, and precompile the application program again.

-103 Literal IS AN INVALID NUMERIC LITERAL

The indicated 'literal' begins with a digit, but is not a valid integer, decimal, or float literal.

-104 STATEMENT CONTAINS THE INVALID CHARACTER
OR TOKEN [token-1]. TOKEN [token-2] WAS EXPECTED

A syntax error in the SQL statement was detected at the specified token 'token-1'.

As an aid to the programmer, a partial list of valid tokens is provided in SQLERRM as 'token-2'. This list assumes that the statement is correct up to that point, and only as many tokens are
listed as will fit.

```
THE NAME [name] IS TOO LONG. THE MAXIMUM
       ALLOWABLE SIZE IS [size]
```

The name returned as 'name' is too long. The maximum permissi-
ble length for names of that type is indicated by 'size'.

The names for columns, tables, views, indexes, and synonyms
can be a maximum of 18 characters (20 including SQL escape
characters, if present).

A maximum of 8 characters is permitted for a table or view qualifier, or the names for storage groups, data bases, tablespaces,
application plans, database request modules (DBRMs), or library
members specified in an INCLUDE statement.

Host variable names must not exceed 64 characters in length.

Volume serial numbers must not exceed 6 characters.

```
-111 A COLUMN FUNCTION DOES NOT INCLUDE
           A COLUMN NAME
```

The specification of a column function (AVG, MAX, MIN, or SUM)
was invalid because such functions must include a column name
in the operand. If the column name is that of a view, it must not be
a derived column, that is, derived from a constant, expression, or
function.

```
-112 THE OPERAND OF A COLUMN FUNCTION IS
  ANOTHER COLUMN FUNCTION OR DISTINCT
        FOLLOWED BY AN EXPRESSION
```

The operand of a column function is another column function, or DISTINCT followed by an expression. Only expressions without functions or DISTINCT followed by a column reference (not an expression) are permitted as operands of a column function. In a SELECT list, the operand of an arithmetic or string operator cannot be a function that includes the keyword DISTINCT.

```
-115 A PREDICATE IS INVALID BECAUSE THE
COMPARISON OPERATOR [operator] IS FOLLOWED
BY A PARENTHESIZED LIST OR BY ANY OR ALL
             WITHOUT A SUBQUERY
```

A simple comparison like ">" must not be followed by a list of items. ANY and ALL comparisons must be followed by a subselect, rather than an expression or a list of items.

```
-117 THE NUMBER OF INSERT VALUES IS NOT
THE SAME AS THE NUMBER OF OBJECT COLUMNS
```

The number of insert values in the value list of the INSERT statement is not the same as the number of object columns specified.

```
-118 THE OBJECT TABLE OR VIEW OF THE
INSERT, DELETE, OR UPDATE STATEMENT IS ALSO
         IDENTIFIED IN A FROM CLAUSE
```

The table or view specified as the object of an INSERT, DELETE, or UPDATE statement also appears in the FROM clause of a subselect within the statement.

The table or view that is the object of an INSERT, UPDATE, or DELETE cannot also be used to supply the values to be inserted or to qualify the rows to be inserted, updated, or deleted.

-119 A COLUMN IDENTIFIED IN A HAVING CLAUSE IS NOT
INCLUDED IN THE GROUP BY CLAUSE

A column identified in a HAVING clause (possibly within a scalar function) does not appear in the GROUP BY clause. Columns specified in a HAVING clause must appear within column functions or also be specified in the GROUP BY clause.

-121 THE COLUMN [name] IS IDENTIFIED MORE
THAN ONCE IN THE INSERT OR UPDATE STATEMENT

The same column 'name' is specified more than once, either in the list of object columns of an INSERT statement, or the SET clause of an UPDATE statement.

-131 STATEMENT WITH LIKE PREDICATE
HAS INCOMPATIBLE DATATYPES

If the column name at the left of LIKE or NOT LIKE is of type character, the expression at the right must be of type character. If the column name is of type graphic, the expression at the right must be of type graphic.

-150 THE OBJECT OF THE INSERT, DELETE,
OR UPDATE STATEMENT IS A VIEW FOR WHICH
THE REQUESTED OPERATION IS NOT PERMITTED

The view named in the INSERT, UPDATE, or DELETE statement is defined in such a way that the requested insert, update, or delete operation cannot be performed upon it.

Inserts into a view are prohibited if:

The view of definition contains a join or a GROUP BY or HAVINGclause,

The SELECT clause in the view definition contains the DISTINCT qualifier, an arithmetic expression, a built-in function, or a constant.

Two or more columns of the view are derived from the same column, or

A base table of the view contains a column that does not have a defined value and is not included in the view.

Updates to a view are prohibited if:

The view definition contains a join or a GROUP BY or HAVING clause, or

The SELECT clause in the view definition contains the DISTINCT qualifier or a function.

Also, a given column in a view cannot be updated (that is, the values in that column cannot be updated) if the column is derived from an arithmetic expression, a constant, or a column that is part of the key of a partitioned index.

Deletes against a view are prohibited if:

The view definition contains a join or a GROUP BY or HAVING clause, or

The SELECT clause in the view definition contains the DISTINCT qualifier or a built-in function.

```
-151 THE COLUMN [column-name] CANNOT BE UPDATED
BECAUSE IT IS EITHER INCLUDED IN THE PARTITIONING
  KEY OF A PARTITIONED TABLESPACE OR DERIVED
      FROM A SQL FUNCTION OR EXPRESSION
```

The specified column cannot be updated because either:

The object table is partitioned (that is, resides in a partitioned tablespace) and the column is included in the partitioning key, or

The object table is a view, and the specified column is defined (in the definition of the view) in such a way that it cannot be updated.

The values for columns occurring in the partitioning key of a partitioned table cannot be updated.

Individual columns in a view cannot be updated for the following reasons:

The column is derived from a SQL function, arithmetic expression, or constant.

The column is defined on a column that is in the partitioning key of a partitioned table.

The column is defined on a column of an underlying view that cannot be updated.

```
-158 THE NUMBER OF COLUMNS SPECIFIED FOR THE
      VIEW IS NOT THE SAME AS THE NUMBER OF
      COLUMNS SPECIFIED BY THE SELECT CLAUSE
```

The number of column names specified for a view in a CREATE VIEW statement must equal the number of elements (column names, SQL functions, expressions, etc.) specified in the following AS SELECT clause.

```
-160 THE WITH CHECK OPTION CANNOT BE
     USED FOR THE SPECIFIED VIEW
```

The WITH CHECK OPTION cannot be used in a view definition under the following circumstances:

The view is defined in such a way as to be "read-only" (for example, the view is defined on more than one base table or other view), or

The SELECT statement of the view contains a subselect, a GROUP BY or HAVING clause, or the DISTINCT keyword.

```
-161 THE INSERT OR UPDATE IS NOT ALLOWED
     BECAUSE A RESULTING ROW DOES NOT
       SATISFY THE VIEW DEFINITION
```

The WITH CHECK OPTION was specified in the definition of the view that is the object of the INSERT or UPDATE statement. Consequently, all attempts to insert or update rows in that view are checked to ensure that the results will conform to the view definition.

```
-198 THE OPERAND OF THE PREPARE OR EXECUTE
     IMMEDIATE STATEMENT IS BLANK OR EMPTY
```

The operand (host variable or literal string) that was the object of the PREPARE or EXECUTE IMMEDIATE statement either contained all blanks or was an empty string.

```
-203 A REFERENCE TO COLUMN
   [column-name] IS AMBIGUOUS
```

Two or more of the tables specified in a FROM clause in the statement contain columns with the specified 'column-name'. The column name needs further qualification to establish which of the possible table columns it is.

```
-204 [name] IS AN UNDEFINED NAME
```

The object identified by 'name' is not defined in the DB2 subsystem. This return code can be generated for any type of DB2 object.

```
-205 [column-name] IS NOT A COLUMN
     OF TABLE [table-name]
```

No column with the specified 'column-name' occurs in the table or view 'table-name'.

```
-206 [column-name] IS NOT A COLUMN OF AN
   INSERTED TABLE, UPDATED TABLE, OR ANY
   TABLE IDENTIFIED IN A FROM CLAUSE
```

This return code is used to report either of two types of errors:

In the case of an INSERT or UPDATE statement, the specified column is not a column of the table or view that was specified as the object of the insert or update.

In the case of a SELECT or DELETE statement, the specified column is not a column of any of the tables or views identified in a FROM clause in the statement.

```
-208 THE ORDER BY CLAUSE IS INVALID
   BECAUSE COLUMN [name] IS NOT PART
        OF THE RESULT TABLE
```

The statement is invalid because a column ('name') specified in the ORDER BY list does not appear in the result table (that is, is not specified in the SELECT-list). Only columns that are to appear in the result table can be used in ordering that result.

```
             -301 THE VALUE OF A HOST VARIABLE
               CANNOT BE USED AS SPECIFIED
                 BECAUSE OF ITS DATATYPE
```

A host variable cannot be used as specified in the statement because its datatype is incompatible with the requested function.

```
             -302 THE VALUE OF AN INPUT VARIABLE
               IS TOO LARGE FOR THE TARGET COLUMN
```

The value of a host variable was found to be too large to fit in the corresponding column of the table. One of the following has occurred:

The column is defined as string and the host variable contains a string that is too long for the column.

The column is defined as numeric and the host variable contains a numeric value too large for the definition of the column.

```
             -303 A VALUE CANNOT BE ASSIGNED TO A HOST
                VARIABLE BECAUSE THE DATA TYPES
                    ARE NOT COMPATIBLE
```

A FETCH or SELECT into a host variable cannot be performed because the datatype of the variable was not compatible with the datatype of the corresponding SELECT-list element. Both values must be numbers, both must be characters, or both must be graphic strings. If the datatype of a column is date, time, or timestamp, the datatype of the variable must be a character string with an appropriate minimum length.

```
-304 A VALUE WITH DATATYPE [data_type 1]
 CANNOT BE ASSIGNED TO A HOST VARIABLE
  BECAUSE THE VALUE IS NOT WITHIN THE
 RANGE OF THE HOST VARIABLE IN POSITION
[position_number] WITH DATATYPE [data_type2]
```

A FETCH or SELECT into a host variable list or structure, position number ['position number'] failed because the host variable having datatype ['data_type2'] was not large enough to hold the retrieved value having datatype ['data_type1'].

```
-305 THE NULL VALUE CANNOT BE ASSIGNED
   TO A HOST VARIABLE BECAUSE NO
      INDICATOR IS SPECIFIED
```

A FETCH or embedded SELECT operation resulted in the retrieval of a null value to be inserted into a host variable for which no indicator variable was provided. An indicator variable must be supplied if a column can return a null value.

```
-309 A PREDICATE IS INVALID BECAUSE
   A REFERENCED HOST VARIABLE
        HAS THE NULL VALUE
```

The statement cannot be processed because a host variable appearing in a predicate such as

column-name = host-variable

has the NULL value. Such a predicate is not permitted in the case in which the host variable contains the NULL value - even though the object column may in fact contain nulls.

```
-312 UNDEFINED OR UNUSABLE HOST
   VARIABLE [variable-name]
```

The host variable 'variable-name' appears in the SQL statement, but either no declaration for a variable of that name appears in the program or the attributes are improper for the specified usage.

```
-313 THE NUMBER OF HOST VARIABLES SPECIFIED
      IS NOT EQUAL TO THE NUMBER
         OF PARAMETER MARKERS
```

The number of host variables specified in the EXECUTE or OPEN statement is not the same as the number of parameter markers (question marks) appearing in the prepared SQL statement.

```
-401 THE OPERANDS OF AN ARITHMETIC OR
COMPARISON OPERATION ARE NOT COMPARABLE
```

An arithmetic operation appearing within the SQL statement has a mixture of numeric a nonnumeric operands, or the operands of a comparison operation are not compatible.

```
-402 AN ARITHMETIC FUNCTION OR OPERATOR
   [arith-fop] IS APPLIED TO CHARACTER
            OR DATETIME DATA
```

A nonnumeric operand has been specified for the arithmetic function or operator 'arith-fop'.

```
-404 THE UPDATE OR INSERT STATEMENT
   SPECIFIES A STRING THAT IS TOO
        LONG [column-name]
```

An INSERT or UPDATE statement specifies a value that is longer than the maximum-length string that can be stored in the indicated column.

```
-406 A CALCULATED OR DERIVED NUMERIC
     VALUE IS NOT WITHIN THE RANGE
         OF ITS OBJECT COLUMN
```

A value that was derived or calculated during processing of the SQL statement was outside the range of the data type of its object column.

```
-408 AN UPDATE OR INSERT VALUE IS NOT
   COMPARABLE WITH THE DATATYPE OF ITS
       OBJECT COLUMN [column-name]
```

The datatype of the value to be inserted into or set in the column 'column-name' by an INSERT or UPDATE statement is incompatible with the declared datatype of that column. Both must be numeric or both must be graphic string; or both must be either:

Dates or character

Times or character

Timestamps or character

However, Dates, Times, or Timestamps cannot be assigned to a character column that has a field procedure.

```
-413 OVERFLOW OCCURRED DURING
     DATATYPE CONVERSION
```

During processing of the SQL statement, an overflow condition arose when converting from one datatype to another.

```
-419 THE DECIMAL DIVIDE OPERATION IS
   INVALID BECAUSE THE RESULT WOULD
       HAVE A NEGATIVE SCALE
```

The decimal division is invalid because it will result in a negative scale.

The formula used internally to calculate the scale of the result for decimal division is:

$$\text{Scale of result} = 15 - np + ns - ds$$

where "np" is the precision of the numerator, "ns" is the scale of the numerator, and "ds" is the scale of the denominator.

```
-421 THE OPERANDS OF A UNION OR UNION
     ALL DO NOT HAVE THE SAME NUMBER
               OF COLUMNS
```

The operands of a UNION or UNION ALL must have the same number of columns.

```
-501 THE CURSOR IDENTIFIED IN A FETCH
     OR CLOSE STATEMENT IS NOT OPEN
```

The program attempted to either: (1) FETCH using a cursor, or (2) CLOSE a cursor at a time when the specified cursor was not open.

```
-502 THE CURSOR IDENTIFIED IN AN OPEN
        STATEMENT IS ALREADY OPEN
```

The program attempted to execute an OPEN statement for a cursor that was already open.

```
-503 A COLUMN CANNOT BE UPDATED BECAUSE
   IT IS NOT IDENTIFIED IN THE UPDATE CLAUSE
     OF THE SELECT STATEMENT OF THE CURSOR
```

The program attempted to update (using a cursor) a value in a column of the object table that was not identified in the FOR UPDATE clause in the cursor declaration.

Any column that is to be updated must be identified in the FOR UPDATE clause of the cursor declaration.

```
-504 THE CURSOR NAME [cursor-name]
          IS NOT DEFINED
```

One of the following conditions is true:

The cursor 'cursor-name' was not declared in the application program before it was referenced;

The 'declare-cursor' statement is static and the 'where-current-of' statement is dynamic;

or the 'where-current-of' statement is static and the 'declare-cursor' statement is dynamic.

```
-507 THE CURSOR IDENTIFIED IN THE
UPDATE OR DELETE STATEMENT IS NOT OPEN
```

The program attempted to execute an UPDATE or DELETE WHERE CURRENT OF cursor statement at a time when the specified cursor was not open.

```
-510 THE TABLE DESIGNATED BY THE CURSOR
   OF THE UPDATE OR DELETE STATEMENT
            CANNOT BE MODIFIED
```

The program attempted to execute an UPDATE or DELETE WHERE CURRENT OF cursor statement against a table or view that is defined in such a way that the requested operation (update or delete) is not permitted. For example, this can occur for a delete from a read-only view or for an update in which the cursor was not defined with the FOR UPDATE clause.

```
-511 THE FOR UPDATE CLAUSE CANNOT BE
SPECIFIED BECAUSE THE TABLE DESIGNATED
    BY THE CURSOR CANNOT BE MODIFIED
```

The result table of the SELECT statement can not be updated. This can occur if the SELECT specifies more than one table or view in the FROM clause, if the SELECT-list contains a built-in function or DISTINCT, or if the statement contains an ORDER BY or GROUP BY or HAVING clause. This can also occur if a view is specified in the FROM clause and the view cannot be updated.

```
-552 [auth-id] DOES NOT HAVE THE PRIVILEGE
     TO PERFORM OPERATION [operation]
```

Authorization ID 'auth-id' has attempted to perform the specified 'operation' without having been granted the authority to do so.

```
-601 THE NAME OF THE OBJECT TO BE CREATED
 IS IDENTICAL TO THE EXISTING NAME [name]
     OF THE OBJECT TYPE [obj-type]
```

The CREATE statement sought to create an object 'name' of type 'obj-type' when there is already an object of that type with the same name defined in the DB2 subsystem.

```
-603 A UNIQUE INDEX CANNOT BE CREATED
BECAUSE THE TABLE CONTAINS ROWS WHICH
 ARE DUPLICATES WITH RESPECT TO THE
    VALUES OF THE IDENTIFIED COLUMNS
```

The index defined in the CREATE INDEX statement cannot be created as unique because the specified table already contains rows that are duplicates with respect to the values of the identified columns.

```
     -604 A COLUMN DEFINITION SPECIFIES AN
   INVALID LENGTH, PRECISION, OR SCALE ATTRIBUTE
```

A column definition in the CREATE or ALTER TABLE statement contains an invalid length, precision, or scale attribute specification. Alternatively, the specification of data type may be incorrect or invalid.

```
   -612 [column-name] IS A DUPLICATE COLUMN NAME
```

The CREATE TABLE or CREATE VIEW statement specifies the same 'column-name' for two (or more) columns of the table or view. Column names must be unique within a table or view.

```
   -616 [obj-type1 obj-name1] CANNOT BE DROPPED
  BECAUSE IT IS REFERENCED BY [obj-type2 obj-name2]
```

An object cannot be dropped if there are other objects that are dependent upon it. For example, a storage group cannot be dropped if there are one or more existing tablespaces that use that storage group.

Execution of the specified DROP statement will drop object 'obj-name1' of type 'obj-type1' on which object 'obj-name2' of type 'obj-type2' is dependent.

```
  -803 ONE OR MORE INSERT OR UPDATE VALUES ARE INVALID
 BECAUSE THE OBJECT COLUMNS ARE CONSTRAINED SUCH THAT
   NO TWO ROWS OF THE TABLE CAN BE DUPLICATES WITH
      RESPECT TO THE VALUES OF THOSE COLUMNS.
```

The table that is the object of the INSERT or UPDATE operation is constrained (by one or more UNIQUE indexes) to have unique values in certain columns or groups of columns. Completion of the requested insert or update would result in duplicates with respect to the values occurring in those columns.

Alternatively, if a view is the object of the INSERT or UPDATE statement, then it is the table on which the view is defined that is thus constrained.

```
       -811 THE RESULT OF AN EMBEDDED SELECT
     STATEMENT IS A TABLE OF MORE THAN ONE ROW,
      OR THE RESULT OF THE SUBQUERY OF A BASIC
          PREDICATE IS MORE THAN ONE VALUE
```

Execution of an embedded SELECT statement has resulted in a result table containing more than one row. Alternatively, a subquery contained in a basic predicate has produced more than one value.

```
       -818 THE PRECOMPILER GENERATED TIMESTAMP
          X IN THE LOAD MODULE IS DIFFERENT
     FROM THE BIND TIMESTAMP Y BUILT FROM THE DBRM
```

The SQL precompiler places timestamp Y in the DBRM, and time stamp X in the parameter list in the program for each SQL statement. At BIND time, DB2 stores the DBRM timestamp for run-time use. At run-time, timestamp X for the SQL statement being processed is compared to timestamp Y derived from the DBRM at BIND time. If the two timestamps do not match, the DBRM and the program were not the result of the same precompile.

```
     -911 THE CURRENT UNIT OF WORK HAS BEEN ROLLED
        BACK DUE TO DEADLOCK OR TIMEOUT REASON
   [reason-code], TYPE OF RESOURCE [resource-type]
         AND RESOURCE NAME [resource-name]
```

The current unit of work was the victim in a deadlock, . . . or experienced a timeout, and had to be rolled back.

The reason code indicated whether a deadlock or timeout occurred. Refer to message DSNT500I under "Service Controller and Install Messages (DSNT. . .)" for an explanation of resource type and resource name.

```
      -913 UNSUCCESSFUL EXECUTION CAUSED BY
  DEADLOCK OR TIMEOUT. REASON CODE [reason-code]
      TYPE OF RESOURCE [resource-type], AND
          RESOURCE NAME [resource-name].
```

The application was the victim in a deadlock or experienced a timeout. The reason code indicates whether a deadlock or timeout has occurred.

Refer to message DSNT500I under "Service Controller and Install Messages (DSNT. . .)" for an explanation of resource type and resource name.

```
      -925 COMMIT NOT VALID IN IMS/VS OR
              CICS/OS/VS ENVIRONMENT
```

An application executing in either an IMS/VS or CICS environment has attempted to execute a COMMIT statement. The COMMIT statement can be issued only in a TSO environment.

Appendix 4

SQL/DB2 Limits and Capacities

The table below describes limits imposed by SQL.

ITEM	SQL LIMIT
Longest synonym, correlation-name, or name of a column, table, view, or index.	18
Longest authorization-id or name of a plan, database, table space, or storage group.	8
Maximum number of columns in a table or view (the value depends on the complexity of the CREATE VIEW statement)	300 or fewer
Longest row of a table, in bytes, including all overhead	for 4K pages, 4056 for 32K pages, 32714
Maximum size of a VARCHAR or VARGRAPHIC column; in bytes	for 4K pages, 4046 for 32K pages, 32704
Largest INTEGER value	2147483647
Smallest INTEGER value	-2147483648
Largest SMALLINT value	32767
Smallest SMALLINT value	-32768
Largest FLOAT value	Approximately 7.2E + 75
Smallest FLOAT value	Approximately -7.2E + 75

(Part 1 of 3). SQL Limits

ITEM	SQL LIMIT
Smallest positive FLOAT value	Approximately 5.4E-79
Largest negative FLOAT value	Approximately -5.4E-79
Largest DECIMAL value	999999999999999
Smallest DECIMAL value	-999999999999999
Smallest DATE value (shown in ISO format)	0001-01-01
Largest DATE value (shown in ISO format)	9999-12-31
Smallest TIME value (shown in ISO format)	00.00.00
Largest TIME value (shown in ISO format)	24.00.00
Smallest TIMESTAMP value	0001-01-01-00.00.00.000000
Largest TIMESTAMP value	9999-12-31-24.00.00.000000
Maximum number of table names in an SQL statement. (In a complex SELECT, the number of tables that can be joined may be significantly less.)	15 or fewer, depending on the SQL statement.
Longest SQLDA	13216 bytes
Maximum total length of host and indicator variables pointed to in an SQLDA	32767 bytes
Longest host variable used for insert or update	32704 bytes
Longest SQL statement	32765 bytes
Maximum number of elements in a select list	300
Maximum number of predicates in a WHERE or HAVING clause	300

(Part 2 of 3). SQL Limits

ITEM	SQL LIMIT
Maximum totla length of columns in a GROUP BY clause	4000
Maximum total length of columns in an ORDER BY clause	4000
Maximum number of columns in an index key	16
Longest index key for a non-partitioned table space, in bytes	254 less the number of key columns that allow nulls
Longest index key for a partitioned table space, in bytes	40 less the number of key columns that allow nulls
Maximum number of partitions in a partitioned table space	64
Maximum number of volume ID in a storage group	133
Longest referential constraint name	8

(Part 3 of 3). SQL Limits

The limit for items not mentioned above is system storage. Examples of such items are most host variables in a source program, most indexes on a table, and most host variables, tokens, or functions in an SQL statement.

SQL
Reserved Words

The following words are reserved words in SQL. They may not be used as ordinary identifiers in forming names. They may be used as delimited identifiers by enclosing them in double quotation marks.

ADD	EDITPROC	LIKE	TABLE
ALL	END-EXEC*	LOCKSIZE	TABLESPACE
ALTER	ERASE		TO
AND	EXECUTE	NOT	
ANY	EXISTS	NULL	UNION
AS		NUMPARTS	UPDATE
	FIELDPROC		USER
BETWEEN	FOR	OF	USING
BUFFERPOOL	FROM	ON	
BY		OR	VALIDPROC
	GO	ORDER	VALUES
CLUSTER	GOTO		VCAT
COLUMN	GRANT	PART	VIEW
COUNT	GROUP	PLAN	VOLUMES
CURRENT		PRIQTY	
CURSOR	HAVING	PRIVILEGES	WHERE
			WITH
	IMMEDIATE		
DATABASE	IN	SECQTY	
DELETE	INDEX	SELECT	
DESCRIPTOR	INSERT	SET	
DISTINCT	INTO	STOGROUP	
DROP	IS	SYNONYM	

The following word is not now reserved in SQL, but is set aside as a possible reserved word in future releases. We suggest that you not use it as an ordinary identifier in names that will have a continuing use.

KEY

---

* COBOL only

Appendix 6

Guide to the DB2 Reference Manuals

DOCUMENTATION IDENTIFICATION NUMBERS

- — Application Design and Tuning Guide (R) (GG24-3004-00)
- — Application Programming Guide for CICS (SC26-4080)
- — Application Programming Guide for IMS/VS (SC26-4079)
- — Application Programming Guide for TSO and Batch (SC26-4081)
- — Database Planning and Administration Guide (SC26-4077)
- — DB2 Reference Manual (SC26-4078)
- — Diagnosis Guide (LY26-3862)
- — Diagnosis Reference 1 (LY26-3862)
- — Diagnosis Reference 2 (LY26-3863)
- — Diagnosis Reference 3 (LY 26-3952)
- — Guide to Publications (GC26-4111)
- — General Information Manual (GC26-4073)
- — Installation Guide (SC26-4084)
- — Introduction to SQL (GC26-4082)
- — Messages and Codes (SC26-4113)
- — Operation and Recovery (SC26-4083)
- — Relational Concepts (R) (GG24-1581)
- — Sample Application Guide (SC26-4086)
- — Security Authorization Guide (R) (GG24-1599)
- — System Performance Monitoring and Tuning (R) (GG24-3005)
- — Utilities Guide (R) (GG24-3130-00)

(R) = Red Cover Manual published by International Systems
        Center Publications.